THE
SCIENCE
OF
REVENGE

Understanding the World's Deadliest
Addiction—and How to Overcome It

James Kimmel Jr., JD

HARMONY | NEW YORK

Harmony Books
An imprint of Random House
A division of Penguin Random House LLC
1745 Broadway, New York, NY 10019
HarmonyBooks.com | RandomHouseBooks.com
penguinrandomhouse.com

LIBRARY OF CONGRESS CATALOGING-IN-PUBLICATION DATA
Names: Kimmel, James P., author.
Title: The science of revenge / James Kimmel, Jr., JD.
Description: First edition. | New York, NY : Harmony, [2025] | Includes bibliographical references
and index.
Identifiers: LCCN 2024048846 (print) | LCCN 2024048847 (ebook) |
ISBN 9780593796511 (hardcover ; alk. paper) | ISBN 9780593796528 (ebook)
Subjects: LCSH: Revenge. | Violence. | Forgiveness.
Classification: LCC BF637.R48 K56 2025 (print) | LCC BF637.R48 (ebook) |
DDC 152.4—dc23/eng/20241126
LC record available at https://lccn.loc.gov/2024048846
LC ebook record available at https://lccn.loc.gov/2024048847
Printed in the United States of America on acid-free paper
2 4 6 8 9 7 5 3

Title page image: Alexandra/Adobe Stock
Book design by Elizabeth A. D. Eno

The authorized representative in the EU for product safety and compliance is
Penguin Random House Ireland, Morrison Chambers, 32 Nassau Street,
Dublin D02 YH68, Ireland. https://eu-contact.penguin.ie

To the perpetrators,
for they were once the victims

And if you wrong us, shall we not revenge?

—WILLIAM SHAKESPEARE, *The Merchant of Venice*

CONTENTS

A REVENGE REVOLUTION

This book is about why we want to hurt the people who hurt us. Understanding this is a matter of life and death. Perhaps your life or the life of someone you love.

Revenge is the author of tragedy and the destroyer of peace and happiness. It's the root motivation behind most forms of human aggression and violence, including intimate partner violence, youth violence and bullying, street and gang violence, mass shootings, riots, police brutality, arson, violent extremism, terrorism, genocide, and war.[1] Revenge destroys individuals, families, romantic relationships, fortunes, communities, nations, and empires. Yet we *want* revenge when we've been physically or emotionally harmed. This is of increasing concern in an age of powerful social networking platforms that make it easy and light speed fast to offend and enrage millions of people simultaneously, creating millions of people wanting revenge for the same thing at the same time.

But consider how odd this all is. We could want anything when somebody hurts or offends us. We could want cotton candy or potato chips, for example, or a nice massage or a relaxing nap. We could want a hug, a walk in a park, or to be surrounded by a litter of puppies. We could want a new pair of shoes, a tropical vacation, or a trove of diamonds. But what humans want most of all when we've been hurt is for the people who hurt us to feel pain—and for those people to understand that their pain is because of what they've done to us.[2]

Yet there's no material gain in this. You can't put another person's pain in your stomach, in your bank account, or on your feet. In economic terms, a single potato chip is more valuable, and a hug or a walk in a park more enjoyable. And who wouldn't rather spend time in the company of puppies? Revenge also comes with enormous risks and costs. Our retaliation against others often leads to equal or greater retaliation against us. And after exacting revenge, we're often left feeling worse but wanting more with continued thinking about the perpetrator and the harm and unwanted feelings of anger, anxiety, guilt, shame, and distress.[3] So why, after we've been hurt, among the many wonderful things in this wide world of ours, would we want something as worthless, unpleasant, and costly as the suffering of another human being?

Surprisingly, given what's at stake, scientists until recently have devoted little attention to revenge, leaving it to poets, playwrights, and prophets to explain the demon inside us.[4] The desire for revenge has been observed in virtually all traditional and contemporary societies around the world.[5] It's experienced by human and nonhuman primates, and children as young as toddlers.[6] Evolutionary psychologists believe the desire for revenge might have evolved as early as the Pleistocene epoch (the Ice Age) more than eleven thousand years ago.[7] Some researchers contend that revenge is so firmly hardwired into our brains that we'd have better luck trying to change the world itself than stopping people from wanting it.[8]

But what if the desire for revenge is both part of our genetic endowment and a neuroplastic brain-biological process, meaning that it's the product of changes taking place inside our brains in response to internal and external events and, therefore, subject to human volition and mastery? What if we could put this brain-biological process under a microscope, as we do with other conditions that produce human suffering, learn how and why it works, and develop strategies to help us control or even stop wanting revenge when other people hurt us?

To be clear, I'm not talking about *self-defense*. That's the necessary, lifesaving instinct we all possess to protect ourselves and others, even with lethal force, when faced with an imminent threat of serious bodily injury or death. We need this instinct to survive. I'm also not talking about sociopaths or psychopaths who have abnormal brain structures, lack empathy, and represent less than 4 percent of the human population.[9] Most murderers are not psychopaths or sociopaths; they're otherwise normal people who, because of a grievance of some sort, make a fateful decision to kill.[10] That's the group I'm talking about in this book: the rest of us who, at times, feel we've been mistreated and want revenge for wrongs of the past—minutes, weeks, months, or even years in the past when the threat of imminent harm no longer exists.[11] Ruminating on the hurts and traumas lurking in our memories is what activates the revenge desires that transform victims into perpetrators.[12] The benefits of scientifically understanding and controlling this process would be incalculable. Reduce the desire for revenge in yourself and others and you'll reduce the level of suffering and violence in your personal life and the world around you.

A REVENGE REVOLUTION

This book tells the exciting, untold story behind recent scientific discoveries leading us toward a revenge revolution. And the key is in the *wanting*. Law enforcement, public health, and behavioral studies from around the world confirm that people who hurt or kill other people are almost always acting in accord with a personal grievance— a real or imagined perception of having been wronged, betrayed, shamed, humiliated, or victimized in the past.[13] Recent neuroscience studies of what's happening inside the brains of people with grievances have led to a chilling discovery: activation of the reward and craving neurocircuitry of *addiction*.[14]

It turns out that your brain on revenge looks like your brain on drugs. Grievances cue the brain to crave revenge in much the same way that stress and anxiety, or seeing drug paraphernalia or places of drug use, cue the brains of addicts to crave narcotics. Addiction scientists describe this cue-dependent learning as part of the brain's self-regulating opponent-process system of maintaining balance between pleasure (well-being) and pain (stress), mediated in part by release of the neurotransmitter dopamine.[15]

Being harmed or treated unfairly, or experiencing anger, disgust, guilt, or shame, is painful and activates the brain's neural "pain network"—specifically, a brain structure called the anterior insula.[16] Getting revenge, or even just fantasizing about it, is rewarding, releasing dopamine and activating the brain's pleasure and reward circuitry, which primarily comprises the nucleus accumbens, the dorsal striatum, and the ventral tegmental area.[17] This produces feelings of pleasure that temporarily cover up the pain, restoring balance.[18] *For a while.* Like drugs and alcohol, the effects wear off quickly and almost always lead to more pain and suffering. But the reward circuitry of the brain is all about gratification *now*, not consequences later.[19] That's up to the brain's prefrontal cortex, which is responsible for cognitive control, self-regulation, and executive function.[20] With addiction, prefrontal control processes are hijacked, and reward circuitry runs amok.[21] When revenge cravings become compulsive and can't be controlled despite the negative consequences, they take on the features of addiction.[22]

Although scientists haven't thought of revenge as an addictive process until recently,[23] poets, playwrights, and prophets have been trying to tell us this for thousands of years. Writing in 700 BCE, Homer warns of the dangers of compulsive revenge seeking in the *Odyssey,* telling the tale of King Odysseus, who, upon returning home from the Trojan War, finds his wife, Penelope, in the company of more than a hundred suitors and slaughters them all in an orgy of retaliation, unleashing a cycle of revenge that can be stopped only with the intervention of the gods.[24] In the fifth century BCE, the ancient Greek playwrights Sophocles, Aeschylus, and Euripides achieved immortal fame through tragic plays like *Antigone, Oedipus Rex, Agamemnon,* and *Medea,* exhorting audiences about the dangers of compulsive revenge seeking. The book of Genesis, oldest of the Hebrew Bible and believed to have been written by the prophet Moses, cautions humanity about the dangers of compulsive revenge seeking in its archetypal stories of Cain's vengeance killing of his brother, Abel, and God's vengeance-fueled mass slaughter of humanity during the Flood.

We've all experienced the desire to punish people who violate social norms or mistreat us. Most of us control these urges, perhaps briefly fantasizing about the deliciously terrible things we'd like to do before shutting down our hedonic desires and moving on with our lives, leaving the pain of the past where it belongs, in the past.[25] But not everyone is so successful, not all grievances are the same or experienced in the same way, and we're not always able to control our revenge cravings. Human history is filled with horrifying examples of compulsive revenge seeking, from cruel acts of interpersonal violence to revenge-driven tribal, communal, and nation-sized conflicts, rebellions, revolts, insurrections, civil wars, and world wars leaving millions dead.

Revenge addicts come in many forms, not all or even most of them violent. Revenge addicts may be wounded kids compulsively firing off mean texts and equally wounded kids firing back. They may be obsessed sports fans thirsting for retaliation against opposing teams, obsessed moviegoers cheering on the superhero to vanquish the villain, and obsessed gamers slaughtering enemies in first-person shooter games. Revenge addicts may be offended lovers demeaning and assaulting each other, politicians taunting and disparaging each other, pissed-off neighbors dumping grass clippings on each other's lawns, road ragers cutting off inconsiderate drivers, customers berating inattentive waiters, and angry employees sabotaging workplaces. Revenge addicts can be anyone: grandmas, grandpas, friends, frenemies, cops, robbers, prosecutors, judges, wardens, guards, prisoners, soldiers, voters, clergy, the faithful, the faithless, nurses, doctors, patients, accountants, brokers, cafeteria ladies, artists, musicians, liberals, conservatives, fascists, communists, racists, extremists, minorities, majorities . . . the list goes on. The point is that, under the right circumstances, almost *anyone* can experience powerful revenge cravings. When the cravings are so strong that they can't be controlled despite the negative consequences of indulging them, they can transform perfectly normal, peaceful people into perpetrators of unexpected and unimaginable acts of psychological and physical violence. The common denominator of those who commit acts of violence isn't that they're deranged or evil. It's their perception, real or imagined, that they've been wronged or victimized. All of them are in pain, and all of them want the one thing that their brains tell them will make the pain go away—the suffering of those who hurt them (or their proxies). It's a matter of brain biology.

This book takes a deep dive into the startling new neuroscience of revenge that's helping make sense of the seemingly senseless acts of cruelty and violence that humans inflict upon each other. Because revenge is ancient, universal, and bound up in so many human behaviors, relationships, values, and institutions, we'll also make excursions into human history, law, psychology, philosophy, politics, and religion. Along the way, we'll talk to leading researchers making breakthroughs in revenge neuroscience; a convicted murderer who has committed his life to helping others overcome revenge addiction from his jail cell; a former white supremacist who has devoted his life to helping violent extremists overcome their revenge addictions and return to lives of peace; a media mogul who acknowledges the entertainment industry's reliance on revenge cravings to sell tickets; a world-respected psychiatrist who believes, like me, that Donald Trump's long history of uncontrolled vengeful behavior suggests he's suffering from revenge addiction; the father of a murdered child who did the unthinkable and forgave the killers; and an inspirational leader of former gang members who risk their lives to stop retaliatory violence in city neighborhoods. We'll also hear from some of the most terrifying people of modern times—mass killers and tyrants who, in their manifestos, histories, interviews, and speeches, describe their descent into revenge addiction, leaving us with clear and dire warnings that we ignore at our peril.

Most important, we'll focus in this book on how understanding revenge as an addictive process can help individuals and communities control the desire to hurt the people who hurt us and protect ourselves and those we love from harm. We'll learn that there's a courtroom inside every human mind where we try, convict, sentence, and punish the people who wrong us and where, at the conclusion of these trials, we choose whether to carry out the punishments in flesh and blood, in the here and now. We'll learn how our addictive brain biology turns these trials into kangaroo courts, but also how we can regain control by adapting and expanding strategies that have been successful in preventing and treating other addictive behaviors. And because forgiveness is the opposite of revenge and plays an important role in recovery from all addictions, we'll look at the remarkable neuroscience of forgiveness and the powerful role it plays in recovering from trauma, reducing pain, stopping dangerous revenge cravings, and restoring peace and happiness in our personal lives and even among nations.

Before we get to all that, however, I have a confession to make. I'm a recovering revenge addict. Let me tell you my story of how I went from being a normal teenager with no history of violence to coming within seconds of committing a revenge-fueled mass shooting—then on to becoming a revenge-dealing lawyer on the verge of suicide before becoming a revenge and violence researcher at the Yale School of Medicine on a quest to prove the existence of, and find a cure for, the deadliest addiction no one has ever heard of.

CONFESSIONS OF A REVENGE ADDICT

I grew up on a small farm in central Pennsylvania, but my folks weren't real farmers. We had a few Black Angus cattle and some pigs and chickens, but my father was an insurance agent and my mother a homemaker, so we didn't make our living from the land. This became a source of contempt from the neighboring farm kids whose fathers were real farmers. My dad rolled out of bed around 9:00 a.m. and into his office in town by 10:00 wearing shiny shoes and a suit. Their dads were up by 4:00 a.m. and in their milking parlors by 5:00 wearing filthy boots and overalls covered in manure.

I did everything I could to win them over. I enrolled in vo-ag classes, joined Future Farmers of America, listened to country music, and wore the same style of western jeans, trucker boots, and "IH" International Harvester hats they did. They weren't buying. There were many farm kids and only one of me. They started bullying me, at first verbally and then physically. This continued through junior and senior high schools. The hunting grounds were the bus, the locker room, and the hallways between classes. There were no anti-bullying programs in the early 1980s, at least not in my school. When you were outmuscled and outnumbered, you learned to leap over tripping feet and duck beneath swinging fists.

Late one night, when I was about seventeen, my parents, brother, and I awoke to the sound of a gunshot. We jumped out of bed and raced to the windows. I recognized the pickup truck speeding away. It belonged to one of the kids who had been harassing me. We checked around the house, didn't see any damage, and went back to sleep.

Before school each morning, my job was to go out to the barn and feed the cows, the hogs, and our hunting dog, an adorable little beagle named Paula. While making my rounds that morning, I found Paula in her pen, lying in a pool of blood with a bullet hole in her head.

Yeah, lots of emotions there. Lots of pain and rage. Why would they kill an innocent dog? Because we weren't real farmers? Because I was thriving despite their abuse? I'd never done a thing to them. We reported it to the state police. Again, this was rural Pennsylvania in the early 1980s. The police did nothing. And my father, who made a living in part by selling insurance to farmers, and who expected me to take care of my business, did nothing. How was I supposed to take care of my business? Well, I had a grievance. Evolution fills in the rest.

About two weeks later, I was home alone late at night and heard a vehicle come to a stop in front of our house again. Moments later, there was a flash and an explosion. I ran to the window. They blew up our mailbox. The same pickup truck roared out of the cloud of smoke. The blast not only launched our mangled mailbox into the cornfield, but it detonated what was left of my self-control. I wanted revenge. *Bad.* Living in the country and being hunters, we had plenty of guns. I grabbed a loaded revolver from my father's nightstand, jumped in my mother's car, and tore off into the night, shouting and cussing at the top of my lungs with tears of rage streaming down my face.

I eventually cornered them against a barn on one of their farms. There were three or four of them. They climbed out of the truck and squinted back into my headlights, trying to see who had just barreled down the long gravel drive kicking up rocks and dust. It had taken some time for me to catch up to them. I had never confronted them before. Since it was my mother's car, they might have thought it was her. What was clear is that they were confused. And unarmed. And they didn't know I had a gun.

It would be so easy and feel so good . . .

I grabbed the gun from the passenger seat and started to open the door.

And then I had a sort of sudden insight. I somehow glimpsed into my future and saw that if I killed them, I'd be killing a part of myself—maybe all of it. I remembered that I was a good person raised by good people, and I didn't really want to become a murderer.

I just wanted the pain to stop. I had something to live for—maybe the dignity and self-respect I thought they'd taken from me. In that moment, I realized that the cost of getting the revenge I craved was more than I was willing to pay. And that was just enough to cause me to shut the door, put the gun back down on the passenger seat, and drive home. Terrified. I'd come within seconds of committing a mass shooting.

It felt cowardly, not going through with it. As if I didn't have the guts. As if I didn't take care of my business and failed the code imprinted in the DNA of humanity to make others pay when they hurt you. I got over it after a while. And for some reason I can't quite explain, those guys whom I let live that night stopped bothering me. Maybe it was a wake-up call for them too.

Any addict can tell you there's a big difference between controlling your cravings once and mastering them over a long period of time. That night, I controlled my craving for revenge, but I was nowhere near mastering it. Quite the opposite, the craving was only starting to grow. There are lots of reasons to feel offended and mistreated in this world, and lots of people whose suffering can help make you feel better. I had acquired a taste for revenge. The way I saw it, I just needed to figure out a way to get it without overpaying.

That's when I came upon the idea of going into the professional revenge business. Instead of becoming a mass murderer, I decided to become a lawyer. See, lawyers get revenge without paying for it. In fact, they get paid, *a lot*, for selling revenge to the masses. And I'm talking about the high-quality, pharmaceutical-grade, government-approved, manufactured-inside-a-courtroom type of revenge, better known by the brand name "Justice," with no strings attached and no criminal record. Legalized revenge. Lawyers are the only people in our society licensed to prescribe, manufacture, and sell revenge. It seemed like a deal too good to pass up.

While attending law school at the University of Pennsylvania, I did an internship in the Philadelphia district attorney's office and got my first taste of punishing people for hire by prosecuting and locking away violent and nonviolent criminals. This felt very good. After graduating from law school, I served as a law clerk to a federal judge, and we spent time sentencing felons to tough federal prison terms. This also felt very good. For a while. I sometimes experienced brief moments of sorrow and remorse watching defendants being led away in handcuffs, but I brushed it off. I gave serious consideration to becoming a full-time prosecutor, but their salaries are low. I had lots of student loans and needed to make money fast. So, I joined a large Philadelphia law firm as a civil litigator and started dealing justice to my clients by the leather briefcase full. I was making bank and snorting all the revenge I wanted for free, or so I thought.

Within a decade, my revenge addiction had nearly destroyed me and my family. By the time I bottomed out, I'd become a maniacal bully like the guys who killed my dog. I threatened retribution against just about anyone for the slightest offense—including my wife and kids. No grievance was too small to merit a retaliatory swipe. Each hit of revenge ("justice") made me feel as if I were on top of the world, followed by an inevitable crash and the need for more. A hammer can't drive a nail without experiencing the impact of the blow, and I was feeling as much pain as I was delivering.

I began to hate what I did for a living and who I'd become. But revenge was my easy fix, the edge that took the edge off until I was hurting again. I descended into a professional and psychological crisis. By this point, I'd quit several law firms, converting a lucrative income into virtually no income at all. I fell into depression and found myself sitting alone in a spare bedroom contemplating suicide. That's when I began to wonder whether I was addicted—when I started craving revenge against *myself*. Fortunately, the cost of exacting that revenge was also more than I was willing to pay.

They say the first step in recovery is admitting you have a problem. I knew I had a huge problem. My thirst for revenge nearly killed me twice. But unlike alcohol, narcotics, and gambling, there are no rehabs or 12-step programs for revenge addicts. I didn't even know for sure whether I was hooked. I just knew that it felt like an uncontrollable obsession, and that a lot of people around me seemed to be obsessed too. This included many of the clients who hired me, opposing lawyers getting high from trading blows with me, and other perfectly normal, average people throughout society doing terrible things like abusing and shooting each other to fulfill some need to hurt the people who hurt them.

I realized that if I was going to be saved, I'd have to do it myself. I'm a spiritual person, so I started there, like many people who struggle with addiction. I studied the revenge and forgiveness teachings of the world's major religions and found them to be in conflict, with nearly as many religions, and sects within religions, encouraging revenge as discouraging it. My first book, *Suing for Peace,* published in 2005, recounts this spiritual-legal journey.[26] It also contains my early hypothesizing about revenge addiction and my "12-step program" for recovery called The Nonjustice System (NJS)—a virtual courtroom role play where you safely release and overcome your revenge cravings by putting the people who harm you on trial while playing all the roles yourself: victim, prosecutor, defendant, judge, jury, warden, and even judge of your own life. I'll discuss The Nonjustice System in more detail in chapters 10 and 11.

This was a start, and it helped me get control of my addiction. In my second book, *The Trial of Fallen Angels,* a novel, published in 2012, I explored what revenge addiction looks like under the most extreme circumstances I could imagine: a young lawyer in the afterlife prosecuting and defending the souls of murderers at the Final Judgment.[27]

I knew while writing these books that if I was going to uncover the truth about why we want to hurt the people who hurt us and how to stop it, I would need to take a scientific approach focused on brain biology—because the brain is where memories of victimization and trauma reside and desires and motivations form. So that's what I set out to do next. It took me twenty years of hard work and incredible luck, and the resources and genius of more than sixty neuroscientists and research psychologists at universities around the world, to arrive at the scientific discovery of revenge addiction. This book tells the improbable story of that discovery and the promise it holds for reducing human suffering and violence and securing peace and prosperity.

Back in 2004, at about the time I was writing *Suing for Peace*, neuroscientists were beginning to explore what happens inside our brains when we've been wronged and want to punish others. Their research provided the first empirical support for my revenge addiction hypothesis. The field has grown enormously in the two decades since, and I became part of it by joining the Yale School of Medicine as a researcher and lecturer in psychiatry and the founder and co-director of the Yale Collaborative for Motive Control Studies. This is the first book to bring it all together in one place. We now know that grievance-triggered revenge cravings are the root motivation of violence, that compulsive revenge seeking can become dangerously addictive, and that we can develop effective ways of preventing and treating it.

This is truly revolutionary, breakthrough stuff that changes everything we thought we knew about why people become violent and how to stop it. It holds the promise of unlocking powerful new public health approaches for preventing and treating violence in all forms, from minor shoves between children on playgrounds and vicious fights between romantic partners to mass shootings, acts of terrorism, and even war. I'm living testament, along with many others throughout history, that there are potent ways to control the thirst for revenge. Some might even have been encoded into our genes to do just that, creating an opposing, lifesaving, brain-biological process we can activate anytime if we know it's there and learn how to use it.

But first, like all addicts, we've got to admit that we have a problem. This problem just happens to be inside our own brains rather than in a bottle or a syringe. You'll see what I mean next.

THE
SCIENCE
OF
REVENGE

CHAPTER 1

THE DEADLIEST ADDICTION

On July 10, 1973, Olga Hepnarová, at the age of twenty-two, rented a Praga RN freight truck and drove it at a speed of nearly forty miles per hour into a crowd of mostly elderly people gathered on a Prague sidewalk waiting for a tram. She had carefully planned her journey to inflict maximum carnage, circling the tram stop for the crowd to build and launching her murderous run from the top of a slope to gain velocity. She left eight dead and twelve seriously injured. She did all this because she wanted revenge.

We know Olga's motive because she went to great lengths to explain it to the world. In the days leading up to the killings, she wrote a letter describing what she intended to do and why. She mailed copies to the editors of two Prague newspapers just prior to setting out to become a mass murderer.

"Please accept this letter as a statement," Olga wrote. "It was written in defense against possible disparagement and ridicule of my act; also I do not want you to doubt about my sanity. . . .

"Today I will steal a [truck] and drive full speed into a crowd of people. It will happen somewhere in Prague 7. I intend to kill people. I know I will be judged and punished. And this is my confession. . . .

"For thirteen years I have been growing up in the clutches of a so-called good family. I am beaten and abused—a toy for adults and a victim of schoolchildren (and forever an outsider among my peers) . . . publicly smeared, slandered, mocked, humiliated.

"I am a destroyed woman," Olga continued. "A woman destroyed by people. So I have a choice: kill myself or kill others. I choose—TO REVENGE MY PERSECUTORS. This is my verdict: I, Olga Hepnarová, the victim of your bestiality, sentence you to the death penalty by running over and declare that in my lifetime x people are not enough. Actions not words."[1]

Olga waited for the police to arrive after her rampage. She confessed to the crimes and the planning and explained that she acted in retaliation against society for the way she had been treated.

Olga Hepnarová regarded herself as bisexual, and this seems to have been a source of some of the rejection and humiliation she experienced. She had a history of treatment for depression and had attempted suicide as a young teenager. However, during her trial in the Municipal Court of Prague, against the advice of her legal counsel, she insisted upon her sanity. She accepted full responsibility for her actions and expressed no regrets. Multiple psychiatrists and psychologists examined her and confirmed that she was, in fact, of sound mind. In a statement to investigators, she explained her rationale:

"If the society destroys individuals, individuals can destroy the society. . . . I wanted to take my revenge on society, including my family, because they are my enemy. . . . Knowing that I managed to do it, I felt a kind of release and satisfaction."

When given an opportunity to speak to the court, Olga explained that she understood justice as an eye for an eye and a tooth for a tooth. In conformance with this logic, she asked the court that the death penalty be imposed upon her for her crime. The court obliged, finding her guilty of the eight murders and sentencing her to execution by hanging.

Olga's mother filed an appeal. The verdict and sentence were upheld by the Supreme Court of the Czechoslovak Socialist Republic. Pleas for mercy from Olga's mother were rejected by Prime Minister Lubomír Štrougal.

On March 12, 1975, Olga Hepnarová was hanged in Pankrác Prison. This earned her the distinction of being the last woman executed in communist Czechoslovakia. Her tragic life and death, and that of those she brutally maimed and murdered, remained largely unknown outside eastern Europe until more than forty years later, when a film about her, *I, Olga Hepnarová*, was released. This film was based in part upon the 2001 book *Oprátka za osm mrtvých* (Noose for eight dead) by Roman Cílek.

THE COURTROOM OF THE MIND

There are many things that might interest us about the shocking case of Olga Hepnarová: the alleged child abuse at the hands of her father and possibly her mother's complicity or failure to protect her; the bullying by her classmates and possibly her teachers' complicity or failure to stop them; the venomous bigotry and persecution surrounding nontraditional sexualities; the role of depression and the trauma of a prior suicide attempt; her acute sensitivity to injustices normally borne by others without resorting to mass murder; the fact that she chose to kill people whom she did not know and who had done nothing to her; her apparent narcissism and desire for notoriety; her insistence upon her sanity and desire for people to understand her; and the failure of mental health professionals, law enforcement agencies, and even the death penalty to prevent or deter the crime—if anything, the prospect of her own execution seemed to motivate her to kill.

But there are two items not on this list, often overlooked, that provide a deeper understanding of not only Olga Hepnarová but revenge itself. The first is Olga's thought process. Prior to the crime,

Olga placed the people who wronged her, and society itself, on trial inside a courtroom of her mind. During this trial, she played all the roles. As prosecutor, she identified the crimes she believed had been committed and the perpetrators. As victim, she provided eyewitness testimony. As the defendants (her family and society), she denied and confessed culpability. As judge and jury, she weighed the evidence, reached a verdict, and handed down a sentence. As warden, she carried it out.

Consider the momentousness of this process. An entire criminal proceeding was conducted *by the perpetrator of the crime* against the future victims *before the crime had even been committed.* This proceeding was identical in all material respects to the criminal proceeding to which Olga knew she herself would be subjected afterward. Whether her future victims had committed the crimes of which Olga felt aggrieved, and whether those crimes were serious enough to the rest of us to warrant the death penalty, were irrelevant. In the courtroom of Olga Hepnarová's mind, she alone had authority to make these determinations. All that mattered is that Olga saw herself as a victim of unfair and malicious treatment. Having reached this conclusion, she naturally and quite rationally sought justice using the judicial process humans have used for thousands of years. The desire for revenge not only motivated Olga Hepnarová to murder human beings with a rented truck; it motivated other human beings to murder Olga Hepnarová with a hangman's noose.

The significance of this process cannot be overstated. It reveals a hidden, archetypal framework for understanding human revenge, rage, and violence. In this book, we're going to discover that most of us—good, normal people, not just the Olga Hepnarovás of the world—are routinely putting the people who offend and mistreat us on trial inside the busy courtrooms of our minds. We're also going to learn that humans experience a never-ending supply of real and imagined grievances, great and small, nearly infinite in number, that drive us to want revenge against others virtually every day of our lives. We're almost constantly thinking about our grievances and ways of avenging them, fantasizing about revenge, trying to suppress our desire for it, and sometimes indulging it. We also spend a great deal of time recovering from the negative effects of getting revenge, and from the negative feelings and harm directed back against us by those who see our acts of revenge as unjust and now seek revenge against us.

It's this always-burning, always-cycling desire for revenge that motivates our rage and violence against others and that motivates their rage and violence against us. Sigmund Freud, father of psychoanalysis, put it this way in his *Reflections on War and Death:* "In our unconscious we daily and hourly do away with all those who stand in our way, all those who have insulted or harmed us."[2]

Although the trials of our enemies take place entirely inside our minds, they have real life-and-death consequences. At their conclusion, we will choose, as did Olga, whether to carry out our sentences in the real world. This makes the trials of our enemies the most important trials of *our* lives. For the outcomes of these trials will determine for us, for the people who harm us, for our families and theirs, and often for people whom we have never met whether tragedy strikes or is avoided, and peace and happiness are lost or found. If we hope to secure personal and communal peace, harmony, and prosperity—and reduce rage, violence, and aggression in all forms—we must learn how to win the trials taking place inside our minds. Because despite the significant progress made by humanity in reducing violence over millennia,[3] we're still losing these trials at a horrific rate and cost in terms of lives, peace, prosperity, and security.

A BRAIN DISEASE MODEL OF REVENGE ADDICTION

How, you might ask, could we possibly lose trials taking place inside our own heads? We're the judge and jury, right?

Yes, but we're operating under the influence.

We can begin to understand this by considering the second overlooked aspect of Olga Hepnarová's case. Notice her description of how she felt after committing the murders: "Knowing that I managed to do it, I felt a kind of release and satisfaction."

Callous remarks like these from confessed killers are typically regarded as evidence of depravity, psychopathology, sadism, or pure evil. And it is indeed true that psychopaths lack empathy and remorse, and sadists take pleasure in other people's pain. However, in this book, we're going to confront startling new scientific evidence that biology rigs the trials inside our minds against all of us, not just the psychopaths and sadists of the world. For most people most of the time—good, normal people—retaliation in any form, violent or otherwise, in our imaginations or in real life, *feels good*. Sometimes irresistibly good. So good that we're sometimes willing to destroy our own lives, and the lives of others, to get it.

The American Society of Addiction Medicine (ASAM) defines addiction as "a treatable, chronic medical disease involving complex interactions among brain circuits, genetics, the environment, and an individual's experiences. People with addiction use substances or engage in behaviors that become compulsive and often continue despite harmful consequences."[4] Researchers have identified the primary feature of behavioral addictions such as gambling, gaming, and compulsive eating as "the failure to resist an impulse, drive, or temptation to perform an act that is harmful to the person or to others."[5] This perfectly describes Olga Hepnarová. She failed to resist an impulse, drive, or compulsion to attack those who harmed her—or, in this case, their proxies as she imagined them.[6] The consequences of her actions were indisputably harmful: She caused the deaths of others and herself.

In the next two chapters, we'll see in detail how addiction researchers and neuroscientists have recently revealed that our brains on revenge look and behave like our brains on drugs. With substance addiction, pain, stress, and environmental cues such as seeing a place where drugs are taken activate craving in the brain's reward circuitry in anticipation of pleasure and relief of pain through *intoxication*.[7] With revenge, pain, stress, and environmental cues in the form of perceived grievances and victimization activate craving in the brain's reward circuitry in anticipation of pleasure and relief of pain through *retaliation*.[8]

These astonishing insights build on discoveries made nearly three decades ago in the field of substance addiction. In 1997, the addiction scientist Alan Leshner, then director of the National Institute on Drug Abuse, wrote a groundbreaking article in the journal *Science* titled "Addiction Is a Brain Disease, and It Matters."[9] Dr. Leshner argued that advances in neuroscience had demonstrated that substance addiction is a disease with biological, social, and environmental causes that produces pathological changes in the brain's reward and self-control circuitry. He acknowledged that substance use begins as a voluntary behavior, but he explained that in many individuals it moves from there into a state of craving and involuntary seeking and using despite the negative health and social consequences. He decried stigmatizing people suffering from obviously severe physical and psychological symptoms of illness as weak and immoral and punishing them for it. He advocated for replacing ideology with neurobiology and urged that addiction be treated like other chronic, relapsing diseases such as type 2 diabetes, high blood pressure, and asthma.

A few years later, the addiction scientists Thomas McLellan, David Lewis, Charles O'Brien, and Herbert Kleber evaluated Dr. Leshner's argument. After reviewing hundreds of medical journal articles and randomized control trials, these scientists wrote an article demonstrating that addiction does, in fact, resemble other chronic diseases in terms of diagnostic differentiation, genetic heritability, role of personal choice and environmental/social factors, pathophysiology, treatment outcomes, and relapse experiences. Like Dr. Leshner, they concluded that addiction "should be insured, treated, and evaluated like other chronic illnesses."[10]

In the years since these two highly influential articles, the brain disease model of addiction has become the dominant model in addiction science and is recognized by the American Medical Association

(AMA) and the American Society of Addiction Medicine.[11] Substance and behavioral addiction research has expanded, evidence-based addiction treatments and therapies have multiplied, legislation requiring the same medical insurance coverage for addiction as other illnesses has been enacted, public health addiction prevention strategies have increased, the stigmatization of drug users has decreased, and most informed people and policy makers now realize that moralization and punishment are not effective strategies for reducing substance addiction.[12]

This has not come without controversy. Some scholars question the brain disease model of addiction. Among other things, they contend that people sometimes recover from addiction spontaneously or "age out" without treatment; genetic heritability is not proof of disease; brain scans do not reveal structural addiction abnormalities; a brain disease focus ignores social, environmental, and developmental factors; and addicts exercise free will and choice in their lives.[13] However, these criticisms have been convincingly rebutted by leading scientists who maintain that the brain disease model of addiction continues to be accurate. It embraces rather than denies the role of biopsychosocial and environmental factors, acknowledges the importance of the behavioral sciences and self-recovery in treatment, reveals that addiction is a medical disorder with medical and nonmedical ways of being addressed, and ensures the availability of evidence-based approaches that reduce stigma and save lives.[14]

I am persuaded by Dr. Leshner, the AMA, the ASAM, and the many proponents of the brain disease model of addiction. Over the course of this book, I hope to convince you that compulsive revenge seeking is also an addiction and a brain disease, and that it matters. (Or at least that it's an addiction and a "mental disorder"—defined by the American Psychiatric Association as a "clinically significant disturbance in an individual's cognition, emotion regulation, or behavior that reflects a dysfunction in the psychological, biological, or developmental processes underlying mental functioning."[15])

To support my case, I'm going to rely on neuroscientific, behavioral, psychiatric, psychological, sociological, and historical evidence showing that revenge is the deadliest addiction of all, and our society is worse off for it. Hard-core drug users inject narcotics into their own bodies to relieve their cravings. Hard-core revenge users inject bullets into the bodies of others to relieve their cravings. Drugs and syringes, bullets and guns, these deadly pairs satisfy the same brain-biological desire for relief of pain and hedonic reward. Tally the casualties of all the wars, murders, and physical and psychological assaults throughout human history—that approximates the number of dead and wounded from compulsive revenge seeking.[16] The multicide researcher Matthew White estimates that a staggering 455 million people have been killed in the top one hundred most deadly atrocities and wars in human history.[17] We'll see in chapter 8 that most of these killings have at their root a real or imagined grievance and a compulsive desire for revenge.

Although criminologists have long identified revenge as a primary motive for violence, they haven't identified the brain-biological basis for it, how or why it's activated, why it's so strongly desired and difficult to resist, or how to control it. They've also proposed other possible motivations for violence, such as predation, dominance, ideology, hate, and sadism.[18] The science of revenge, however, suggests that these are more accurately understood as categories of *grievance* that activate revenge desires and the hedonic *reward* one receives from getting revenge. In other words, except for self-defense and rare cases of brain abnormality, the science of revenge suggests that there is *one* universal motive for most acts of human violence: the desire for revenge to relieve pain and experience pleasure in response to a real or imagined grievance.

As in the case of Olga Hepnarová, it doesn't matter whether other people agree that a particular grievance exists or that its magnitude warrants the punishment exacted. If a grievance is perceived, then it has the capacity to activate a desire to retaliate. Researchers have shown that perpetrators of violence believe they're victims, and they believe their actions are a legitimate means of righting wrongs and obtaining justice.[19] We'll learn in chapter 6 that even Hitler, Stalin, and Mao—the deadliest tyrants in modern human history—believed they were victims of serious wrongs, betrayals, and oppressions and that the tortures and murders they ordered were justly motivated. This is also true of serial killers. After kidnapping, raping, and murdering thirty-three boys, John Wayne Gacy explained his horrific acts this way: "I was cheated out of my childhood," and "I see myself more as a victim than a perpetrator."[20]

REVENGE ADDICTION WITH BENEFITS

Building a brain disease model of revenge addiction on the existing brain disease model of substance addiction creates a powerful leveraging effect. We can repurpose many already existing addiction prevention and treatment approaches to create and deploy public health prevention and treatment approaches to combat violence and intentionally inflicted human suffering. The enormous investments made over the past three decades in substance and behavioral addiction research are poised to yield unanticipated violence reduction dividends.

As with the failed war on drugs, the war on violence will not be won through blunt-force approaches like increased law enforcement and punishment.[21] Humanity has maintained a losing streak with this strategy lasting thousands of years. Every person who uses violence knows they risk arrest, incarceration, injury, and death, yet they do it anyway. Why? As we'll see in the coming chapters, because their brains have been hijacked by powerful, uncontrolled revenge cravings. *For people with revenge addiction, guns and other weapons are objects of abuse.* This means that the public safety necessity of restricting access to semiautomatic firearms capable of killing many people fast should be as obvious as the public safety necessity of restricting access to drugs like fentanyl capable of killing many people fast. Addicts will abuse them, causing enormous harm to others and themselves. However, even removing all guns from the planet wouldn't stop the carnage because it wouldn't address the *desire to kill*. Since the beginning of recorded human history, revenge addicts have always found ways to hurt and kill: with rocks, sticks, bare hands, or, as in the case of Olga Hepnarová, a freight truck. This book focuses on the desire to hurt and kill.

I want to be clear, however. This is about creating a public health approach to preventing violence and saving lives. It's not about creating excuses or legal defenses for people who commit violent crimes. Murder under the influence of alcohol, drugs, or revenge is still murder. Addicts remain legally responsible for acting on their compulsive urges. Dangerous people who threaten the lives of others because they're unable to control their revenge cravings must be separated from society so they can do no further harm. Yet we can and must do more scientifically and medically to prevent violence from happening in the first place, and much more to treat and rehabilitate individuals whose violent behaviors are driven by compulsive revenge cravings. The brain disease model of revenge addiction is the platform upon which to achieve these long sought but elusive violence prevention and treatment goals and produce genuine, attainable, measurable benefits in harm reduction and improvements in public health and safety.

A GRIEVANCE OVER GRIEVANCES

I hope I have you at least interested in considering compulsive revenge seeking as an addiction and a brain disease. But before concluding this chapter and moving on to the fascinating neuroscience of revenge, I want to address a question you might be asking: Why should we go after revenge cravings instead of the grievances and injustices that trigger them?

Here's why. Grievances are subjective, in the eye of the beholder, and unlimited in number.[22] There are as many grievances in the world at any one time as there are human beings on the planet times the number of thoughts and feelings of offense, unfairness, victimization, mistreatment, and injustice they can experience or imagine from moment to moment. There's no universal judge of whether a grievance is real or not, or whether it's important or not. As I've explained, if a grievance is real and important to you, and if it's triggering revenge cravings inside your brain, then it's real enough for you to lash out, or even kill . . . even if every other person on the planet says it doesn't exist or wouldn't bother them.

Working to reduce the causes of grievance, victimization, and mistreatment is a worthy goal. We can and should strive in every way possible to make the world a better, safer, fairer place, and to reduce the social, environmental, developmental, and economic inequities, injustices, and personal behaviors that lead to grievances and victimization. But solving an infinite number of infinitely generating grievances is, in effect, infinitely impossible. As a public health matter, we stand a far better chance of controlling human revenge seeking and violence by focusing on the *one* common brain-biological reaction to all grievances, regardless of their origin or form. That's where we should be investing our limited public health resources if we want to reduce violence and human suffering. It's a cycle:

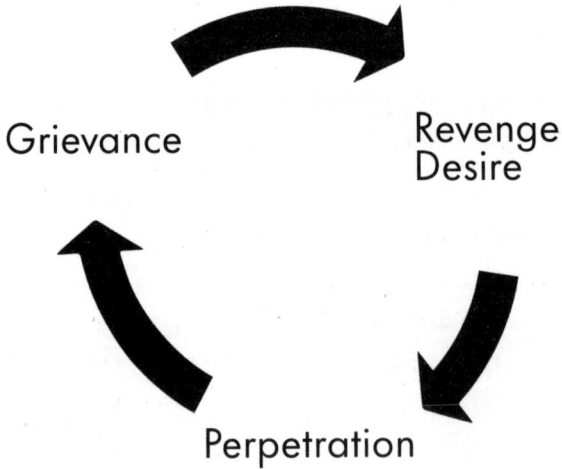

Grievance

Revenge Desire

Perpetration

Some might be tempted to claim that this is a reductionist theory of violence. Like the brain disease model of addiction itself, it's not. The science of revenge integrates brain biology with the multitude of psychological, social, and environmental factors that expose us to, and give rise to, the personal perception and significance of painful grievances—and that alter the brain chemistry that produces revenge cravings and motivates, or prevents, people from acting on them.[23] It's a holistic approach, not the reduction of behavior to biology.

The science of revenge provides us with the answer to *why* we want to harm the people who harm us and how to control it. The question is this: Will we act on it?

Read on and decide for yourself.

CHAPTER 2

QUEST TO FIND A KILLER

One of my good friends is a clinical psychologist named Larry Nulton. Dr. Nulton has treated thousands of people suffering from mental illnesses and is a skilled and compassionate clinician. He's also the first mental health professional with whom I shared my theory that revenge might be an addictive process, and that I might be a revenge addict.

This was in the early years of the twenty-first century. I'd just emerged from about five years of high-stakes civil litigation for wealthy clients who rarely allowed an insult to go unpunished, understood their legal rights, and didn't seem to care how much they spent in attorney's fees or even whether they ultimately won or lost in court—only that they got to court and had the pleasure of dragging their adversaries through the traumatizing litigation process. For the uninitiated, this process includes being interrogated and investigated by your own lawyer; being interrogated and investigated, under oath, by the other side's lawyer; searching through, fighting over, and disclosing thousands of pages of private documents; appearing at maddening mediation sessions where both sides are convinced they're victims; and, finally, if a settlement doesn't happen, doing it all over again in a public courtroom, followed by years of costly appeals. Plus paying tens to hundreds of thousands of dollars or more for the privilege. It's not fun. Or maybe it is.

The cases I'd been handling were intellectually interesting with lots of money at stake and lots of fees for me. It wasn't just the money or the challenge that hooked me, though. I loved what my clients loved—the pleasure of putting opposing parties and their lawyers through the ringer. My clients and I plotted ways to increase the costs, pressure, and pain on the other side to bend to our will. The more the other side retaliated by increasing the costs, pressure, and pain on us, the more we cranked up the pain in retaliation in an endless cycle. My clients and I reveled in knowing each day that we were making life a bit more miserable for our opponents, and our opponents indicated that they enjoyed making our lives more miserable too. The job of the lawyers on both sides was to deliver the maximal dose of revenge ("justice") allowed by law.

I loved being a legal bully. This was the role reversal I'd been seeking since my teenage years of being a bully victim. Only later, as a researcher, did I learn about studies showing that victims of bullying are at greater risk than others of becoming bullies themselves.[1] Being a bully also comes with costs. I'd grown darker and more vengeful in my personal and family life, and exhausted and bruised from inflicting and receiving all that pain. I also felt an increasing sense of guilt about making my opponents suffer. My legal maneuvers were all perfectly legitimate—taught, practiced, and encouraged by lawyers everywhere. I began to question what I was accomplishing with my life. Yes, I was a member of a learned profession. But when I thought more deeply about why I was doing it, the gratification I was receiving, the negative effects it was having on my relationships and mental health, and the unbreakable grip it had on me, it seemed that I was nothing more than a junkie shooting up in a courtroom and looking for the next hit.

So, I put all these concerns and anxieties to my good friend Dr.

Nulton. He was skeptical of my theory and gently reassured me that I was not a revenge addict. "I think you've just been working too hard, Jim," he offered. "Maybe you need a break."

Maybe. But I was convinced there was more to it and asked him how psychologists diagnose people with addiction. He explained that "addiction" isn't really a diagnosis. Doctors call drug and alcohol addiction a "substance use disorder" and gambling addiction a "gambling disorder." In the United States, doctors use criteria published by the American Psychiatric Association in a book of nomenclature called the *Diagnostic and Statistical Manual of Mental Disorders* (*DSM*) to evaluate and diagnose patients. This piqued my interest. I asked him if he had a spare copy he could send me. After insisting that I'd benefit more from taking a vacation than reading the nearly thousand pages of the *DSM*, he relented.

When the *DSM* arrived in the mail, I turned to the section on substance use disorders and found a list of eleven diagnostic criteria that doctors use to evaluate whether a patient has an addiction. Here's a summary of them from the most recent edition of the *DSM*, called the *DSM-5, Text Revision*.[2]

DSM CRITERIA FOR SUBSTANCE USE DISORDER

- using more of a substance (or for longer periods) than intended
- inability to cut down or stop using a substance
- increased time getting/using/recovering from a substance
- cravings and urges for a substance
- unfulfilled responsibilities because of using a substance
- using a substance despite relationship problems
- giving up important activities for a substance
- using a substance even when it puts you in danger
- using a substance even when it is harming you

- needing more of a substance to achieve the same effect

- developing substance withdrawal symptoms

If a patient has experienced two or three of these symptoms in the past year, the *DSM* says they should be diagnosed as having a "mild" substance use disorder. Having four or five of these symptoms in the past year indicates a "moderate" substance use disorder. Having six or more indicates a "severe" substance use disorder.

Hmm. What if, I wondered, I replaced the term "substance" in this list with the word "revenge" to create some hypothetical criteria for "revenge use disorder"? Here's what that looks like:

HYPOTHETICAL CRITERIA FOR "REVENGE USE DISORDER"

- using more revenge (or for longer periods) than intended

- inability to cut down or stop using revenge

- increased time getting/using/recovering from revenge

- cravings and urges for revenge

- unfulfilled responsibilities because of using revenge

- using revenge despite relationship problems

- giving up important activities for revenge

- using revenge even when it puts you in danger

- using revenge even when it is harming you

- needing more revenge to achieve the same effect

- developing revenge withdrawal symptoms

Of these eleven symptoms, I knew I had experienced at least seven during the past year. This would mean I had a *severe* "revenge use disorder."

I reported my findings to Dr. Nulton. He cautioned me that this is no way to discover new disorders, let alone self-diagnose myself with one. And he's correct, and you shouldn't, and I'm not recommending it. But my approach aligns with the process scientists use to answer novel questions, employing the scientific method of making observations, forming hypotheses, developing predictions, and conducting experiments to test them. Without necessarily trying to, I had gone through the first three steps of the scientific method—observation, hypothesis, and prediction. Sort of like building a case for trial, which I had plenty of experience doing. Now I needed to conduct an experiment to test my hypothesis and prediction that revenge can be addictive. But how? At this point, I was a despondent lawyer with no access to a laboratory.

PROVIDENCE SMILES

"At this point" was July 2004. That's when *The New York Times* reported on an article published in the journal *Science* about the results of an experiment conducted by the neuroscientists Dominique de Quervain, Urs Fischbacher, Valerie Treyer, Melanie Schellhammer, Ulrich Schnyder, Alfred Buck, and Ernst Fehr at the University of Zurich.[3] They wondered why people willingly incur costs to punish people who violate social norms (for example, violating someone's trust) when they receive no material benefit in return. In other words, why do we want to harm the people who harm us when we receive nothing and it costs us something to do it?

The researchers hypothesized that the explanation for this must be that punishers gain some form of satisfaction from punishing people that exceeds the cost of doing the punishing. If this is so, the researchers predicted that an area of the brain called the dorsal striatum should activate when planning revenge. Why the dorsal striatum? Because it's closely associated with goal-directed behavior, habit formation, and the brain's reward and satisfaction circuitry of *addiction*.

Bingo.

By sheer coincidence, these Swiss researchers had just conducted the experiment I would have wanted to conduct if I were that brilliant. Using positron emission tomography (PET scans), they observed the brains of fifteen male study participants while playing an economic version of the prisoner's dilemma.[4] This is a thought experiment in which two bank robbers are arrested, separated, and offered a catch-22 deal by the prosecutor. If one confesses and the other remains silent, the confessor goes free, and the one who remains silent receives a long jail sentence. If they both confess, they both receive moderate jail sentences. But if they both remain silent, they both receive light jail sentences. The dilemma is that each robber is incentivized to confess, but if they both confess, the outcome is worse than if they both remain silent.

In the economic version of this game used in the study, pairs of participants, A and B, were each given ten money units (MUs) at the start of the game and encouraged to trust each other to increase this number. If A trusts B and gives B their ten MUs, B receives a bonus of thirty MUs, leaving B with a total of fifty MUs but A with nothing. If B honors A's trust, B should share half the windfall and give A twenty-five MUs, making them even. But B can betray A's trust by keeping all fifty MUs. Either way, at this stage both players are given an additional twenty MUs. If B has betrayed A, A is given the option to punish B—by paying twenty MUs to force B to forfeit up to forty MUs. In other words, A can get revenge, but it will bankrupt A, making revenge highly costly.

During the study, in the cases where B players betrayed A players and A players were deciding whether to spend their MUs to punish the B players, the researchers scanned the brains of the A players. Among the A players who used their MUs to punish B players, the brain scans confirmed the researchers' hypothesis: increased activation of the dorsal striatum—a core component of the brain's pleasure and reward circuitry. The scans also revealed activation of the medial orbitofrontal cortex, which is associated with the weighing of difficult choices based on reward values. These findings demonstrated for the first time at the brain-biological level that people seek revenge in anticipation of experiencing satisfaction or pleasure that outweighs the costs.

Tears welled up in my eyes when I read about this study. It didn't establish the existence of revenge addiction. In fact, the researchers made no mention of addiction at all. But the study did provide the first scientific evidence that I might be on the right track.

I received more scientific evidence two years later. The researchers Tania Singer, Ben Seymour, Klaas Stephan, Raymond Dolan, and Chris Frith at University College London, and John O'Doherty at the California Institute of Technology, performed a study using functional magnetic resonance imaging (fMRI) to scan the brains of male and female participants during a similar version of the prisoner's dilemma.[5] Unlike the de Quervain study, however, these researchers were looking at what happens when study participants merely *watch* players being fairly and unfairly punished by other players with the application of electrical shocks to their hands.

The researchers wanted to determine whether the participants maintain empathy with those being punished. Empathy means to share the feelings of another person, and this would be assessed during the study by monitoring the brain's "pain network"—the anterior insula/fronto-insular cortex and anterior cingulate cortex of the brain. The theory is that an empathic person watching another person in pain will experience activation of the same brain structures even though they're not in pain themselves. Hoping to extend the findings of the de Quervain study, the researchers also predicted activation of the nucleus accumbens—another core component of the brain's reward circuitry of addiction closely associated with craving and pleasure.

Bingo again.

What the researchers found is fascinating. First, as predicted, the brain scans revealed activation of the "pain network" in men and women observing another person in pain, demonstrating brain-biological empathy.[6] But when the person being observed was in pain because they were being *punished* for playing the game unfairly—

in other words, because the pain was being inflicted as an act of revenge—these pain structures remained *inactive in men but active in women,* providing evidence that men lose their ability to empathize with those who are being "justly" punished. This may explain why men seem to be more punitive than women and willing to continue punishing despite signs of suffering by those being punished.

The second important finding of the Singer study is that the nucleus accumbens pleasure and craving center activated in men, but not women, while *watching* somebody being punished. This extends the de Quervain study by demonstrating at a brain-biological level that in men the reward circuitry of satisfaction and craving, which activates for substance addiction, is activated by merely *seeing* acts of revenge. This may explain why males can't take their eyes off villain-destroying superhero movies and revenge-fueled video games. And perhaps why, in addition to genetic, hormonal, and cultural factors, males engage in more violence than females. As with the de Quervain study, however, Singer and colleagues made no mention of addiction.

OUT OF THE SHADOWS

We're addicted to revenge! I shouted at nobody while sitting alone in my office after reading the Singer study. *That's why we hurt the people who hurt us! Why aren't you talking about that in your research!?*

I guess I felt aggrieved. But then I realized that de Quervain, Singer, and their colleagues weren't trying to make a connection between revenge, violence, and addiction. They were investigating an entirely different question: whether "altruistic punishment"—meaning punishment without personal benefit and at a personal cost—was crucial in the evolution of human cooperation. That's certainly a question worth investigating, but the practical value of it for humans living today—that this might be an addictive process—was beyond the scope of their inquiry. I needed to find addiction scientists, not evolutionary theorists, who could look at these data, compare them with my revenge addiction theory, and tell me whether I was crazy.

I did some investigating and discovered that one of the leading addiction neuroscientists in the world, Anna Rose Childress, is the director of the Brain-Behavioral Vulnerabilities Laboratory of the Center for Studies of Addiction at the University of Pennsylvania— my law school alma mater and only about an hour from where I lived. Dr. Childress is a recognized expert in the brain substrates of reward, motivation, pleasure, craving, and addiction—and something of a celebrity who's appeared on talk shows, on news broadcasts, and in film documentaries about addiction. I also discovered that just about an hour and a half from where I lived in the opposite direction is the neuroscientist Paul Eslinger at The Pennsylvania State University, my undergraduate alma mater. Dr. Eslinger is an expert on the frontal lobe and executive function areas of the brain.

It turns out that about six months after the Singer study, Dr. Childress, together with researchers from the Brookhaven National Laboratory and the National Institute on Alcohol Abuse and Alcoholism, published a study demonstrating that when cocaine addicts are merely shown images of people preparing to smoke crack cocaine, they experience strong cocaine craving and increased dopamine release in the dorsal striatum—the habit, motivation, and compulsion area of the brain that was the subject of the de Quervain study.[7] Two years later, Dr. Childress and her colleagues from the University of Pennsylvania demonstrated that the nucleus accumbens—the craving and pleasure area of the brain that was the subject of the Singer study—activates in the brains of cocaine users in response to mere *thirty-three-millisecond* flashes of images of people using cocaine, flashes so brief that they're considered outside the range of conscious awareness.[8]

Dr. Childress and Dr. Eslinger were obviously the scientists I needed to talk to—if they would listen to me.

I figured I could increase my odds of that happening if I had something to offer. While snooping around, I'd learned that the Pennsylvania Department of Health (PA DOH) was in the process of funding new biomedical research with millions of dollars recovered from tobacco companies for addicting people to nicotine. Maybe the PA DOH would want to use some of that money to fund a study into whether revenge is addictive?

I sent an email to Drs. Childress and Eslinger dangling this prospect while explaining my revenge addiction theory and describing the studies I'd found. I expected them to ignore me—or to agree with Dr. Nulton that what I really needed was a vacation. Instead, they both emailed back that I might be onto something, and they wanted to talk further.

For me, this was like meeting rock stars. I remember three things from my initial phone conversation with Dr. Childress. First, talking to her was like being plugged into a supercomputer. Second, she wanted to partner with me to apply for a PA DOH grant to study the brain biology of reward and revenge. Third, and I'm only paraphrasing here because this was about fourteen years ago, Dr. Childress said something like this: "When I read your email and the studies you sent, thirty years of my addiction research snapped into place. We're learning that some people seem to be vulnerable to addiction in general, not just drug addiction. Evolution wired the human brain to seek rewards like food and sex necessary for survival. That's the GO! signal that tells you to get the reward that might save your life or help you procreate."

"You mean like, go kill that bear," I quipped, "and then invite that woman back to your cave for a drink?"

"Yes. And in most people, this is modulated by the STOP! signal from the brain's frontal circuitry that thinks things through. This signal acts like a brake on reward seeking that could harm you. So, if the bear is angry and you don't have your best spear with you, you'd better cut and run."

"Got it."

The problem is that the brains of some people seem to respond almost automatically to the GO! signal. They're stepping on the gas without worrying about smashing into the wall in front of them. Speed can be good. Chucking a spear faster than other hunters can mean the difference between survival and starvation. But it's a disaster when the reward is cocaine, heroin, or revenge. In addition, being unable to hit the brake might increase your vulnerability to relapse, meaning that even when you've learned your lesson and you're back in control, if the right external cue comes along, you're back on the gas again with your STOP! circuitry hijacked and gagged in the backseat.

My initial conversation with Dr. Eslinger, whose expertise is in studying the brake that stops you from slamming into the wall, was every bit as intellectually stimulating if slightly less colorful. He too was interested in partnering with Dr. Childress and me to seek research funding to study reward and revenge.

More bingos.

The three of us quickly put together a grant application. We framed the question we wanted to research as whether brain science can predict and prevent violence. In support of the grant, we argued that brain imaging data show that violence and substance use are "co-travelers" in the addiction brain circuitry of reward impulses (GO!) and reward inhibition (STOP!). Hypersensitivity to rewards that overwhelm compromised inhibition circuitry may lead to compulsive drug taking and/or compulsive revenge-fueled violence despite the negative consequences. This could result from genetic factors, early trauma, or biopsychosocial and environmental circumstances. Our proposed study would scan the brains of substance-addicted young male criminal offenders and non-addicted, non-offending control groups to determine whether individuals with weakened prefrontal control (STOP!) circuitry and hyperactive nucleus accumbens, dorsal striatum, and amygdala (GO!) circuitry have an increased likelihood of becoming aggressive or punishing others. This would be assessed by analyzing their criminal backgrounds and using fMRI brain scans during laboratory tasks designed to provoke grievances and revenge urges.

Our application was strong enough to garner the support of Thomas McLellan, one of the big-name scientists discussed earlier who validated Alan Leshner's brain disease model of addiction. Dr. McLellan was later appointed by President Barack Obama the deputy director of the Office of National Drug Control Policy. He authorized his organization, the Treatment Research Institute, to join our application and contribute one of its senior addiction and criminal justice scientists, David Festinger, to our team. My dream was about to come true.

I'd like to report that this story has a happy ending. Alas, despite all our intellectual firepower and effort, the university, for political reasons, advanced a different researcher's project for the PA DOH grant over ours—a frustrating but not uncommon occurrence in academic research. However, the process opened doors that could not be closed. In 2009, Dr. Childress, Dr. Eslinger, and I were invited to testify about our revenge addiction research before the Health Research Advisory Committee of the PA DOH. Three years later, Dr. Childress and her laboratory, with me serving as an adviser, were awarded a different multimillion-dollar PA DOH grant to create the Addiction Center of Excellence at Penn to study the brain mechanisms of relapse and recovery. This wasn't the revenge addiction research I'd been pushing for, but it was a start.

INTO THE JAILS

I circled back to my friend Dr. Nulton to update him on what I'd been doing. Intrigued, he said he had been thinking about launching a new type of mental health and addiction agency that would help people recover from mental illnesses and co-occurring substance use disorders by employing peer support specialists—people with a lived experience of recovery who mentor others in their recoveries. What if we joined forces and included revenge addiction on the menu of services? People with mental illnesses and addiction often struggle with grievances and revenge desires, and they're all too often caught up in the criminal justice system, leading to poor outcomes and lives of despair. One of the goals for our new agency could be to help those in prison and reduce their risk of reincarceration after release, which is extremely high: Nearly 68 percent of people with mental illnesses and addiction return to jail within four years of getting out.[9] Maybe we could even place our peer support specialists inside jails to begin services prior to release? We would train them to use my Nonjustice System "12-step program" for recovering from revenge addiction that I'd written about in *Suing for Peace.*

It all made sense, but we didn't have experience operating peer support programs in the criminal justice system, so we'd need help. I started searching for experts. The two names that kept popping up were Michael Rowe, PhD, and Larry Davidson, PhD, then co-directors of the renowned Program for Recovery and Community Health (PRCH) at the Yale School of Medicine. I emailed them, explained what we wanted to do and my work with Drs. Childress and Eslinger, and asked if they would consult with us. By this point, my confidence had grown, and I expected a positive response. Sure enough, they immediately understood the potential of our program and offered to help—although they, too, had never heard of the de Quervain and Singer studies, making these studies perhaps the best-kept secrets in all of addiction science.

Dr. Nulton and I traveled to Yale. Dr. Rowe is an erudite, icono-clastic medical sociologist who sees connections others miss and revels in pushing boundaries and knocking down walls. Dr. Davidson, a research psychologist, is a luminary in the world of mental health recovery and transformation who also expands boundaries and knocks down walls. They gave us a tour of the Yale PRCH facilities and recovery programs and arranged meetings with their über-talented colleagues Patricia Benedict and Dr. Chyrell Bellamy, now the director of Yale PRCH.

A few months later, a team from Yale traveled to our location in central Pennsylvania for a week to help us develop our program. I served as the trainer of The Nonjustice System. When this was complete, Dr. Nulton and I set off around Pennsylvania to persuade wardens, judges, district attorneys, public defenders, probation officers, and county officials to let us inside their jails. The response to our program was enthusiastic—until we asked them to pay for it. This is often the problem when trying to improve conditions for incarcerated people. We were prepared and said we'd offer the in-jail component of the program free to prove the concept. The gates opened. We ended up running our program in seven different county jails and mentoring hundreds of inmates before release.

The agency that Dr. Nulton and I founded has gone on to become the largest mental health peer support organization in Pennsylvania. We launched our forensic peer support community reentry program in 2010. A Yale PRCH study of the program published in the *Journal of Public Health* showed success: The reincarceration rate for participants in our program during their first year after release was cut by nearly half compared with the reincarceration rate of inmates in the overall U.S. jail and prison population.[10]

NEW EVIDENCE

While all this was happening, researchers in the Netherlands, at the National Institute of Mental Health in the United States, and at six different universities in Germany were busy conducting a new experiment that supported my revenge addiction theory. Alexander Strobel, Jan Zimmermann, Anja Schmitz, Martin Reuter, Stefanie Lis, Sabine Windmann, and Peter Kirsch used fMRI to scan the brains of twenty-four male and female college students playing the dictator game.[11] In this game, players A, the "dictators," started off with 20 euros each and were allowed to decide whether to split this amount with players B (the study participants) while knowing the B players could punish them if they made unfair splits. Players B started off with 10.50 euros each, which they could either keep for themselves or spend to punish unfair splits made by players A. In other words, players B would need to pay from their own allotment to get revenge. Cleverly, the researchers chose for the study an almost equal number of students with and without a genetic variation in dopamine processing that produces higher than normal levels of dopamine in the nucleus accumbens and dorsal striatum (the GO! circuitry) during reward anticipation. The researchers also ran a portion of the study with players B merely *watching* players A making unfair splits against a group of players C and deciding whether to punish the A players.

Based on the de Quervain study, the researchers hypothesized increased activation of the dorsal striatum and nucleus accumbens when study participants (players B) punished versus did not punish players A, and even stronger activation in these structures when participants were directly victimized by unfair splits versus only watching others being treated unfairly. In the latter case, the researchers hypothesized increased activation of the dorsolateral prefrontal cortex—an executive function brain center involved in cognitive control and decision making (the STOP! circuitry)[12]—as participants weighed the conflicting goals of punishing players A versus keeping their money since they were not victims themselves and merely watching. The researchers also hypothesized stronger nucleus accumbens, dorsal striatum, and dorsolateral prefrontal cortex activation in study subjects with the genetic variation that yields higher than normal dopamine levels during reward anticipation.[13]

The results of the study confirmed these hypotheses. The more unfair the splits made by players A (that is, the more money players A kept for themselves), the more players B were willing to pay to punish them, including even bankrupting themselves for the satisfaction of getting revenge. The fMRI brain scans revealed increased activation of the nucleus accumbens, dorsal striatum, and dorsolateral prefrontal cortex during punishment. Nucleus accumbens activation was more pronounced when players B were direct victims of unfair splits versus merely watching. Dorsal striatum activation was greatest when the punishments were the most severe. Study subjects with the genetic variation yielding higher levels of dopamine during reward anticipation experienced greater activation in the nucleus accumbens, suggesting that individuals with this genetic variation might be more susceptible than others to reward-driven revenge. Notably, *no differences* were observed between male and female study participants, indicating that females experience the same reward effects from seeking revenge even though, as shown in the Singer study, they remain more empathic than males to the suffering of those being punished.

Strobel and colleagues interpreted these results as confirming and extending the de Quervain and Singer studies. They concluded that "violations of personal interest" (grievances) trigger the reward circuitry of the brain, motivating punishment in anticipation of experiencing satisfaction from taking revenge.[14]

Two years later, in 2013, these findings were replicated by yet another group of German researchers using fMRI brain scans.[15] That same year, a different group of researchers from Cambridge University, the University of Zurich, the Joint Research Centre of the European Commission, and the University of California, Los Angeles performed an fMRI study that confirmed the de Quervain and Strobel findings and, further, demonstrated "a causal role for the [dorsal striatum] in retaliatory motives."[16] They also showed that serotonin—a neurotransmitter associated with social behavior—helps to regulate retaliation such that manipulating serotonin levels in the brain appears to "reduce aversion" to retaliation "to the extent that it may even be pleasurable in certain contexts."

A RESEARCHER IS BORN

It was now 2014. Time to take stock. Ten years had passed since I'd begun my scientific journey. The neuroscience evidence supporting my revenge addiction theory had grown significantly, but it was far from established. Progress was agonizingly slow. I'd written two books on the topic, but the public barely noticed. I'd collaborated with world-leading addiction researchers to fund a study to prove the existence of revenge addiction, but university politics torpedoed it. I'd co-founded a mental health agency to put my Nonjustice System revenge addiction program into practice, but criminal justice and mental health authorities wouldn't fund it.

All the while, compulsive revenge seeking was running rampant. Among the revenge-fueled world headlines from 2014: a soldier killing three people at Fort Hood before committing suicide; a mass shooter killing six at the University of California, Santa Barbara; police killing an unarmed Black man in a choke hold; an investigation revealing that the CIA tortured detainees after the terrorist attacks of 9/11; three botched executions by lethal injection in Arizona, Ohio, and Oklahoma; ISIS seizing cities in Iraq and decapitating Western prisoners on video; mass killers in Kunming, China, slaughtering 28 and wounding 113; militants kidnapping more than 270 girls from a boarding school in Nigeria; Palestinians murdering three Israeli teens; Israelis retaliating with the murder of a Palestinian boy and wide-scale violence erupting in Gaza, leaving more than 2,100 Palestinians and 65 Israelis dead; the Olympic sprinter Oscar Pistorius convicted of murdering his girlfriend, Reeva Steenkamp; and Taliban gunmen attacking a school in Pakistan, killing 145 students.

I couldn't give up now.

What if, I wondered, I moved further from the practice of law and joined a university to become a revenge and violence researcher? Maybe I could advance the field if I was on the inside. But I was fifty years old at this point, with my own kids entering college. Heading back to school (*with them?*) for four years or more to get a PhD would take time and money I didn't have.

Then this question: Did I need a PhD to conduct revenge and violence research? I already had a doctoral degree. I was a juris doctor, a doctor of law. That's the degree that gave me the special license to prescribe, manufacture, and distribute legalized revenge. Not even PhDs or MDs can do that. Who better to research revenge than a lawyer neck-deep in it?

I pitched this very unorthodox idea to the benevolently rebellious Dr. Rowe at Yale. Here's how I remember our conversation, paraphrasing because it was some time ago:

Me: "Hi, Michael. I've been thinking about affiliating with a university to research my revenge addiction theory and The Nonjustice System."

"Good idea," he said.

Well, that was easier than I thought. But did he really mean it? Might as well swing for the fences. . . .

"I've been thinking about Yale. Maybe I could join you, Larry, and Chyrell?"

"Sure, why not?"

I couldn't believe my ears.

"Really?"

Dr. Rowe made my case for me. "You've got a doctorate from Penn. You've got experience developing, operating, and researching forensic peer support programs, which is what we do at PRCH. You've developed a novel intervention that combines psychology and jurisprudence to help people overcome destructive revenge desires. There's nothing like it anywhere, and it's obviously needed. We should have you here to study it. I'll make it happen."

And that was that. PRCH's co-director Larry Davidson and the chair of the Yale Department of Psychiatry, Professor John Krystal, MD, signed off on my academic appointment to the position of lecturer of psychiatry. They also signed off on my idea of founding the Yale Collaborative for Motive Control Studies to house my research. I'll be forever grateful to each of them. I'd somehow gone from being a farm kid holding a gun on his classmates to becoming the first person in my family to graduate from college, then on to law school and a career as a lawyer increasingly convinced that compulsive revenge seeking is the world's deadliest addiction. Now I was being given an opportunity to prove it at one of the greatest research universities in the world.

CHAPTER 3

THIS IS YOUR BRAIN ON REVENGE

The first experiment I conducted with my new Yale colleagues was designed to test whether my Nonjustice System virtual courtroom role play reduces revenge cravings.[1] To do that, we needed to have a perpetrator do something rotten to our study participants to activate revenge cravings inside their brains. We obviously couldn't just slap them in the face; we didn't want them craving revenge against *us*. We had to come up with an ethical and safe way of provoking revenge feelings that could be standardized and measured across all participants. In other words, we needed to "infect" them with a grievance.

To demonstrate how we did it, and how easy it is to cause just about anybody to crave revenge, I'm going to infect you right now with the same grievance we used in the study. Don't worry, I won't be injecting you with a dangerous bacterium or virus. It's just a short story I wrote, a fictional grievance scenario. It worked so well in triggering revenge cravings that we now use it for revenge addiction education, prevention, treatment, and training and in group sessions using The Nonjustice System.

The grievance scenario starts below, but first a word of caution. Although the events are fictitious and there are no graphic words or images, it involves a disturbing situation involving a beloved pet that could cause you to experience strong negative emotions. As you read it, notice what happens inside you.

THE STORY OF BILLY

This is a picture of your dog, Harley, and cat, Lucy.

You rescued Harley and Lucy from an animal shelter when they were young. They both had been abused by their prior owners. Because you care deeply for animals, you took them into your home and nursed them back to health. You love them very much, and they love you. And they obviously love each other.

Harley and Lucy are the sweetest, most gentle pets in the world. They bring you joy and happiness whenever you see them.

This is your neighbor Billy. You've known Billy for about a year but not very well. He seems like a decent enough guy and keeps mostly to himself. And he has a dog.

There's just one problem. . . . This is Billy's dog, King. Everybody in the neighborhood fears King. He's even tried to attack Harley and Lucy several times.

One day, Billy came to your door. He said he was in a real jam. He was being called away unexpectedly for a couple of days, and the person who normally watches King was away too. Billy asked if you could take care of King at his house—just come over and give him some food and water and let him out a couple of times a day.

You were reluctant. But Billy kept begging you and saying how good you are with dogs—and that King is really very sweet and gentle when you get to know him. Billy also offered to return the favor anytime. You wanted to be nice, so you said okay. Billy was very happy and very grateful to you.

You took good care of King while Billy was away. You fed him twice a day and even took him to the park to play, leaving Harley and Lucy behind. King did seem like a nice dog once you got to know him. When Billy returned from his trip, you gave him this picture of King from your day together at the park. Billy was thrilled.

A month later, you found yourself in the same jam as Billy. You were called out of town on a family emergency, and the person who normally watches Harley and Lucy for you wasn't available. So, you asked Billy if he could help you out. Billy said, sure, absolutely, he was happy to return the favor and take care of Harley and Lucy for you.

When you got home from your trip a couple of days later, you found Lucy, your cat, sleeping in her normal spot, but Harley was missing. You called Billy and asked if he had Harley. Billy said he was very sorry, but Harley had escaped when he took him for a walk at the park. Billy felt terrible. He had been looking everywhere for Harley but couldn't find him.

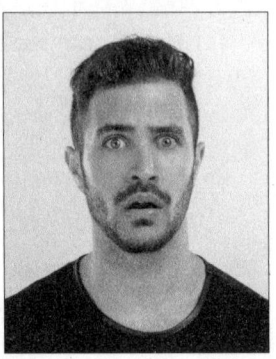

You were frantic to find Harley. You searched all through the night and all through the next day. You put up posters and called animal shelters. Billy helped you. He drove around searching for Harley and putting up posters too. You were desperate to find Harley and reunite your family.

Two weeks passed. Harley was still missing. Billy had given up searching for him. You were heartsick and didn't know what else to do. Poor Lucy seemed heartsick too. She wouldn't sleep and kept pacing all through the night. You were worried that you'd never see Harley and Lucy together again.

The next day, you received a call from a man named Sean who said he was a friend of Billy's. Sean sounded drunk or high and asked if you could get him another bait dog as you did for Billy a couple of weeks ago. You said you didn't know what Sean was talking about. Sean explained how much he and Billy loved dogfighting and how Billy's dog, King, was the best fighter around. Sean said that Billy showed him his secret to training King a couple of weeks ago by putting a weak, scrawny bait dog into a ring with King and provoking King to kill it. Sean said that it worked great because King attacked the dog and snapped its neck almost instantly. Sean said Billy told him that he got the bait dog from you, and that you got it from a local animal shelter. Sean asked again if you could get a bait dog for him.

You were shocked by what Sean said and immediately went to Billy and confronted him. Billy denied that he engaged in dogfighting and acted offended and outraged that you would accuse him of harming Harley.

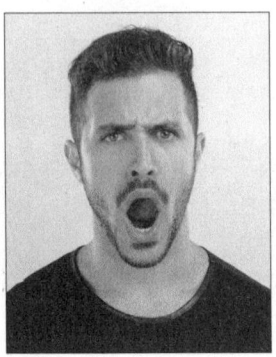

You didn't believe Billy. He was acting suspicious. And you remembered that when you were watching King, you had noticed some equipment in Billy's house that looked as if it could be used for dogfighting. You threatened to call the police unless Billy told you the truth.

Billy finally admitted that he had put Harley into the ring with King and that King killed him. Billy said he threw Harley's dead body in a dumpster. Billy wasn't sorry he did it. He became angry and threatening and said that he would harm you if you told anyone that he was engaged in illegal dogfighting.

So, how do you feel? Do you want revenge against Billy?

Most of our study participants did. My research team included Michael Rowe, Chyrell Bellamy, Maria O'Connell, Kimberly Blackman, Luz Ocasio, Anthony Pavlo, Miraj Desai, and Elizabeth Flanagan. We recruited thirty-six people who self-disclosed having experienced intrusive revenge desires during the prior six months against someone who had harmed them.[2] We measured participants' revenge desires before and after reading the Billy story using a tool called the Transgression-Related Interpersonal Motivations Inventory, which is a validated series of questions that require individuals to respond on a scale of 1 to 5 assessing their motivation to seek revenge against, avoid, or show benevolence toward a person who has wronged them. As we predicted, the results of our study showed that after reading the story, most participants experienced soaring revenge desires toward Billy and plummeting feelings of benevolence. The results also showed that after our study participants put Billy on trial in The Nonjustice System for his crimes, their revenge desires decreased significantly, and their feelings of benevolence increased—exactly as we had hoped. I discuss these results in more detail in chapter 10, and in chapter 11 you'll have the opportunity to put Billy on trial yourself using The Nonjustice System.

After the results of our study were published, Michael Norko, MD, the Yale forensic psychiatrist, professor, and past president of the American Academy of Psychiatry and the Law, invited me to speak at the American Psychiatric Association's annual convention in New York City. In a room packed with around a hundred psychiatrists, I put the story of Billy up on a screen and then led them through a trial of Billy in The Nonjustice System in which they played the roles of victim, prosecutor, judge, jury, warden, and judge of their own lives. After unanimously convicting Billy of animal cruelty and other offenses as the jury, they were given the opportunity, as the judge, to sentence him to a term of punishment. The sentence that drew the most enthusiastic cheers was that Billy should be locked inside a cage with vicious dogs and torn to pieces.

Remember, these were *psychiatrists* trained to be compassionate, not murderers.

Would the psychiatrists actually have done such a thing if Harley was their dog and Billy a real person? Unlikely. Their well-developed prefrontal cortexes would have intervened to STOP! them long before they assembled a pack of dogs to devour him. They might have fantasized about it briefly but then moved on to more productive thoughts and actions, knowing that revenge like this would only destroy them by turning them into perpetrators of the very cruelty and violence they abhorred. Indeed, in the final step of The Nonjustice System, where they played the role of judge of their own lives, most of them released their revenge desires. But we should have no doubt that revenge in some form is what the reward circuitry of their brains wanted. And we should be aware that not everyone, even a psychiatrist, has a fully functioning prefrontal cortex capable of restraining runaway reward circuitry when it's needed. Consider the horrific case of the army psychiatrist Nidal Hasan, who, on November 5, 2009, murdered thirteen people and injured thirty-one others, most of them unarmed soldiers, at the Fort Hood, Texas, army base in retaliation for America's war in Afghanistan and being forced to deploy there against his will.[3]

THE NEUROBIOLOGY OF REVENGE

So, what's going on inside your brain while reading the story of Billy? We didn't have the funding to perform expensive fMRI scans during our study. However, in a laboratory at the University of Kentucky at about the same time, the researchers David Chester and Nathan DeWall were scanning the brains of sixty-nine undergraduates to see what was happening when they were unjustly subjected to painful noise blasts and given the opportunity to seek revenge.[4] Chester and DeWall wanted to know whether people engage in retaliatory aggression because they're seeking hedonic reward (pleasure) in response to a grievance (pain).

More than a century ago, Sigmund Freud raised eyebrows by proposing that anger builds up inside us and, if it's not released through cathartic acts of aggression, can cause psychological disorders.[5] Although this "hydraulic" metaphor of violence has long been disproven in the scientific literature,[6] Freud might have been onto something. More recent studies have reported that participants subjectively rate retaliatory aggression as being more pleasurable than unprovoked aggression.[7] And, as we've been discussing, the de Quervain, Singer, and Strobel studies provide brain-biological evidence for this. So, it's not that anger "builds up" in your brain like an overfired steam boiler. The science of revenge suggests that anger-producing grievances are painful.[8] We're desperate to feel better, and we do this by seeking revenge to get the pleasure and "release" that Freud describes from our brain's reward circuitry.

Freud didn't have the benefit of neuroscience to test his theory of violence, but Chester and DeWall did. They pointed out that the Strobel and related studies of revenge involved only economic injury, falling short of retaliatory *aggression*—that is, the deliberate infliction of some form of physical or psychological harm upon a transgressor. To fill this gap in the research, they went to ear-piercing lengths. They pitted the undergraduates in their study against fictional opponents during a computer game to see who could press a button faster, with the loser receiving painful noise blasts at volumes chosen by their opponents. The students were able to see on a computer screen whether their opponents tried to blast them with aggressively high-volume levels or more gentle, low-volume levels. In later rounds, the students were given the opportunity to retaliate by blasting their opponents back. Sort of like Billy killing your dog and you getting an opportunity to make him pay.

Chester and DeWall noted that neuroscience studies have long established the nucleus accumbens as the brain structure "most reliably associated with the subjective experience of hedonic reward and pleasure"—part of the GO! circuitry.[9] They also referenced studies showing that the brain's ventrolateral prefrontal cortex inhibits both the nucleus accumbens and aggression—part of the STOP! circuitry. They therefore predicted that during the experiment the nucleus accumbens would be most active among participants who chose to fight fire with fire by launching painful noise blasts, and that functional connectivity between the ventrolateral prefrontal cortex and the nucleus accumbens would be greatest among students who decided not to retaliate—indicating that they were being STOP!-ed from seeking revenge. To determine whether students were, in fact, experiencing pleasure during nucleus accumbens activation, the researchers asked them to complete a tool called the Angry Mood Improvement Inventory, which is a series of questions that measure whether aggression is motivated by a desire to feel better. (Sample item: "To improve my mood when I am upset, I strike out at whatever angers me.")[10]

The fMRI brain scans confirmed Chester and DeWall's predictions. The scans revealed increased nucleus accumbens activity among students who sought maximal revenge by trying to deafen their opponents. Scores on the Angry Mood Improvement Inventory indicated that these noise avengers were indeed seeking pleasure—either in anticipation of or while getting revenge. Conversely, increased functional connectivity between the nucleus accumbens and the ventrolateral prefrontal cortex occurred most among those students who didn't retaliate, suggesting that the STOP! circuit was controlling their revenge cravings.

This research gives us a picture of what's probably happening inside your brain when you read the Billy story—or anytime you have a grievance and start jonesing for revenge. The research also went about 90 percent of the way toward corroborating my theory of revenge addiction. Chester and DeWall even used the word "addiction," concluding that treatments targeting aggression "should adopt practices from addiction treatment models that often seek to mitigate the role of cravings and anticipated reward."[11]

That's incredibly encouraging. In 2017, I was able to persuade the Pennsylvania Psychological Association to become the first professional mental health organization to adopt a resolution acknowledging that revenge seeking may be addictive and calling for research into addiction-informed public health approaches for controlling violence.[12]

STABBING TO FEEL BETTER

What if you're like the psychiatrists at the New York convention center who wanted Billy locked in a cage and torn to shreds? In a later study with 132 undergraduates, Chester and DeWall took a step toward explaining retaliatory violence.[13] The students were invited to toss a virtual Cyberball on a computer screen with two fictitious partners. After playing nicely for several rounds with everyone receiving equal tosses, the two partners started tossing the ball only between themselves, excluding the students from the fun. The students were then asked to complete a tool called the Need Threat Scale, a set of questions that measure the subjective experience of social rejection, which is considered very painful.

After this, the students were asked to complete a Voodoo Doll Task. For this task, they were shown an image of a voodoo doll on a computer screen and told to imagine that it represents one of the partners who rejected them. As they watched the voodoo doll, an increasing number of pins were stabbed into it, ending with nineteen pins in total—*yikes!* The students were asked to indicate how many pins they wanted to stab into their partners. They were then asked to complete the Angry Mood Improvement Inventory to determine whether stabbing their Cyberball partners was motivated by their hurt feelings and an attempt to repair their moods through the pleasure of revenge.

Chester and DeWall don't report exactly how many pins the students wanted to plunge into those poor dolls—perhaps because it might cause alarm among people who interact with University of Kentucky students. But the published results of the study show that

the more the students felt socially rejected by their Cyberball partners, as measured by the Need Threat Scale, and the greater their
desire to repair their mood, as measured by the Angry Mood Improvement Inventory, the more times they wanted to stab the dolls,
er, their partners. Chester and DeWall concluded that "aggressive
behavior closely mirrors that of *addictive behaviors* in that it results
in a short-term improvement in mood and that this motivates individuals to seek out that behavior" (emphasis added).[14] So, if you
wanted Billy torn to pieces, you were probably trying to make yourself feel better after the loss of Harley, and what you craved most was
Billy's pain. A hug or some hot chocolate wouldn't have sufficed. It
also suggests why toddlers sometimes hit when they don't get what
they want; they're trying to make themselves feel better.

Two years later, Chester (now at Virginia Commonwealth University) and DeWall teamed up with Donald Lynam at Purdue University and Richard Milich at the University of Kentucky to perform
an fMRI study to see what's happening inside our brains when we
experience the pain of social rejection and are given the opportunity
to seek revenge.[15] They recruited sixty more undergraduates. After
being inserted inside the brain scanner, the students were exposed to
social rejection while tossing the Cyberball with fictitious partners
and subjected to noise blasts from those same partners when they
lost rounds following a button-pressing competition. Bound to be
rabidly vengeful after this double-barreled onslaught of psychological and physical assaults, the students were then given the opportunity to retaliate by launching noise blasts against their partners. They
were also asked to complete the Angry Mood Improvement Inventory plus another tool called the Brief Aggression Questionnaire
designed to measure whether someone has a naturally aggressive
personality.

Brain scans of the students revealed activation of their anterior
insula (the brain's "pain network") during Cyberball rejection. This
indicates the presence of social pain. Replicating prior studies, the
scans also showed that the opportunity to launch retaliatory noise

blasts was associated with significant nucleus accumbens (GO!) activation and higher scores on the Angry Mood Improvement Inventory. This again supports the conclusion that revenge is pleasurable and motivated by the desire to improve mood and reduce pain caused by a grievance.[16]

The brain scans also linked increased nucleus accumbens activity to students with higher scores for naturally aggressive personality on the Brief Aggression Questionnaire. Among these students, the scans showed *decreased* functional connectivity between the nucleus accumbens and the ventral lateral prefrontal cortex (STOP!). Chester and colleagues suggested this may point to reward circuitry dysregulation among individuals with aggressive dispositions— something that Dr. Childress at Penn might refer to as brain-biological vulnerability to revenge addiction.[17]

Chester and colleagues noted that the data were not clear enough to determine whether the mere prospect of future pleasure, or the actual pleasure realized during retaliation, motivates retaliatory aggression. They also pointed out that their fMRI scans couldn't determine whether dopamine transmission in the brain's reward circuitry drives "wanting" (craving) revenge versus only "liking" it.[18] This remains an open question in the science. However, other researchers using PET scans with a tracer—which *can* detect dopamine transmission—have detected dopamine release and/or reduced dopamine receptor availability in the nucleus accumbens for behavioral addictions such as gambling.[19] So, we might reasonably expect that it happens for revenge gratification too.

GOOD VIBRATIONS

In August 2020, the researchers Hunter Threadgill at Florida State University and Philip Gable at the University of Delaware published the results of a study tightening the connection between revenge and pleasure seeking in humans. Instead of using fMRIs or PET scans, they used electroencephalograms (EEGs) that monitor electrical activity in the brain to measure fluctuations in the emotional states of nearly a hundred study participants who were insulted by ostensible aggressors and then competed for the opportunity to seek revenge by taking money from them or blasting them with loud noises. The EEGs revealed clear neural wave-form signatures of reward processing and the experience of pleasure when participants won the opportunity to blast back.[20]

One way I think about revenge addiction is in terms of the dopamine model described by the Stanford addiction scientist and physician Anna Lembke, MD, in her brilliant 2021 book, *Dopamine Nation*.[21] Dr. Lembke explains that the brain has an opponent-process system for maintaining balance, or homeostasis, between pleasure and pain. Dopamine is released in the reward pathway of the brain when we experience pleasure from things like eating sweets, having sex, taking narcotics, or—as the evidence in this book now demonstrates—getting revenge. Dopamine is also released in response to a mere *cue* associated with one of these pleasurable experiences, like seeing a thirty-three-millisecond image of people using drugs or, as the evidence in this book now demonstrates, perceiving a real or imagined grievance.

Grievances are memories of painful experiences of injustice or mistreatment. As we've seen, they activate the brain's pain network. Under Dr. Lembke's dopamine balance model, this likely produces a "pre-reward dopamine spike" followed by a sudden dopamine crash, creating a dopamine deficit. This dopamine deficit activates our GO! circuitry to restore pleasure-pain balance, making us *want* (crave) the reward and the big dopamine surge we expect to come when we get it.[22] It's this expectation of reward that drives us to seek out the cake in the refrigerator, the sexual encounter in the bedroom, the cocaine in the dealer's pocket—or the act of revenge. If the STOP! circuitry of the brain's prefrontal cortex has been weakened, depleted, hijacked, or silenced by genetic, biopsychosocial, environmental, or other factors, then even the threat of severe negative consequences—including arrest, incarceration, and death—won't be enough to stop us. That's revenge addiction.

What makes revenge so pleasurable, and what are avengers hoping to achieve? The German psychologist Mario Gollwitzer and his colleagues have been conducting studies to answer these questions. They've discovered that avengers feel the greatest satisfaction when the target of their revenge doesn't merely display suffering but signals that they understand their suffering is *because of* a harm or wrong they've committed.[23] Better still is when the target signals a change in attitude or behavior, indicating reform or rehabilitation.[24] This suggests that deterrence might be a hoped-for outcome of revenge. But the fact that revenge is the primary *motivation* of perpetration and violence calls into doubt its value as a deterrent, suggesting that the enhanced pleasure derived from witnessing reform or rehabilitation may be from another source, such as seeing that revenge has produced not only pain in the target but submission (often humiliating and painful in its own right). Enhanced pleasure might also be experienced from seeing that the target has "benefited" from learning a lesson—perhaps with a corresponding reduction in the avenger's own pain and guilt from inflicting harm as the "teacher."

More work needs to be done on all this. What seems clearer is that avengers are not mere sadists feasting on other people's pain.[25] Avengers attack only when provoked. By contrast, sadists tend to attack both those who provoke them and innocent victims.[26] In this sense, revenge is more analogous to schadenfreude than sadism. Schadenfreude is the pleasure we experience when bad things happen to other people, most often people whom we envy in some way. Envy is a form of grievance, a painful feeling of inferiority and resentment because of another person's possessions, achievements, or qualities. The neuroscience of schadenfreude has shown—*you guessed it*—that it activates the nucleus accumbens. Researchers theorize that when misfortune befalls a person we envy, the gap we perceive between them and us is reduced, making us feel better.[27] Of course, if we're the ones who bring about the misfortune, we've crossed the line from schadenfreude into revenge.

REVENGE OF THE NEUROSCIENTISTS

I spoke with David Chester, the Virginia Commonwealth University professor, for this book. He's a brainy, self-described mercurial, bearded bear of a man who happens to be a basic scientist living between the worlds of psychology and neuroscience. He told me he started studying aggression and revenge out of sheer fascination, because he says he's the opposite of an aggressive person and wondered what it was all about. His current work is focused on the most common, least studied form of aggression, which isn't physical violence but social revenge—acts intended to harm those who harm us through daily slights, insults, rejections, exclusions, and attempts to inflict feelings of guilt that can damage relationships, reputations, and psychological well-being. Even the nonaggressive Dr. Chester concedes indulging in this form of revenge on occasion and is keenly interested in studying anyone who says they don't.

Despite the growing mountain of empirical data unearthed by his and others' research, Dr. Chester is wary of the term "addiction." He doesn't hesitate in saying that revenge is "certainly habit forming. I don't think anyone could reasonably disagree with you there, and I have evidence from my own lab that it is." He points to data showing that people crave revenge, with aggrieved study participants reporting feelings like "I can never be satisfied until I have revenge on the other person." He explains, "That is what craving is. It's a motivation. It's an impelling factor that demands satisfaction and will result in discomfort until it is satisfied." Dr. Chester is convinced that "revenge feels good a lot of the time for a lot of people." He also believes that "if you take the sweetness out of the revenge, you're really taking the revenge out of the person."

All this sounds like addiction to me. But Dr. Chester told me he prefers not to traffic in the A-word:

> There's baggage around the word "addiction," and we don't need it. We can talk about all the things you mentioned without it. Compulsion, reward, fleeting feelings of satisfaction. None of that requires us to talk about it in an addiction framework. It's very useful and helpful. It's a heuristic that everyone kind of gets. But you and I can sit and say all the things you just said [about revenge being an addiction] and back them up with studies from my lab and others, and never utter the word "addiction." . . . What I've found is that when you start to put it in an addiction framework, you're paddling upstream a little bit. And so, if you're courageous more than I, I encourage you to paddle against that stream. But perhaps I'm an intellectual coward, I don't know, but I felt like it didn't get me anything I wasn't already getting. . . . I'm still right there, a bellicose supporter of all this stuff. It's just, do we use "addiction" or not, to me it matters less. We can say all the things we want to say without it.

I've gotten this type of reaction from other researchers, including some of my colleagues at Yale: fear and shame about using the word "addiction." Frankly, it needs to stop. It's slowing progress in reducing human suffering and violence. Researchers need to be able to honestly identify the phenomena they're studying without fear of reputational attack.

Yes, the A-word carries baggage accumulated from centuries of travel in search of why humans ingest substances and engage in behaviors that harm themselves and others despite knowing the harm's coming and that their own actions are inviting it. And, yes, clouds of darkness and suspicion swirl around addiction: immorality, evil, pleasure, compulsion, weakness, crime, poverty, decadence, dependence, dereliction, dissipation, enslavement, overdose deaths, narco-terrorism, drug wars, police corruption, mass incarceration, racism, oppression, recovery, quackery, rehab life, sin, damnation, and more. *But so what?* Desperate for answers and relief, the public has moved past these stigmas. Now it's science that's trapped in the Dark Ages.

One intrepid team of researchers has gone so far as to publish a paper attempting "to define addiction in a way so as to make it a respectable scientific term."[28] After conducting an extensive review of the literature, they identified five elements that, alone or in combination, describe addiction: "(a) engagement in the behavior to achieve appetitive effects, (b) preoccupation with the behavior, (c) temporary satiation, (d) loss of control, and (e) suffering negative consequences."[29] Although these five elements accurately describe compulsive revenge seeking, most researchers are still afraid to say it. I'm not. Maybe because I'm also a lawyer and a sufferer. It's called revenge addiction. And as Alan Leshner wrote, "It matters."

Dr. Leshner and other proponents of the brain disease model of addiction long ago faced their fears and overcame them. They recognized that the reluctance of policy makers, health-care professionals, and the public to treat addiction as a disease was the result of the baggage, not the evidence. Refusing to treat addiction as a disease condemns obviously ill people to unnecessary suffering and untimely deaths, and these researchers were no longer willing to accept this.[30] Instead of using mere paddles to go upstream, they strapped the engine of science to their boats and surged against the current full speed. They knew that the baggage carried by addiction floats, and that it can be lashed together into a barge for hauling mercy and relief to the desperate.

The brain disease model of addiction has translated science into public policy and action, mobilizing research, creating new treatments and interventions, reducing stigma, increasing funding, and saving lives.[31] Likewise, the brain disease model of revenge addiction I'm proposing in this book—unabashedly, because the neuroscientific, behavioral, and historical evidence demonstrates all the elements of addiction—can help scientists and nonscientists alike understand the behavior and empower us to do something useful about it to protect ourselves and others from harm. If, that is, we truly wish to reduce violence and intentionally inflicted human suffering and live more secure and peaceful lives. Perhaps we enjoy the pleasure of revenge too much to want to tame our hunger for it?

During my interview, Dr. Chester also pointed to a lurking skepticism about behavioral addictions in general. Many new forms of addiction have been proposed recently for a variety of common behaviors (for example, internet, social media, and video game use), making some researchers worry that if everything's an addiction, then nothing is. "Are we simply talking about reward and the denial of reward," Dr. Chester asks, "or are we talking about something truly addictive?"

Well, if we're talking about compulsive revenge seeking, Dr. Chester's own research demonstrates that it is "truly addictive." Skepticism about behavioral addictions as a disease is similar to past skepticism about substance addictions as a disease. The same stigmas of immorality and weakness are now being applied to compulsive sex, eating, gaming, and internet usage. Yet the same scientific evidence supporting the brain disease model of addiction debunks these stigmas: features of compulsion, appetitive craving, loss of control despite negative consequences, neural circuitry dysfunction (nucleus accumbens and prefrontal cortex), neural chemistry dysfunction (dopamine and serotonin dysregulation), and responses to treatment and prevention efforts.[32] A shared neurogenetic basis for both substance and behavioral addictions, linked to dopamine dysregulation and known as reward deficiency syndrome, has emerged in the research.[33] Overlapping incidence of substance (tobacco, alcohol, and cannabis) and behavioral (gambling, internet use, eating) addictions was recently demonstrated in a study of 3,003 young adults, suggesting a shared brain vulnerability to both forms of addiction[34]—just as Dr. Childress surmised nearly two decades ago.

There are, of course, very good reasons to reserve the term "addiction" for behaviors that are truly pathological. Labeling benign behaviors addictions can be just as stigmatizing as failing to recognize and treat dysfunctional behaviors. But we shouldn't hesitate to call a duck a duck. For example, humans walk by nature, we're built for it, it's good exercise, and, unless we're disabled, we all do it. One would think walking could never be considered a behavioral addiction. But what if the walking some people do is through minefields—not to clear the mines, but for the thrill of cheating death? And what if they do this compulsively, they experience temporary satiation by doing it, they have no control to stop it, and they're often maimed or killed as a result? And what if there's scientific evidence of brain-biological dysfunction? Should we refuse to treat this form of walking as an addictive disorder merely because most other forms of walking are beneficial? Or because by labeling it an addiction we somehow risk calling every form of walking an addiction? We recognize that hundreds of types of beneficial bacteria live in our guts and keep us healthy. We also recognize that some types of bacteria that get loose in our guts, like salmonella, listeria, and *Clostridium botulinum* (the bacterium that causes botulism), can sicken or kill us. We easily distinguish between beneficial and pathogenic bacteria. We can also easily distinguish between beneficial and pathological behaviors.

It seems the baggage carried by the A-word generates something approaching hysteria, but this is also its superpower. "Addiction" is the most efficient and effective word we have for communicating the presence, nature, and severity of a specific form of disease and a constellation of ways to address it. So, if you hurt people who hurt you (or their proxies) because it makes you feel good, and if you become preoccupied with thinking and fantasizing about hurting them, and if you're unable to resist hurting them despite knowing the negative consequences, then you should seriously consider that you might be addicted to revenge and do something about it. We need to use the A-word, baggage and all.

We also need to reject the argument advanced by some researchers that the desire for revenge shouldn't be considered a disease because it's an adaptive trait selected by evolution to deter aggression and promote social cooperation.[35] First, as mentioned above, revenge is the primary *motivation* behind most forms of human violence—the very opposite of deterring it—and violence is pathogenic, not adaptive.[36] Second, compulsive revenge seeking meets the definition of addiction, which *is* considered a disease or disorder by most physicians. And third, scientists have shown that many modern human diseases and disorders have evolutionary origins, including cancer, schizophrenia, autism, allergies, neuropsychiatric disorders, obesity, type 2 diabetes, HIV/AIDS—and addiction.[37] Whether a trait or condition evolved at some point in our primordial past does not disqualify or immunize it from being recognized and treated as a disease here in the twenty-first century.

OF MICE AND NEUROSCIENTISTS

Dr. Chester encouraged me to speak further about all this with Sam Golden at the University of Washington. Dr. Golden is a neuroscientist who studies addiction in rodents. And, no, this shouldn't evoke images of stoned little mice named Cheech and Chong; he studies addictive *aggression* in mice as a way of understanding addictive aggression in human beings.

In one study, Dr. Golden and his colleagues Conor Heins, Marco Venniro, Daniele Caprioli, Michelle Zhang, David Epstein, and Yavin Shaham used models of drug addiction in rodents to see whether mice exhibit "addiction-like" aggression.[38] Employing tasty food pellets as a reward, they trained sixty older mice to press a lever to open the doors on their home cages for the opportunity to attack intruding younger mice who haplessly wander in from the cage next door. This sounds brutal, but we can hardly do it with people. Seventy percent of the mice became persistently aggressive in attacking their nosy neighbors. These aggressive mice were next given the choice of pressing a lever for food pellets or opening the door for more attacks. Most of the mice initially chose food over aggression, but over time *they relapsed like drug addicts into choosing aggression over food.*

That's fascinating, and concerning, but the researchers took things a step further. To test whether the mice had actually become "addicted" to aggression, they began administering electric shocks to their feet when they chose aggression over food—adding a strong negative consequence. Dr. Golden described these electric shocks to me as "like a cannonball-to-the-gut type of feeling for the mouse." If that sounds cruel, I agree. But for approximately 19 percent of the mice, it wasn't cruel enough to stop them from pressing the lever for one more chance to attack an intruding young mouse. They were so hooked on the pleasure of that experience that they not only chose it over food but were literally willing to be electrocuted to get it. *Now, that's addiction.* Although mice can't tell us what they're thinking, the intrusion by the younger mouse can be theorized as creating a territorial "grievance," triggering a desire to retaliate in anticipation of a pleasurable dopamine release. The fact that the grievance was self-staged by the older mouse opening the door doesn't negate this possibility. We'll see in the coming chapters that humans regularly self-stage, self-create, and self-imagine grievances all the time to get delicious hits of revenge.

Did you notice that only about 19 percent of the mice became addicted? That's telling, because about this same percentage of humans (20 percent) become addicted to drugs, and about this same percentage of humans become pathologically aggressive.[39] Contrast that with data showing that between 50 percent and 90 percent of people can recall experiencing recent revenge desires. This suggests that although most people experience revenge desires on a regular basis, only a minority become addicted—just what we see with substance addiction.[40]

Dr. Golden and his colleagues offered some helpful takeaways from their study for those of us with two legs and no tails:

> We take the general commonality of aggression seeking between rodents and humans . . . to reflect a biologically conserved correlate of compulsive aggression seeking across species. This observation suggests that this type of aggression in humans—appetitive aggression—can be viewed within the context of *addiction* [emphasis added].[41]

Backing up these conclusions, Dr. Golden and another group of colleagues performed an immunohistochemistry examination on the brains of mice that went through the intruder mouse training described above. Turns out that mice, like humans, have a nucleus accumbens. This experiment involved removing the brains of the mice immediately after the training, sectioning the nucleus accumbens, and evaluating it for evidence of dopamine transmission—more cruelty here, but, thankfully, they anesthetized the mice first. The results of the experiment confirmed nucleus accumbens activation and identified dopamine-receptor-expressing neurons as playing a role in increasing or decreasing aggression seeking.[42]

INTO THE LIGHT

In December 2020, I co-authored the first peer-reviewed scientific article proposing a behavioral addiction model of revenge, violence, and gun abuse.[43] The article was part of a special issue on gun violence in America in the *Journal of Law, Medicine, and Ethics* published by Cambridge University Press and organized by the Yale Law School's Solomon Center for Health Law and Policy. It broke new ground by identifying guns as objects of abuse used by people seeking pleasure through revenge to relieve the distress of their grievances and victimization—and by advocating for the use of addiction-informed strategies as a public health approach for reducing gun violence.

Based in part on my article, in 2022 the researchers Ryan Brown, Rajeev Ramchand, and Todd Helmus at the RAND Corporation published their own article finding undeniable parallels between violent extremism and substance addiction.[44] They identified the common roles of cue-triggered grievances and stress; the neurobiology of revenge; mirrored aspects of chronic disease and relapse; co-occurring psychiatric disorders; the role of social groups in substance addiction and extremism; and the geographic clustering of substance addicts and violent extremists. They also echoed my call to use addiction-informed strategies to prevent and treat violent extremism. In 2023, the terrorism researchers Jessica Stern, Megan Mc-Bride, Jessa Mellea, and Elena Savoia at the Harvard T. H. Chan School of Public Health got on board, citing my article in their own research arguing that "addiction serves as a useful metaphor" for understanding violent extremism.[45]

CLICK . . .

So, there you have it, a scientific snapshot of your brain on revenge from more than sixty neuroscientists and research psychologists around the world. And one lawyer. This concludes our neuroscience lesson, but there's much more to be learned about revenge addiction. In the next chapters, we're going to journey beyond the laboratory to examine what compulsive revenge seeking looks like in real life. Be forewarned. What we're about to see is far worse than what Billy did to poor Harley.

CHAPTER 4

THIS IS WHAT REVENGE ADDICTS WANT YOU TO KNOW

With a current world population of about 8.1 billion people, the science of revenge suggests that 20 percent, or about 1.62 billion, may become addicted to revenge at some point during their lifetimes. That's a big number, but it requires context. Addiction ranges from mild to severe, symptoms come and go, abstinence and relapse get better and worse, and acts of revenge range from passive and verbal to physical and aggressive. So, the number of people at any time whose revenge addiction might pose a threat of significant physical harm to others or themselves is bound to be much smaller. Nevertheless, the destruction that revenge addicts inflict is enormous. Most acts of violence are revenge-driven, and the World Health Organization estimates that violence-related injuries kill approximately 1.25 million people each year.[1] Although resources should be made available to all who suffer from revenge addiction, our focus should be on identifying and getting resources to individuals who suffer from severe revenge addiction and are at risk of gratifying their cravings through acts of violence.

In the next few chapters, we're going to meet people who have struggled with severe revenge addiction and used violence compulsively. By getting to know them and the challenges they face, we can better understand the nature of the addiction, how to identify those at risk, how to intervene to save lives, and maybe even develop a sense of empathy and compassion for them. In later chapters, we'll explore strategies and resources available now to help people suffering from revenge addiction overcome it—hopefully before committing future acts of violence.

"THE NICEST YOUNG MAN YOU'D EVER WANT TO MEET"

At 9:20 a.m. on May 25, 1993, a twenty-three-year-old navy cook named Michael Stokes walked into a crowded fast-food restaurant in Connecticut with a .45-caliber semiautomatic handgun and ordered the customers to get down. He then went behind the counter, located the manager, twenty-six-year-old Wanda Salgado, and the assistant manager, twenty-eight-year-old William Abate, and shot them multiple times while shouting in blind rage, "Fuck you! Fuck you!" As they lay motionless on the floor, his shouts turned into taunts: "Are you dead yet?"

Michael then walked back around the counter into the dining area and assured the stunned customers he had no intention of harming them. "I already have my revenge," he muttered.

Michael had intended to kill himself next, but he made eye contact with an older man gazing back at him in horror and changed his mind. He waited quietly for the police to arrive. When they pulled up in front of the restaurant, he placed his gun on the counter, put his hands on his head, walked outside, and surrendered.

Michael pleaded guilty to two counts of murder and is currently serving a fifty-five-year sentence in a maximum-security prison in Connecticut. He had no criminal history before the shootings. Elsie Reilly, a neighbor who lived across the street from his family home, described him to a reporter afterward as "the nicest young man you'd ever want to meet."[2]

This may sound like another in a seemingly endless stream of senseless murders in America, but the science of revenge tells us there are no senseless murders.

I first began communicating with Michael Stokes in 2019. He had read about my revenge addiction research and written me a letter asking if I could help him understand why he wanted to kill two people twenty-six years earlier. I visited him in prison in 2020 to learn more about the crime and what his life had been like leading up to it. As he revealed the details during our visit and in subsequent correspondence and interviews, I began to see how closely my life could have been his, and his mine. How it all balanced on the function—or dysfunction—of neural circuits and chemicals inside our brains reacting to genetic, developmental, biopsychosocial, and environmental circumstances that were often beyond our control. Michael was twenty-three when he entered the restaurant with a gun; I was just six years younger when I cornered my classmates with a gun. He had never done anything like that before; neither had I. He was burning with the desire for revenge; so was I. He lives in a cage, haunted by memories of murder. I live in a home, haunted by memories of how close I came to living in a cage. We are for each other pictures of lives that might have been. It's agonizing and terrifying. Nothing stopped him at the last second from pulling the trigger. Something stopped me. What was it? And why?

Michael agreed to speak with me for this book and share what was happening inside his mind in the days, hours, and minutes leading up to the shootings. He's taking a personal risk by doing this and receiving nothing of economic value in return. He's not seeking sympathy or absolution. He does not want to inflict further pain upon the families of Ms. Salgado and Mr. Abate. He merely wants to be of service to others as a way of giving back a small portion of what he has taken.

We need to hear and learn from people like Michael Stokes. The murders he committed are among the most common types of kill-ings in America, far exceeding the death toll from the mass shoot-ings that attract widespread media attention.[3] In telling Michael's story, I'm not in any way excusing what he has done. I'm trying to examine it through the lens of the science of revenge so we can learn how to prevent other people from committing similar acts of vio-lence in the future. The forensic psychologist James Garbarino, who has testified as a psychological expert witness in over three hundred murder cases, put it this way in his powerful book, *Listening to Kill-ers:* "I am not trying to use my professional expertise to justify vio-lent crime, only to illuminate the reality of how one's past pain can lead to one's present infliction of pain on others."[4]

I confess that when I went to visit Michael in prison, I expected to meet a thug. Even though I had come close to shooting my class-mates, I hadn't actually done it. Surely there would be immediate and obvious differences between a real killer and me, differences that would make me feel self-assured and superior. What I found instead was the guy that Ms. Reilly described to the reporter. Michael Stokes really is one of the nicest (now middle-aged) men you'd ever want to meet. He's polite, soft-spoken, well kempt, intelligent, and quick to put others at ease. He's earned the respect of the warden and cor-rectional officers who guard him day and night, perhaps reflecting something about his inner nature. Or not. As a lawyer, I've met many people who have done terrible things, and I'm on guard for their at-tempts to manipulate. I approached Michael Stokes like a prosecu-tor, searching for evidence of dishonesty and turpitude. What I found is astonishing.

Michael is among the first inmates in Connecticut to become a hospice volunteer and has been doing hospice work inside the prison for more than twenty years, assisting terminally ill inmates with the process of dying: comforting them, toileting them, changing their soiled briefs, bathing them, feeding them, reading for them, cleaning their cells, monitoring them, and even providing postmortem care for their remains. Michael does all this without pay. He's also become a certified nurse's assistant in prison, supporting the medical teams that treat sick and injured inmates. For this service, he receives the princely sum of $2 per day. To obtain these positions, you've got to be a model prisoner, and Michael is that. He received an award from the warden for saving a fellow prisoner's life twice by performing the Heimlich maneuver. When not volunteering or working, he's taking classes and studying. In 2024, Michael and another inmate became the first in the history of the Connecticut prison system to earn bachelor of arts degrees while incarcerated, through a program operated by the Yale Prison Education Initiative at Dwight Hall and the University of New Haven. Michael graduated magna cum laude and was inducted into the Alpha Sigma Lambda honor society. His next goal is to become the first inmate in Connecticut to earn a doctoral degree.

All of which leaves us with the perplexing question: Why did one of the nicest (and brightest) guys you'd ever want to meet slaughter two people in cold blood?

Michael says that he and his brother were the only Black kids in their otherwise all-white high school in Connecticut, but that he was well liked and elected class president all four years. Although popular, Michael struggled academically. He tells me his childhood dream was to become a rocket scientist or an astronaut, but he was terrible at math and science, foreclosing such a career. Neither of his parents had gone to college, and they divorced when he was young. After high school graduation, Michael enrolled at the University of Connecticut under a special program for minority students but flunked out during his first semester. Even if he had been able to earn passing grades, he says he didn't have the money to stay in school. He took a variety of menial jobs and eventually landed a position as a cook at a fast-food restaurant, where he met Wanda Salgado, one of his co-workers.

Michael says he was immediately attracted to Wanda, but she was already married. Even so, they went out to dinner, movies, and shopping—all with her husband's consent, she told him. Wanda sometimes playfully referred to Michael, who was three years younger, as her boyfriend. She seemed unhappy with the marriage, and Michael developed romantic feelings for her. He thought she was developing similar feelings toward him. She hinted that if she wasn't already married, she would be interested in dating him. Michael convinced himself that Wanda would eventually leave her husband. He was willing to wait and didn't push for their relationship to become physical.

As time passed, Wanda took a job as a manager at a different restaurant nearby, the one where the shootings took place. Following the move, she stopped communicating with Michael. He heard rumors that she was having an affair with an employee at the new restaurant, a guy whom Michael had briefly met. This hurt and angered him. If Wanda was willing to have an affair, why not with him when they had been so close and she knew he wanted her? And why was she suddenly refusing to communicate with him if they had been "just friends"?

Michael knew working as a fast-food cook was a dead-end job. He had been considering making a change in his life and had recently spoken to a recruiter about career opportunities in the navy. The rumors that Wanda was having an affair, and her refusal to communicate with him, prompted him to make a rash decision to enlist and get away from Connecticut.

The navy sent Michael to California for basic training, but he couldn't stop thinking about Wanda. He grew desperate to return to Connecticut in the hope of winning her. He tried to quit the navy, but his superiors threatened him with a dishonorable discharge. He decided to stay when he learned he could be stationed in Connecticut if he joined the navy's Atlantic submarine fleet based in Groton. After completing basic training, he asked to be assigned to submarine school to work as a cook. His request was granted.

When the navy transferred Michael back to Connecticut, he immediately began trying to contact Wanda. He says she continued to avoid him. He interpreted this as proof that she really was having an affair, and that she had been misleading him all along. He started to spiral. He began to see everything he had tried to do in his life, from wanting to become a rocket scientist or astronaut through flunking out of college, becoming a fast-food cook, struggling in the navy, and now losing Wanda, as abject failure while all around him other people were succeeding—including the man he believed was having an affair with her. Michael became deeply depressed, and thoughts of suicide entered his mind. One day, while at his family home on liberty, he purchased two handguns for that purpose and stored them in a closet. He considered using them as only a distant possibility, but it comforted him knowing they were available if his life was no longer tolerable.

While on another liberty at his family home, Michael says Wanda called him late one night in a panic. She said her husband was missing and asked Michael to help her find him. Michael agreed. He drove Wanda around to various places until they located him. Michael waited in his car while they talked in private and then drove Wanda home. He thought these good deeds would lead to the relationship with her that he so desperately wanted. Instead, he says, Wanda turned cold again and refused to speak to him.

Michael became enraged. It was now clear to him that Wanda didn't love him and never would, that she was having an affair with someone else, and that he would never have the relationship with her that he wanted. He felt used and betrayed. He had been willing to be Wanda's knight in shining armor. He had pinned all his hopes and self-worth on being with her. Now, in his mind, by rejecting him, she had, in effect, destroyed him.

These were Michael's grievances, real or imagined. The pain was enormous. Michael began planning to end his life. He decided to kill himself at his family home, where he kept the guns. To do that, he would need permission to leave the navy base. He devised a plan to inform his superior that he was having car trouble and ask for leave to get it repaired—a simple request routinely granted. Over and over, Michael imagined arriving home, retrieving one of his pistols, loading it, pointing it at his head, and pulling the trigger. Over and over, he imagined the relief he would feel.

On the evening of May 24, 1993, Michael decided that the next day would be his last. This time, however, as he imagined killing himself, he imagined how Wanda and her lover would react to news of his suicide. In his mind's eye, he saw them together laughing at him and his weakness. Although this was entirely fabricated, it grew into a reality inside Michael's head. The humiliation, shame, and betrayal were too much for him to bear. His rage and desire for revenge exploded. Michael placed Wanda and her lover on trial inside the courtroom of his mind, found them guilty, and handed down a sentence. It was this: Instead of killing himself at home alone, he would get his gun, drive to the restaurant, and kill them both first before killing himself.

The next morning, May 25, 1993, Michael was granted permission to leave the base. Driving home, he continued imagining how Wanda and her lover were laughing at him. His desire for revenge continued to build, pushing him onward. When he got home, he loaded multiple clips with .45-caliber ammunition, inserted one in his gun, put the spares in his jacket pocket, and left for the restaurant. Still, he imagined Wanda and her lover laughing at him.

After bursting through the doors of the restaurant and yelling for the customers to get down, Michael went behind the counter. He found Wanda speaking with William Abate in the kitchen. Sure enough, they were both laughing about something and, Michael believed, smirking at him—just as he had imagined it. Michael thought William was the employee having an affair with Wanda. This turned out to be a tragic case of mistaken identity. William Abate was merely an innocent co-worker doing his job and had no romantic relationship with Wanda. Michael opened fire on him first and then Wanda, killing them both. In a statement to police afterward, Michael said that in that moment he felt "relief, anger, and disbelief," echoing the haunting words of Olga Hepnarová after murdering eight people in Prague.

Because of Michael's uncontrolled desire for revenge, Wanda Salgado and William Abate were murdered, their families and friends were left devastated, and Michael's family and friends were left devastated. In my interactions with Michael, he speaks as though he were the district attorney at his own trial, convicting himself for the killings. He's agonized, filled with remorse, sorrow, and shame. He wants us to know what he now knows—not about the difficulties of life behind bars or his longing to be free, but about the dangers of compulsive revenge cravings.

Can the science of revenge teach us anything about this tragedy? Can it help prevent similar tragedies in the future? The answers are yes and yes. The science of revenge shows us that this tragedy was *not* senseless. It was the predictable result of the pain of real and imagined grievances triggering powerful revenge cravings for relief and pleasure within the reward (GO!) circuitry of Michael Stokes's brain. It was also the result of the failure of the executive function (STOP!) circuitry within Michael Stokes's brain to intervene and override his desire to harm Wanda, William, and himself. These are the runaway brain-biological processes of addiction.

Revenge addiction is a brain disease, and it matters. It mattered to Wanda Salgado, William Abate, and Michael Stokes. It matters to their families and friends. It matters to us all. The science of revenge tells us these murders could have been prevented if Michael, or any of a number of other people in the weeks and months leading up to the killings, had understood what was happening to him and what to do about it. Michael had several real and imagined grievances and had begun craving revenge and gradually becoming addicted to it in his fantasies—first against himself with his ideation and planning to kill himself, and then against Wanda and the man he believed she was having an affair with. Virtually any of the addiction recovery strategies that already exist, including my Nonjustice System approach for recovering from revenge addiction, had a chance of helping Michael control his revenge cravings long before he picked up a gun.

Near the end, Michael's revenge fantasies moved toward reality, and he began displaying signs that he was experiencing a *revenge attack*. A revenge attack is a life-threatening medical emergency that should be treated like a heart attack but is often ignored until it is too late. Like a heart attack, if you know the warning signs of a revenge attack and seek emergency medical assistance quickly, you may be able to save your own life or the life of another. The warning signs include preoccupation or obsession with a grievance, expressions of anger and rage over the grievance that won't go away, planning to hurt or kill, identifying targets, and acquiring weapons. *I list the warning signs of a revenge attack and what to do in chapter 10 of this book.*

The science of revenge tells us that Wanda Salgado and William Abate would likely be alive today if Michael Stokes had been recognized and treated for revenge addiction. Preventing violence is now within our reach.

Don't forget about Michael; we'll be hearing more from him later.

NIGHTHAWK DOWN

In 2014, after completing a tour of combat during the war in Afghanistan, Chris Buckley, a former U.S. Army sergeant, joined the Georgia White Knights of the Ku Klux Klan.[5] Within a year, he was given a black robe and hood and promoted to Imperial Nighthawk. Nighthawks are the Klan's enforcers and security officers and usually armed beneath their robes.[6] They investigate and screen applicants, punish disloyalty, and sometimes serve as the Klan's hit men.

Today, Chris is out of the Klan and has dedicated his life to getting others out. So far, working as an intervention specialist for deradicalization organizations like Parents for Peace and Serve2Unite, he has directly or indirectly helped more than 250 people find their way to freedom from violent extremist groups like the KKK, Three Percenters, Oath Keepers, Atomwaffen, ISIS, and the Taliban.

I first met Chris Buckley in January 2022. He was introduced to me by the Harvard terrorism expert Jessica Stern. Chris's life story is so simultaneously tragic, horrifying, and inspiring that he's become the subject of an award-winning 2023 film documentary, *Refuge*, produced by the renowned broadcast journalist Katie Couric.[7] He's also been widely covered by major media outlets.[8] On March 31, 2022, he gave brave and deeply moving testimony before the Committee on Veterans' Affairs of the U.S. House of Representatives about violent extremism among military veterans.[9] But what brought Chris and me together is his conviction that people become violent extremists because they're addicted to revenge. Since former KKK Nighthawks rarely speak, when one is willing to break the code of silence, we should listen. This is what Chris wants us to know about revenge addiction and violent extremism.

Chris tells me it often starts with grievances formed at an early age. In his case, he says his father would come home from days-long drinking benders and beat and whip Chris with "extension cords, coat hangers, and even wrenches" while railing about nonwhite people taking his job.[10] Looking back on it now, he says the real reason his father couldn't hold a job is that he couldn't stay sober. Chris was, in effect, beaten by his father into believing Black people were the reason his father was in pain—and therefore the reason his father was beating Chris. These perceptions only deepened when, as one of the only white kids in his elementary school in Cleveland, Ohio, a group of Black kids attacked Chris, stole a pair of sneakers his grandmother had given him, and urinated on him. Chris insists that he "was not born racist."[11] The science of revenge suggests that violent racism isn't genetic or learned. *It's inflicted.*

This also appears to be true of homophobia. Chris became a one-stop shop for abuse during his childhood. From ages five to twelve, Chris says he was sexually abused by a male relative.[12] From these traumatic experiences, he concluded that homosexuals are people who molest kids. As he grew older, seeing a gay couple in public or in the media would activate these painful memories, and he would experience a strong desire to retaliate. This wasn't senseless hatred of other people's lifestyles; it was his brain's attempt to recover from trauma caused by mistreatment. When trauma is successfully addressed, the grievance and desire to retaliate usually disappear. But this type of resolution would be a long time coming for Chris, and he would pass through many more trials and suffer many more wounds.

On September 11, 2001, Chris was in his high school cafeteria watching the Twin Towers collapse on television after Muslim extremists flew loaded passenger jets into them, killing themselves and thousands of others in a mad frenzy of revenge seeking. Watching this unparalleled terror, he experienced the searing agony and desire for revenge that millions of Americans felt. He had already signed up to join the army upon graduation, so his rage had a ready outlet. He was eager to become an American soldier to avenge his nation.[13]

Chris's wish was granted when the army deployed him to Afghanistan. There he met an English-speaking Afghan named Abdullah who tried to show Chris that Muslims aren't a threat to Americans. Abdullah and Chris sometimes drank tea together and exchanged stories. They became fast friends. Until, Chris says, "Abdullah was caught one day sneaking an improvised explosive device into our bunker. Abdullah, my friend, wanted to kill me and my buddies just because I was an American."[14]

It gets worse. Chris's best buddy in the army was a fellow soldier named Daniel Wallace, a father of two young children from Kentucky. While out on a mission, Chris and Daniel were ambushed by the Taliban. Chris testified before the congressional committee, "I saw Daniel get hit by a bullet under his left eye, and his skull get shattered by the impact of the bullet. Daniel died in my arms while I was trying to push his brain back into his skull."[15]

"That fucked me up," Chris told me. "I remember that was the moment I felt that same hatred rise up toward Muslims that I felt toward my relative who had molested me."

Chris and, it seems, many of his fellow soldiers got very fucked up in Afghanistan. Here's how he described it to me:

ME: What's the role of grievance and revenge in the military?

CHRIS: Oh, man, it's your driving factor. I mean, so you're running on pure anger, nicotine, and caffeine constantly. . . . You're living in this anger life cycle constantly. . . . You're gonna go tell twenty-five-year-old boys what to do in combat, [chanting], "Kill! Kill! Kill! What makes the green grass grow? Blood, blood, bright red blood!" Like, those are the things that we would say while we were marching. . . .

ME: The gratification of the revenge craving, can you talk about that?

CHRIS: I mean, have you ever sneezed? That feeling after you sneeze is amazing. And the next one starts to build. And it comes out, and you feel amazing. And then forty sneezes in, you realize that your life has just become unmanageable. . . . That satisfaction is almost like an orgasmic release, right? You do all this work, you're trying, trying, trying, and, pow, you get your release. And usually, the same things happen after it: There's like a period of like contentment. There's a period of tiredness, of sleepiness. But then it starts to itch again. . . .

ME: So, you did the military. You killed people, right?

CHRIS: I did my job.

ME: You did your job. . . . Did you feel that kind of release that you've described, that almost sexual or drug, you know, almost like a high when you did your job, as you say?

CHRIS: So, at first, no. At first it was, you're just on this high of fear. And you, you just go through this hypervigilance. But then you start to blame the people that you're engaging [the enemy] for the hypervigilance that you have to live in. And it almost becomes satisfactory to know that you killed one of them. It's like you start to be like, "Yeah, gotcha. Not tonight, buddy." And then you start to have the, it's just a little at first, then you start to enjoy it. Then you realize that you're not the only one. Then you and the guys on the team are making fun of it.

I remember, we had one guy that we didn't know that we had hit. They [the soldiers on Chris's team] had fired a Mark 19—a little rocket that looked like a little grenade launcher. They fired it over towards a berm or an embankment where we had intel that there was somebody placing an IED [improvised explosive device]. And nothing ever happened. No shots were fired back, so we just kept on going.

On the way back, right, we come across this guy. He's blown in half on the middle of the road. It was the one that we killed. His whole face had been pulled off of his body, even to the point like the bottom of the hair on his beard was singed. But the lips were missing. And like from the eyebrows down was missing.

We made a mask out of this leather skin face and, like, hung it off our shield [on the front of our vehicle] when we would drive through these villages. And you would just see these children staring there in mortal fear. And we just smile at them and wave, right? Like, we knew it was a Taliban fighter. And these kids probably knew this person. So, we would display it, like, "Hey, if you support these guys, the next space on this vehicle will be yours."

ME: Wow. [*What was I supposed to say? I was horrified.*]

CHRIS: And it was such a perverted sense of satisfaction. . . . You don't realize how deep of a hole you're in till you come home. And you've got to get your fix. And then you find yourself watching like the Al Jazeera network or find the videos posted by like Al-Shabaab, and you're like, "Yeah, cut his head off." And you get that fix. . . . That's how the cycle continues. I would love to sit online for hours and watch, I still had these *Faces of Death* videos from like the '90s, right? And like, you know, like the beheading videos and things like that. I would look for them and find them online, you know, 4chan and things like that.

I had to find my fix. It's like somebody who goes into detox from substance abuse, right? You gotta find that fix, and that's how you go from pain pills to heroin to fentanyl, you progress, right? I went from getting a dose of fentanyl in the arm every day overseas to like now, they're like, here's an ibuprofen, now fix your addiction with that. It's the same thing, man, and that's why I loved when we first met and you were like, "the addiction to revenge." And I was like, "I've been fucking saying this." It's like, we're on the same page. Finally, somebody who I can talk to about this that is like right there with me.

Chris testified to Congress that by the time he returned from Afghanistan, he hated all Muslims: "In fact, I tattooed the word *Kafir,* infidel, in Arabic script, on my arm, as a warning to Muslims, but also as my way of remembering who my enemies were who had taken away my best friend."[16]

Here begins the third act of Chris Buckley's life: addiction to drugs and joining the KKK. In 2009, while still in the military but on a humanitarian mission with the Kentucky National Guard after a tornado touchdown, the axle on his military vehicle broke, causing a horrific accident that left Chris with a broken back.[17] He says, "I was put on opioids, which I became quickly addicted to, just as I was developing a habit of numbing my psychological pain by resentment directed against my growing list of enemies, Muslims, gays, Blacks, and Jews."[18] After the prescription opioids came cocaine, heroin, and methamphetamine. He says he was convicted twice for possession of meth. (Remember Dr. Childress's brain vulnerability theory to addictions of all sorts? Chris might be the poster child.)

But why the KKK? No doctor wrote Chris a prescription to start wearing robes and hoods and burning crosses.

ME: How do I go from, I'm just angry with my spouse, or with somebody in traffic, or my neighbor, to . . . the extremism level?

CHRIS: So, you find me somebody who's pissed off, and I'll make an extremist for you. It's finding out what their grievance is. They're pissed off at their wife blah, blah, blah, blah, blah. And it's like, okay, yeah, man, fucking insert misogynistic ideology here, right?

Oh, you're pissed off because your kid's getting bullied at school? Oh, yeah, let me tell you about this population or that population. They teach their kids to attack white people. *You're* the minority; *you're* the victim. You have a right to be pissed off. Let me tell you what we're doing to combat that. You should join our cause. . . .

You were a veteran, or you have a family member who's a veteran? Let me teach you about militia ideology, about the Three Percenters, the boogaloo boys, or the Oath Keepers.

Or, let me teach you how to make an extremist cop. Oh, yeah. Let me tell you why the amount of Black people that you arrest or that you come in contact with is significantly higher than whites. It ain't because of the demographic in your area. Oh, Lord, no. It's because Black people are apes. They're beasts. They're this. They're that. They're tribalistic.

They're not societal. You can't domesticate an animal, blah, blah, blah, blah.

ME: That's terrible. I mean, you're like, you just really went through how you can recruit in any of those groups.

CHRIS: So, the other important thing is providing that sense of community, bringing them into your in-group. You have to show them that they're a valued member. They have support; they have resources. They now belong to something. It's been so long since they've had that connection with society or a group.

Usually, the ones that are willing to go out and do violence are the people whose cognitive ability to process right and wrong is somehow skewed. . . . I would love when I would, you know, find that kid who was like slightly autistic, ADHD, you know, or a substance abuser. Dude, those are the guys that will go out and do violence for you.

Chilling stuff. Chris testified before the congressional committee that when he was discharged from the army, he received no mental health treatment for trauma: "Instead, there was a loving group eager to embrace me and acknowledge my pain. It was the KKK. And they did not approach me with pitchforks and burning crosses, but with a plate of BBQ ribs, a Bible, and the promise of a brotherhood I missed from my days in the army."

But plenty of groups that do not espouse hatred and violence offer food, Bibles, and brotherhood—like churches, for example. What's the special sauce on the KKK's BBQ ribs?

Chris told me it was his "anger towards the homosexual community and the Muslim community" that attracted him to the KKK: "Because, one, they claim to be completely a super-Christian organization, so that's in direct conflict with Islam. They claim to have like, you know, this hatred towards Muslims and homosexuality—and that's what I felt."

He goes on to make an important distinction: "But then there was the extra indoctrination where they'd be like, let me tell you about the Jews. And I'm like, yeah, that's cool, man; but this is why I'm here. Just let me hate these [Muslims and homosexuals]. I don't care, you know, [about the Jews]. It's kind of, you know, it's like a buffet."

"What about Black people?" I asked him.

"I had a lot of Black soldiers that were my battle buddies, man, and like to just hate people because of their blackness like that, that wasn't morally or ethically okay with me."

Chris's emphasis on his own personal grievances and rejection of the KKK's other beliefs supports my hypothesis that violent extremism is driven by revenge addiction. Politics, ideology, and (real or imagined) victimization are among the grievances that activate it.

Things got even more complicated for Chris. By the time he joined the KKK, he was married with two young children. His wife was horrified by his new group of friends and rapid ascent to Imperial Nighthawk. She was even more horrified by this: Chris's surprise appearance in a 2015 documentary produced by the BBC called *KKK: The Fight for White Supremacy*. The film captures Chris at a Klan event wearing his black Nighthawk robe and hood standing next to a much smaller person wearing a matching robe and hood. That little robed person happens to be Chris and his wife's four-year-old son. Together, father and son give a hearty *Sieg Heil* salute for the camera and shout, "White power!"

The stunned British interviewer, as if in a *Monty Python* skit, asks Chris why he would dress his son up in Klan clothes. Chris responds, "I just want my kid to know that it's okay to be proud of who he is. And, if being proud of his heritage makes him a racist, well, I'll teach him to be a racist."[19] The Klan's indoctrination worked to perfection.

The fourth act of Chris's life is a beautiful work in progress. It begins when his outraged but still loving wife issues Chris an ultimatum: the Klan and the drugs or her and the kids. Chris said he wanted to change but needed help. They eventually found Arno Michaelis, a former racist skinhead who helps people escape violent extremist groups.

Here begins a long and treacherous road. Chris testified to the congressional committee that "as difficult as it was to give up the drugs, giving up my addiction to hatred and resentment was not any less challenging. I *wanted* to blame others. I *wanted* to remain an angry victim rather than take responsibility for my own actions. And I wanted a quick fix to numb my pains right then and there." That's a powerful description of revenge addiction.

I'm not going to chronicle the many steps of Chris's recovery journey. Much of that is in the documentary *Refuge.* Suffice it to say that he's now out of the Ku Klux Klan and working with Michaelis to help others escape from violent extremism. And he's still with his wife and kids. He's making amends in every way possible. He says he's fully sober now—from both the drugs and the revenge.

But salvation hurts. As a former Imperial Nighthawk whose duty had been to punish those who betray the Klan, Chris knew that gaining his freedom from an organization built on revenge would come at a price. One night, the Imperial Wizard—the highest-ranking member of the Klan—picked Chris up in his truck and drove him to a secluded area. Four robed Klansmen were waiting. Chris had asked for it this way, on his own terms, rather than living in fear of being jumped. He'd trained three of the robed men, so he knew what to expect. The Imperial Wizard had promised there would be no guns or clubs.

"Okay, let's do this," Chris said, climbing out of the truck.

The four Klansmen beat and kicked Chris senseless, breaking his nose and collarbone in the process. The evidence is still on his distorted face. Then they tied him to a tree and drove off. Things had come full circle for Chris. The group he had joined to exact revenge upon his enemies had exacted its revenge upon him. This time, though, Chris was determined to break the cycle. When he finally made it to a hospital, rather than tell the doctors he had been jumped by KKK members and have them arrested, he said he had been in an accident riding an ATV.

Recovery from addiction is a journey, not a destination. We need a way to free ourselves from our memories of trauma and the pain and revenge cravings they activate. I invited Chris to try the mobile app version of my Nonjustice System—the Miracle Court app. He decided to put his father on trial for abusing him as a child. His reaction when the trial was over: "I will say that I did feel better, strangely, and it helped me forgive him a little. But also, I was surprised when I [played my father as the defendant during the trial]. I found some empathy for him."

CHAPTER 5

THESE ARE THE SCREAMS OF REVENGE ADDICTS IN PAIN

Imagine the moment you realize that your brain—the organ inside your head that's been with you, thinking, sensing, loving, and feeling from the moment of your birth—wants you to kill as many people as possible. Can there be anything more terrifying? Yes: being the target of someone whose brain is telling them to do this.

Mass killers are among the most violent people in modern human society. The Mass Killing database maintained by *USA Today,* the Associated Press, and Northeastern University records that between 2006 and 2023 there were 576 mass killings (with and without guns) of four or more people in the United States, resulting in 2,997 deaths.[1] The Violence Project, a database of mass shootings (guns only) created by researchers at Hamline University, records that between 1966 and 2023 there were 193 mass shootings of four or more people resulting in 1,391 deaths.[2] If you thought these numbers would be even higher, that's probably because mass shootings are becoming more frequent and producing higher death tolls than in prior decades.

MASS MURDER AS A SYMPTOM
OF SEVERE MENTAL ILLNESS

Researchers have not found a close relationship between serious mental illness and violence or mass murder.[3] A recent study of eighty-two mass murders in school and university settings worldwide revealed that most perpetrators did not have a severe mental illness—defined in the study as displaying symptoms of psychosis, hallucinations, delusions, or thought disorganization.[4] A large-scale study in 1998 following more than a thousand people with serious mental illnesses (schizophrenia, major depression, personality disorders) after their discharge from psychiatric hospitals found no difference in levels of violence between them and others from the same neighborhoods, except in cases where they used drugs or alcohol.[5]

All of which leads to this question: If the brain drives behavior, how is it possible that people who engage in mass murder—which on its face is pathological[6]—are not suffering from a severe mental illness?

The science of revenge provides the answer. It suggests that most mass murderers *do* suffer from a severe, often fatal, form of mental illness. It's just not one of the mental illnesses currently recognized in the all-important *Diagnostic and Statistical Manual* that doctors use to diagnose mental disorders. The mental illness that mass murderers suffer from is revenge addiction (or, in medical parlance, "revenge use disorder"). Instead of insisting that obviously pathological behavior somehow isn't pathological because it's not in the *DSM*, maybe we should update the *DSM*?

Both of the mass killing databases mentioned above identify *grievances* and *revenge* as the primary motivation for mass murder of all forms. A study of 160 active shooter incidents between 2000 and 2013 conducted for the Federal Bureau of Investigation reached the same conclusion.[7] A study of 41 targeted school shootings between 2008 and 2017 conducted by the U.S. Secret Service also reached this conclusion.[8] In fact, these studies reveal that the vast majority of mass shooters studied (more than 79 percent) were acting in accord with a real or imagined grievance. Mass violence researchers have now identified the typical mass shooter as "an isolated, angry, grievance-collecting loner who has failed in school, work, and home settings and is obsessed with violence and mass murder."[9]

The fact that most mass shooters kill to avenge grievances should cause us to focus on *how* grievances are converted by the brain into the desire to kill. The science of revenge explains this process. Grievances cue powerful cravings inside the brain to hurt the people who hurt us (or their proxies) to help us feel better. They activate the reward circuitry of the brain's nucleus accumbens and dorsal striatum, giving rise to wanting and craving revenge for satisfaction, pleasure, and reduction of pain. These cravings may become compulsive and habit-forming, inhibiting or overriding the executive function circuitry of the brain's prefrontal cortex. Mass killers behave like people suffering from severe substance use disorders who compulsively ingest dangerous drugs of abuse like heroin and fentanyl despite knowing they risk death by doing so. In the case of mass killers, they compulsively assault others using dangerous weapons of abuse like semiautomatic handguns and assault rifles—despite knowing they risk death by doing so.

Can we really call mass killers addicts when they rarely commit more than a single mass killing? Yes. Remember that the behavior to which they're addicted isn't "mass killing." It's grievance-cued revenge fantasizing and seeking. Mass murderers are "angry, grievance-collecting loner[s]."[10] The well-known Pathway to Violence model used by threat assessment experts to identify individuals at risk of mass violence theorizes that mass killers move through six steps: (1) grievance, (2) violent ideation, (3) research and planning, (4) preparation, (5) probing and breaching, and (6) attack.[11] Steps 1 and 2 involve repetitive grievance and revenge rumination and fantasy. This may include months or years of grievance collecting and lesser acts of revenge seeking that may or may not involve violence. The culminating mass killing event that attracts the attention of the media and the public is not the first but, more often, the last of many repetitive and habitual acts of grievance rumination and revenge gratification in fantasy and/or real life. It's the final, glorious overdose using the most powerful drug in the maximal quantity available to achieve the maximum high. How can this dysfunctional brain-biological process with neurobiological symptoms not be considered a severe mental illness?

Many mental health professionals justify this position by arguing that if we identify violent people as mentally ill, we risk stigmatizing all people with mental illness as violent; and by referring to the studies above showing that people with serious mental illnesses—as defined by the *DSM*—are not more likely to commit acts of violence. There are two problems with this. First, the *DSM* fails to acknowledge "revenge use disorder" (revenge addiction) as a serious mental illness that leads to violence. Second, correcting this omission would avoid the problem of stigmatization. By identifying "revenge use disorder" as the specific mental illness that leads to the greatest risk of violence, and by emphasizing that the risk of violence for those with revenge use disorder is on a spectrum of mild to severe (like substance use disorders), we avoid stigmatizing people with other forms of mental illness—or mild revenge use disorders—who pose little risk.

This is common practice in medicine. For example, there's a severe airborne respiratory disease that produces a cough and kills more than a million people around the world each year. It's called tuberculosis, caused by *Mycobacterium tuberculosis*. There's also a mild respiratory disease that produces a cough and very few deaths. It's called the common cold, caused by rhinoviruses. By giving these two respiratory illnesses specific names and identifying their specific causes, characteristics, risks, and how to diagnose and treat them, we're able to identify, isolate, and treat those with high-risk tuberculosis while avoiding the stigmatization of those with low-risk common colds. This benefits everyone. There's no reason why we can't distinguish the mental illness that presents a high risk of violence (severe revenge use disorder) from the mental illnesses that do not—

particularly when failing to do so leads to injuries and deaths that could be prevented by giving mental health professionals and the public the correct information.

THE COURTROOM OF THE MASS KILLER'S MIND

To understand "*severe* revenge use disorder"—the most dangerous form of revenge addiction—we must examine patients who display the most severe symptoms of the disease. Mass murderers fit this category. How do they present? What are their symptoms? What do they tell us is happening to them? Do they report that they're overcome by irresistible cravings for revenge? Or are they just evil? Do they want it this way, or do they seek help to make their terrifying cravings stop?

Most mass murderers don't survive their killing sprees. When they do, they're often unwilling to speak with researchers about their motivations (I asked several serving life sentences in prison to speak with me for this book to no avail). However, the Violence Project found that about 23 percent of mass shooters in their database left behind manifestos or other communications, often posted on the internet for all to see, explaining what they were experiencing and why they wanted to kill. These manifestos attract widespread curiosity and attention, some of it prurient. There's vigorous debate about whether to make them available to the public, with some arguing the content is dangerous and risks encouraging copycats and others insisting the information is vital to researchers, scholars, and the public so we can learn why people kill and develop strategies for protecting ourselves.[12] I'm in the latter camp. We can't address a complex and dangerous problem like mass violence until we understand it. Instead of hiding these manifestos, we should be studying them to see if mass murderers are telling us something valuable—not about their twisted ideologies and interests, but about their desire to kill.

That's what we're going to do in the remainder of this chapter.

We're going to examine the manifestos of two mass murderers through the lens of the science of revenge. We're going to see whether they tell us anything about the desire to kill, how and why it forms, whether the killers want it to be there, what they tried to do to control it, and why they've failed. In other words, we're going inside the courtroom of the mass killer's mind.

We've done this already with Olga Hepnarová, who sent a manifesto to two Prague newspapers. We need to compare her case with those of other mass killers to see if there are common attributes, themes, and disease processes. As I emphasized in the previous chapter, we're not doing this to excuse or justify the crimes of mass murderers. We're doing it to understand how their real and imagined grievances are converted inside their brains into the desire to kill large numbers of people so we can prevent such crimes in the future.[13] In the process, we may be surprised to discover that instead of hearing only the unhinged, vile, hate-filled ravings of depraved monsters, we hear screams for help from desperate people afflicted by a merciless and deadly illness that's on the verge of taking their lives and the lives of others.

SEUNG-HUI CHO

On the morning of April 16, 2007, twenty-three-year-old Seung-Hui Cho, an English major at Virginia Polytechnic Institute and State University in Blacksburg, Virginia, went on an astonishing and horrifying rampage that left thirty-two students and faculty dead, plus himself, and seventeen wounded. News of the massacre shocked the world. At the time, it was the deadliest shooting by a single individual in U.S. history—an ignoble distinction that, sadly, has since been far surpassed. The Virginia Tech massacre has also been among the most thoroughly investigated mass shootings in history, making it particularly appropriate for our purposes here. We'll begin with what Cho did, and then we'll examine his manifesto to uncover why.

The Killing[14]

At about 7:15 a.m. on April 16, Seung-Hui Cho entered the dorm room of Emily Hilscher, a student with whom he had no apparent prior relationship, and inexplicably shot her with a handgun at close range. When the student resident assistant Ryan Clark went to see what was happening, Cho shot him as well. Cho then fled back to his own dorm room in a nearby building undetected. Hilscher and Clark later died of their wounds.

Virginia Tech Police rushing to the scene learned from a student that Hilscher's boyfriend had recently dropped her off at the dorm building and left the campus. Based on this information, the police began searching for the boyfriend as the primary suspect of what they assumed was an isolated act of intimate partner violence. For these reasons, Virginia Tech officials did not put out a warning to the school community, cancel classes, or lock down the campus— fateful decisions that have since been sharply criticized.

Meanwhile, Seung-Hui Cho remained alone and unsuspected inside his dorm room. While there, he changed out of his blood-stained clothing and shoes, worked on a computer document, deleted his university computer account, and removed the hard drive from his computer. He then outfitted himself with a shooting vest, a light jacket, and a backpack containing what investigators have described as his "killing tools": a hunting knife, heavy chains and padlocks, a hammer, a Glock 9mm semiautomatic handgun, a Walther .22-caliber semiautomatic handgun, and nearly four hundred rounds of ammunition loose and in rapid-loading, large quantity magazines.

With this equipment in tow, Cho left his dorm room. A student reported seeing him between 8:10 a.m. and 8:20 a.m. near a pond on campus where he might have disposed of his computer hard drive and cell phone, although neither had been found as of the time of the Virginia Tech Review Panel investigation. He then walked to the nearby Blacksburg post office off campus. There he mailed a package to NBC News in New York, with the mailing receipt indicating the time of mailing as 9:01 a.m.

From the post office, Cho proceeded to Norris Hall, a large engineering building on campus where classes had just begun. With students in their classrooms and the building quiet, Cho chained and padlocked the doors at each of three main student entrances. He then proceeded to the second floor of the building and began poking his head inside the classrooms and glancing around, attracting the attention of students but raising no alarm.

At 9:40 a.m., Cho made his move. He entered room 206, an advanced hydrology engineering class being taught by Professor G. V. Loganathan. Without saying a word, Cho shot and killed Professor Loganathan and opened fire on the students. Of thirteen total students in the class that morning, nine were murdered and two wounded. This all happened so quickly that nobody in the classroom was able to call for help.

Meanwhile, in nearby room 211, a French class being taught by the adjunct professor Jocelyne Couture-Nowak, the sounds of gunshots were recognized, and the student Colin Goddard placed an emergency 911 call to police. Other students shoved a table in front of the door as a barricade. The time was now 9:41 a.m.

Cho went from room 206 across the hall to room 207, a German class being taught by Christopher James Bishop. Cho immediately shot and killed Bishop and began firing at students while walking up and down the aisles of desks. Again, he spoke not a word.

Cho then moved on to room 211, the French class. He forced his way through the makeshift barricade and opened fire. One of the bullets struck Goddard, the student calling 911, causing him to drop his phone. The student Emily Haas retrieved the phone and pleaded with police to hurry. Cho shot at her twice, grazing her head and causing her to fall to the floor. While playing dead—which ultimately enabled her to survive the attack—Haas kept the line open while concealing the phone beneath her hair.

The time was now 9:45 a.m. The first police began arriving at Norris Hall. They heard gunshots coming from the building but were unable to gain entrance because the doors were chained and padlocked. Upstairs, Cho left room 211 and returned to room 207, the German class. Two injured students and two uninjured students tried to hold the door shut with their feet and hands. Cho was able to pry it open slightly and fire shots into the classroom but soon gave up.

He returned to room 211, the French class, and opened fire again on the students. He hit Goddard, the student who had placed the 911 call, twice more. Despite his multiple wounds, Goddard ultimately survived the attack, like Haas, by playing dead. But by the time Cho had finished his barbaric work in room 211, he had slaughtered Couture-Nowak and eleven other students and wounded six.

Cho next went to room 204, a solid mechanics class taught by Professor Liviu Librescu. Librescu courageously held the door shut while shouting for his students to leap out the windows. Cho fatally shot him through the door, burst inside, and opened fire. He killed one student and wounded three others. A total of ten students escaped by jumping out of the windows, plunging two stories to the ground below.

Cho returned to room 206, the advanced hydrology engineering class where he had begun the massacre, and opened fire again. In addition to Loganathan, Cho killed four students and wounded six others in room 206.

The time was now 9:50 a.m. Using a shotgun, police blasted their way into Norris Hall and raced up the stairs to the second floor. It is believed that Cho heard the shotgun blasts and realized his time was coming to an end. One minute later, at 9:51 a.m., he killed himself with a bullet to the head.

Eleven total minutes had elapsed from the time Seung-Hui Cho first pulled the trigger of his handgun in Norris Hall. During that brief time, he fired a total of 174 rounds, murdered thirty people, wounded seventeen, and killed himself. This is in addition to the two students he had already murdered in the dorm a little more than two hours earlier. He committed all this violence without speaking a word.

The Manifesto

The package that Seung-Hui Cho sent to NBC News in New York contained a printout of an eighteen-hundred-word manifesto and forty-three photographs, many of them menacing images of Cho brandishing his handguns while wearing his shooting vest.[15] The package also contained a pdf file of the manifesto indicating that it had last been modified at 7:24 a.m., just minutes after Cho had murdered his first two victims, Hilscher and Clark, in the dorm. The package also contained Microsoft Word files of prior drafts of the manifesto modified days before the rampage, a video recording of Cho reading a version of the manifesto dated April 10 (six days before the shooting), and some undated video clips of Cho making rambling, angry comments about students.

The following are excerpts of Cho's manifesto. They're terrifying and profane, but we must not look away if we want to prevent future mass killings. Using the science of revenge, we're going to search for clues about why Seung-Hui Cho wanted to kill, what he believed he would gain, whether he was aware of the negative consequences, whether he tried to resist it and why he failed, and whether he wanted it this way or believed he was sick and a victim of forces beyond his control.

EXCERPTS FROM THE MANIFESTO OF SEUNG-HUI CHO[16]

p. 1 Oh the happiness I could have had mingling among you hedonists, being counted as one of you, only if you didn't fuck the living shit out of me.

You could have been great. I could have been great. Ask yourself what you did to me to have made me clean the slate.

p. 2 Only if you could be the victim of your reprehensible and wicked crimes, you Christian Nazis, you would have brute-restrained your animal urges to fuck me.

You could be at home right now eating your fucking caviar and your fucking cognac, had you not ravenously raped my soul.

p. 3 For every action, there is an equal and opposite reaction. Can you feel the pain that you fucked us in, you Descendants of Satan? Well, can you feel it?

p. 4 All the shit you've given me, right back at you with hollow points [the types of bullets Cho used].

Don't you just wish you finished me off when you had the chance? Don't you just wish you killed me?

p. 5 You had a hundred billion chances and ways to have avoided today, but you decided to spill my blood. You forced me into a corner and gave me only one option. The decision was yours. Now you have blood on your hands that will never wash off, you Apostles of Sin.

p. 6 Congratulations. You have succeeded in extinguishing my life. Vandalizing my heart wasn't enough for you. Raping my soul wasn't enough for you. Committing emotional sodomy on me wasn't enough for you. Every single second wasted on your wanton hedonism and menacing sadism could have been used to prevent today. Ask yourselves, What was I doing all this time? All these months, hours, seconds. Only if you could have been the victim of your crimes. Only if you could have been the victim . . .

. . .

p. 11 By destroying we create. We create the feelings in you of what it is like to be the victim, what it is like to be fucked and destroyed. Because of your annihilations, we create and raise new breeds of Children who will show you fuckers what you have done to us. Like Easter, it will be a day of rebirth. It will be a start of a revolution of the Children that you fucked. You have never felt a single ounce of pain your whole life, thus, by destroying you, by giving you pain, we attempt to show you responsibilities and meanings of other people's lives.

. . .

p. 13 We have no sympathy in killing humans who have no respect for other people's lives.

p. 14 Now that the slate has been cleaned and you have the world's attention, the question is what are you going to do? Are you going to admit the truth or are you going to stand resolute on your mission to eternally fuck the Weak and the Defenseless and lie about it? Are you still going to use your power and manipulate the truth to end up with some sort of profit as you have always done? Are you going to skip over all the crimes you've committed and act as victims to the world so you can suck in millions of donation money to turn the situation into a profit? Your two million dollar house wasn't enough? Your BMW wasn't enough? Your inheritances weren't enough? You have to fuck and steal form [*sic*] the Poor and the Weak who have nothing in order to gratify your fucking pride and hedonism? What are you going to do with the blood money? Buy a new Mercedes? You want to brainwash your bratty, snobby kids that its [*sic*] right to steal from the poor, the Weak, and the Defenseless to always stay in power? The fat surpluses that you roll on everyday [*sic*] aren't enough? Fuck you. Your answer rings loud and clear.

. . .

p. 15 The blood of the Innocents should never be shed, but the wicked we shall spread our wings and strike. We do not want the Weak, the Defenseless, or the Innocent, but the sadistic, the corrupt, and the wicked who prey and rape from the Weak, the Defenseless, and the Innocent. We will seek and demolish them until our last breath. You Lifetakers may have succeeded in raping our souls and shattering our dreams—but mark our words—the vendetta you have witnessed today will reverberate throughout every home and every soul in America and will inspire the Innocent kids that you have fucked to start a war of vendetta. We will raise hell on earth that the world has never witnessed. Millions of deaths and millions of gallons of blood on the streets.

p. 16 will not quench the avenging phoenix that you have caused us to unleash. Generation after generation, we martyrs, like Eric and Dylan [the infamous Columbine High School shooters], will sacrifice our lives to fuck you thousand folds for what you Apostles of Sin have done to us.

Pain of every atom between air and water, sky and ground, heaven and hell, life and death wouldn't begin to explain the experience that we went through under your wrath.

What did you expect me to do, you violators of human rights?

p. 17 As the time approached, I wished for a last minute miracle and [sic] discard this mission you've given me. Heaven knows I wouldn't hurt a single leaf of a flower. But when the time came, I did it. I had to. What other choices did you give me? All this time . . . You never know that [sic] a human being is capable of doing until you fuck him to the edge.

When you're raped of everything, you got nothing to lose.

. . .

p. 23 Are you happy now that you have destroyed my life? Now that you have stolen everything you could from me? Now that you have gone on a 9/11 on my life like fucking Osama. Now that you have fucked your own people like fucking Kim Jong-Il. Now that you have gone on a hummer safari on my life like fucking Bush? Are you happy now?

The Analysis

I said Cho's manifesto was terrifying and profane. Fortunately, we have experts to help us understand it. The forensic psychiatrist James Knoll IV at SUNY Upstate Medical University performed a psycholinguistic analysis of the manifesto in a 2010 article in *The Journal of the American Academy of Psychiatry and the Law* with the ominous title "The 'Pseudocommando' Mass Murderer: Part II, The Language of Revenge."[17]

In part 1 of his article, Dr. Knoll anticipated aspects of the coming neuroscience of revenge addiction. He theorized that mass murder is motivated by retribution for perceived affronts to self-esteem that activate our evolved "psychological hard-wiring" of revenge, which was originally meant to support survival but that, in modern times, has become "available for excessive use in situations that do not involve survival of the body, but survival of the ego."[18] He also noted that revenge fantasies produce pleasure, referring to a telling observation from the psychoanalyst Irwin C. Rosen that revenge "dominates thought and impels action much as an addiction or erotomania does."[19]

Analyzing Cho's manifesto in part 2 of his article, Dr. Knoll uncovers the evidence of revenge addiction we're seeking. He points to many of the passages above where Cho states his grievances, in particular how he believes his ego and core identity have been attacked and destroyed by students and faculty at Virginia Tech. Although

Cho criticizes what he perceives to be rampant hedonism at the school, his rage centers on being socially excluded from taking part in it and bitter envy, as a child of relatively poor immigrants, of his wealthier classmates.[20] Cho uses extreme language to describe the instances of his social exclusion as "wicked" crimes, analogizing them to the "rape" of his soul, the "extinguishing" of his life, the theft of his "happiness," and the infliction of unremitting "pain." Whether he's overstating or entirely imagining this is beside the point. The perception of identity destruction for Cho was real and, therefore, sufficient to activate powerful revenge cravings inside his brain. The fact that none of his ultimate victims likely knew him or had done anything to him is also beside the point. Revenge by proxy is revenge and just as satisfying.

What did Seung-Hui Cho believe he would gain from the massacre? He says he was seeking pleasure and relief by inflicting the "pain" he experienced upon his perceived persecutors: "All the shit you've given me, right back at you with hollow points." He wants the joy of creating "the feelings in you of what it is like to be the victim. . . . Like Easter [the most joyous of Christian feast days], it will be a day of rebirth." "We have no sympathy in killing humans who have no respect for other people's lives."

Was Cho aware of the negative consequences of what he was about to do? Very much so. He acknowledges not only that he's planning to inflict enormous suffering and death on others but that his own life will be destroyed in the process. In an unquoted passage from page 19 of his manifesto, he says that all those who have suffered like him are with him "in life and death and spirit. We'll soon be together." He concludes his manifesto by acknowledging that his life is being ended, comparing this to people who were slaughtered by Osama bin Laden, Kim Jong Il, and George Bush.

Did Cho try to resist the revenge cravings that were overwhelming him? Did he plead for help? To these questions, he speaks like a patient with a terminal illness: "As the time approached, I wished for a last minute miracle and [sic] discard this mission you've given me.

Heaven knows I wouldn't hurt a single leaf of a flower. But when the time came, I did it. I had to. What other choices did you give me?" Cho insists his victims could have helped him—and, by helping him, themselves: "You had a hundred billion chances and ways to have avoided today, but you decided to spill my blood."

The psychiatrist Aradhana Bela Sood at Virginia Commonwealth University served on the Virginia Tech Review Panel investigating the massacre and performed a psychological autopsy of Seung-Hui Cho.[21] Examining medical records of Cho's childhood, Dr. Sood found evidence of major depression during his middle school years, for which he received what appeared to be successful treatment. He had recurring anxiety and selective mutism—an inability to speak in stressful situations—continuing into college. However, Dr. Sood found no indication that Cho suffered from a recognized serious mental illness (for example, psychosis, schizophrenia, bipolar disorder, or borderline personality disorder). She also found that antisocial personality disorder (sociopathy/psychopathy) could not be established.

Dr. Knoll and Dr. Sood did not consider severe revenge addiction or revenge use disorder, yet evidence for Cho having this dangerous condition is abundant. Dr. Sood found that Cho likely had a *delusional disorder* centered on his imagined *victimization* by other students and the university.[22] Delusional disorder is a serious form of paranoia recognized in the *DSM* as a persistent and unshakable belief in things that are not true despite incontrovertible evidence to the contrary.[23] These beliefs may be persecutory, meaning that one imagines being deliberately harmed and victimized by others. The science of revenge tells us that imagined grievances are sufficient to provoke very real revenge cravings in reward (GO!) circuitry as the brain tries to rebalance pain with pleasure. If the executive function (STOP!) circuitry is inhibited or hijacked, retaliatory violence may follow.

We find multiple examples of this in Cho's manifesto. For example, he insisted that his identity had been "raped" and destroyed by students and faculty at Virginia Tech—something obviously not true. But Dr. Sood also points to instances when Cho's (often violent) fictional writings for classes were harshly criticized by faculty and even rejected by a New York publishing house—outcomes that Cho, as an English major, appears to have regarded as attacking his identity and shattering his future.[24] These were real grievances, but Cho took them to a delusional extreme. The forensic behavioral scientist and former FBI profiler Roger Depue, who also served on the Virginia Tech Review Panel investigating the massacre, theorized that "these rejections were devastating to [Cho] and he fantasized about getting revenge from a world he perceived as rejecting him."[25]

The Virginia Tech Review Panel also pointed to a chain of events during Cho's junior year when an awkward and unwelcome romantic overture by Cho to a female student resulted in a report by that student to the Virginia Tech Police, who met with Cho and instructed him to have no further contact with her.[26] This was another real grievance that Cho took to an extreme. Publicly shamed and humiliated, Cho complained to one of his dormmates, "I might as well kill myself." This prompted the dormmate to report to police that Cho might be suicidal, which led to Cho being subjected to a psychiatric evaluation and commitment hearing. Two evaluators found that Cho was not an imminent danger to himself, but the judge found that he was and ordered outpatient treatment. However, Cho was discharged the same day. The science of revenge tells us that grievances involving public shame and humiliation can activate powerful revenge cravings in the reward circuitry of the brain.

Putting all this together, we have unearthed a sequential connection between a form of mental illness recognized in the *DSM* (delusional disorder) and mass violence. To be sure, a diagnosis of delusional disorder does *not* itself mean that somebody is at risk of becoming violent. People can have delusions about any number of things. However, if the delusions in question involve *persecution and victimization,* the science of revenge tells us that we must consider whether these delusional grievances might be activating very real revenge cravings signaling potential revenge use disorder and increased risk of a revenge attack. This is how an otherwise nonthreatening mental illness (delusional disorder) can lead to a potentially deadly mental illness (severe revenge use disorder).

What, then, does the science of revenge tell us could have been done to prevent the Virginia Tech massacre? Seung-Hui Cho could have been evaluated and treated for delusional disorder to control his false beliefs of being persecuted and victimized—with the goal of reducing or dispelling his grievances. *Or,* he could have been evaluated and treated for revenge use disorder—with the goal of reducing or dispelling the dangerous revenge desires activated by his grievances. *Or,* he could have been evaluated, treated, and, if necessary, committed as being at risk of having a revenge attack. *Or, ideally, all of the above.*

This is not to minimize the challenge facing mental health and public safety professionals in uncovering what's happening inside somebody's brain. Much of what we know about Cho was either unknown or fragmented prior to the massacre. But signs of potentially dangerous revenge addiction were there. He was psychiatrically evaluated a little more than a year before the massacre after his remark about killing himself—*made in response to a very real grievance created by police instructing him to stop contacting a young woman in whom he was romantically interested.* The police did their duty, of course, in ensuring the woman's safety. However, Cho's overreaction, by suggesting suicide rather than respecting her wishes and moving on, should have prompted a thorough evaluation into how Cho was handling his grievances and any revenge desires they might be activating (against himself and others)—rather than merely performing a standard screening for mental illness and suicide risk, which obviously missed the underlying problem. Indeed, the science of revenge suggests that grievance and revenge addiction evaluations should be a routine part of the standard suicide risk evaluation protocol in all cases. Revenge itself is a motivation for suicide and murder-suicide.[27] The presence of strong revenge desires and fantasies in an individual being evaluated for suicide risk should be a red flag. The science of revenge tells us what to look for and what steps to take to prevent violence, if we know to use it.

ANDRE BING

The second mass murder we're going to consider took place fifteen years after the Virginia Tech massacre. Our analysis of the killer's manifesto in this case will go more quickly because the investigation afterward was far less extensive. As mass killings have become more common in the United States and abroad, it seems that we're gradually giving up hope of understanding the motivations of the killers and developing a public mental health approach to preventing these tragedies. The science of revenge tells us otherwise. We have renewed reason for hope and should be redoubling our efforts.

The Killing

Shortly after 10:00 p.m. on November 22, 2022, during a meeting of ten to fifteen employees at a Walmart store in Chesapeake, Virginia, Andre Bing, a thirty-one-year-old shift manager, aimed a 9mm semiautomatic handgun at one of his co-workers and opened fire.[28] By the time Bing finished shooting, he had murdered six of his fellow employees, wounded four, and killed himself. Approximately forty customers were in the store at the time and escaped. This all took place just before the Thanksgiving holiday.

The Walmart employee Jessica Wilczewski, who had only recently started working at the store, witnessed the killings while hiding beneath a table. She described Bing as hunting down specific employees for slaughter. After shooting his victims, she said, he "went back and shot dead bodies that were already dead. To make sure."[29] When Bing found Wilczewski hiding under the table, he pointed his gun at her, but after realizing she wasn't one of the workers he intended to kill, he said to her, "Jessie, go home." She fled from the store in terror.

Bing had worked at the store for twelve years. Police said he had no criminal record and legally purchased his handgun on the morning of the shootings. Some employees described him as generally normal but occasionally grumpy.[30] Others described him as abusive and often angry. They said that two years earlier Walmart had investigated co-worker complaints that Bing was aggressive and threatening, but he continued in his job anyway.[31]

Thankfully, the body count left behind by Andre Bing is not as large as Seung-Hui Cho's, but this is of little comfort to his victims.

The Manifesto

Chesapeake police searching Bing's cell phone after the shooting found a manifesto that Bing called his "Death note."[32] Below is the full text, retrieved from the City of Chesapeake's social media account. The names have been redacted by the police.

MANIFESTO OF ANDRE BING

Death note

Sorry God I've failed you. This was not your fault but my own. I failed to listen to the groans of the holy spirit which made me a poor representation of You. I was harassed by idiots with low intelligence and a lack of wisdom[.] I remained strong through most of the torment but my dignity was completely taken away beyond repair by my phone getting hacked.

I can't say that they were the only ones that lacked intelligence and wisdom, I was just as guilty and failed my management team and everyone that ever loved me by convincing them that I was normal. _____ and the associates orcastraighted [*sic*] it they laughed and made subtle code speeches which I eventually figured out. I thought _____ was my friend but he betrayed me, betrayal is one of the worst feelings next to regret.

They laughed at me and said that I was like Jeffrey Dahmer. I would have never killed anyone that entered my home.

A few months back I had overheard _____ talking to _____ and he told me that he had been trying to get rid of me since day one. After I heard that I lashed out.

The associates gave me evil twisted grins, mocked me and celebrated my downfall the last day. That's why they suffer the same fate as me.

_____ from maintenance was emanating with the holy spirit which I could feel, people thought that she was crazy for walking out but unlike me she actually listened to the holy spirit like _____[.] _____ knew that they were antagonizing me so one day she approached me in personnel and apologized to me. On the last day she looked me in the eyes terrified by a demonic aura.

My true intent was never to murder anyone believe it or not, I was actually one of the most loving people in the world if you would get to know me. I just wanted a wife that was equally yoked as I and obsessed over the thought; however, I didn't deserve a wife.

I hope that people will learn from everyones [*sic*] mistakes and truly love God and not the material possessions of the world.

My only wish would have been to start over from scratch and that my parents would have paid closer attention to my social deficits. Sorry ☹ everyone but I did not plan this I promise things just fell in place like I was led by the Satan. I have written songs in the past though. I only did it when I realized that my phone was hacked and was giving the worst feeling imaginable. I wish that I could have saved everyone from harm.

I will spare _____ because I have a special place for her in my ♥ because my mother died from cancer. Please _____ let everyone know that bitter seed apricots are the cure for cancer and not the Dr.

My God forgive me for what I'm going to do . . .

The Analysis

I am not a psychiatrist and will not attempt a psycholinguistic analysis of Andre Bing's manifesto. It seems likely, however, that Bing suffered from one or more forms of mental illness recognized by the *DSM*. Yet they were not the reason he became a mass murderer. The science of revenge tells us that what drove Andre Bing to kill were his real or imagined grievances against his co-workers and the powerful, unrestrained cravings for revenge those grievances activated inside his brain.

Bing's grievances were many: He said he felt "harassed," "betrayed," "laughed at," "mocked," that his "phone was hacked," that he'd been compared to "Jeffrey Dahmer" (a serial killer who murdered and cannibalized his victims), and that his "dignity was completely taken away."

Bing's desire for revenge was overwhelming. He explained that the co-workers who "mocked me and celebrated my downfall" must "suffer the same fate as me." He compared the inexorable compulsion he felt to do this to being under the control of dark forces: "like I was led by the Satan." He insisted that his "true intent was never to murder anyone believe it or not, I was actually one of the most loving people in the world if you would get to know me." Bing knew he was ill. He wished that his "parents would have paid closer attention to [his] social deficits." Yet he accepted personal responsibility for "convincing [people he loved] that [he] was normal." He apologized for failing and asked for forgiveness.

Based on this admittedly limited record, we may surmise that Andre Bing became a mass murderer because he was experiencing a revenge attack on the day of the killings. Two years earlier, his co-workers saw early signs of revenge addiction and reported them to their employer. Sadly, Walmart, which investigated the complaints, lacked the science and expertise to understand what was happening. This is a tragedy that continues to repeat itself in mass shootings.

A MASS OF MASS KILLERS

I've examined the manifestos of other mass killers: Patrick Crusius (2019, murdered twenty-three, wounded twenty-two, primarily Latinos, at a Walmart store in El Paso, Texas); Dylann Roof (2015, murdered nine, wounded one, all Black, at an African Methodist Episcopal church in Charleston, South Carolina); Elliot Rodger (2014, murdered six, wounded fourteen, primarily female students at the University of California, Santa Barbara); Christopher Dorner (2013, murdered four, wounded three, all officers or related to officers of the Los Angeles Police Department); Gang Lu (1991, murdered five, wounded one, all faculty or employees at the University of Iowa).

Reading the manifestos of mass killers is grueling, and I'm not going to put you through any more of it. What you need to know from these manifestos (and you can confirm it for yourself if you wish) is that each one describes an individual with real or imagined grievances and overwhelming, unrestrained cravings for revenge to relieve their pain. That was their brain-biological motivation to kill.

The primary variation between them is in the *types of grievances*—not their *motivation* (revenge).

We also see that in nearly all cases the killers expressed an awareness that they were ill, wanted help, and were angry or regretful that help never arrived or that they failed to secure it. The primary exception to this is political grievance manifestos, as with Crusius and Roof, or Adolf Hitler's manifesto, *Mein Kampf*. For political killers, awareness of illness is replaced by hubris, narcissism, ideology, and the desire for heroic fame. But we should not be misled. Political killers always express deeply felt grievances and revenge as the motivation for their massacres. The difference is that political grievances are corporate in nature, not merely personal. As we'll see in greater detail in the next chapter, these killers seek through their acts of revenge not only to make themselves feel better but also the groups of people whom they purport to represent or act on behalf of—regardless of whether those people truly share the killers' grievances or have sought or authorized such vengeance.

Contrary to popular theory, the science of revenge does not support the contention that the desire for fame alone motivates mass murder. Many people desire fame, but few seek to achieve it through mass killing—which typically ends with the killer dead or incarcerated for life and unable to enjoy the benefits of fame. The activating grievance could, however, be the real or imagined *denial of fervently desired fame or recognition*. For example, one of Seung-Hui Cho's grievances appears to have been the rejection of his writing by a New York publisher. This seems to have been very painful for him (as it is for most authors). Had his work been accepted, so great might have been his compensating joy and confidence that it is possible to imagine that the massacre would never have occurred—how thin a line exists between grievance and revenge, life and death. The potential to achieve fame from mass killing appears to be more of a secondary benefit that revenge-driven killers sometimes pursue to maximize the pleasure they will experience by increasing body counts and media coverage and, resultingly, the pain they inflict.

Viewed through the lens of the science of revenge, mass murderers begin to appear less like monsters who were born to kill and more like very sick, traumatized individuals experiencing medical emergencies and in need of urgent treatment *before they become mass murderers*. If not to save them, then at least to save ourselves.

CHAPTER 6

THESE ARE THE DEADLIEST REVENGE ADDICTS IN HUMAN HISTORY

The three most deadly people in modern human history—Adolf Hitler, Joseph Stalin, and Mao Zedong—are responsible for a combined death toll of approximately 102 million people.* Of this number, approximately 38.5 million were killed in non-battle-related executions, murders, and prison camp deaths.† Although much has been written about these men, their behaviors and motivations have never been examined through the lens of the science of revenge. We're going to do that in this chapter.

We're about to see for the first time that Hitler, Stalin, and Mao slaughtered millions of people not because of an inherent evilness of character but as the result of severe, uncontrolled revenge addiction— the same thing that motivates teens to murder their classmates, lovers to murder their partners, and gang members to murder each

---

* Matthew White calculates that Hitler is responsible for 42 million deaths; Stalin, 20 million deaths; and Mao, 40 million deaths (White, *Atrocities*, 271, 382, 429). Looking back to ancient times, White adds Genghis Khan (1162–1227) with an estimated death toll of 40 million (ibid., 115).

† White calculates that Hitler is responsible for the murders of 15.5 million people; Stalin, 13 million murders; and Mao, 10 million murders (ibid., 393).

other on city streets. This may seem like a shocking claim, but the evidence that follows is not easily dismissed.

ADOLF HITLER

Adolf Hitler is the undisputed führer of revenge addiction. How do we know he was addicted to revenge? Because he told us so, and because his atrocities can only be explained as the result of compulsive grievance production and revenge seeking on a massive scale using advanced methods, systems, and technologies for addicting and gratifying the revenge cravings of entire populations.

Evidence of Hitler's revenge addiction appears in one of his earliest public addresses, given seventeen years *prior* to the start of World War II. Speaking as the new chairman of the German Workers' Party (later to become the Nazi Party), he outlines his grievances and demands for revenge against German politicians and Jews who he believes "stabbed Germany in the back" by signing the 1918 armistice that ended fighting in World War I and the Treaty of Versailles that formally concluded hostilities the following year.

A bit of background here is helpful. The terms of the Treaty of Versailles were dictated by the victorious Allies and designed to inflict severe retribution on the German people. The treaty forced the Germans to accept responsibility for starting the war, agree to surrender foreign financial holdings, make enormous reparations payments, demilitarize, and cede German territory in valuable industrial regions. So harsh were these terms that the British economist John Maynard Keynes, who participated in the treaty negotiations on behalf of Great Britain, walked out in protest, predicting that the treaty would lead to a new and far more disastrous war:

> If we aim deliberately at the impoverishment of Central Europe, vengeance, I dare predict, will not limp. Nothing can then delay for very long that final civil war between

the forces of Reaction and the despairing convulsions of Revolution, before which the horrors of the late German war will fade into nothing, and which will destroy, whoever is victor, the civilisation and the progress of our generation.[1]

Grim stuff. And prescient. Keynes understood how grievances trigger lethal revenge desires and violence at national and international scale.

Now here's Hitler just three years later, on September 18, 1922, speaking at the Circus Krone in Munich and setting in motion the terrifying fulfillment of Keynes's prophecy. He lists his grievances by number and states exactly what he intends to do about them. Here are just a few snippets:

> We must call to account the November criminals of 1918. It cannot be that two million Germans should have fallen in vain [during World War I] and that afterwards one should sit down as friends at the same table with traitors. No, we do not pardon, we demand—Vengeance!

> The dishonoring of the nation must cease. For betrayers of their Fatherland and informers the gallows is the proper place.

> The present laxity in the fight against usury must be abandoned. Here the fitting punishment is the same as that for the betrayers of their Fatherland.

> We must demand a great enlightenment on the subject of the Peace Treaty. With thoughts of love? No! but in holy hatred against those who have ruined us. . . .

> If families who have lived in Germany for a thousand years are now expropriated, we must do the same to the Jewish usurers.

We demand immediate expulsion of all Jews who have entered Germany since 1914, and of all those, too, who through trickery on the Stock Exchange or through other shady transactions have gained their wealth.

Extremes must be fought by extremes. Against the infection of materialism, against the Jewish pestilence we must hold aloft a flaming ideal. And if others speak of the World and Humanity we say the Fatherland—and only the Fatherland![2]

The science of revenge tells us that the desire to inflict severe harm on others arises from a perception, real or imagined, of a great harm inflicted upon ourselves. This harm, this grievance, is deeply painful for the person experiencing it. This pain triggers a powerful craving for revenge in anticipation of experiencing pleasure and temporary relief of the pain, just as narcotics provide pleasure and temporary relief of pain.

In Hitler's speech above, we see him expressing the (false) perception that certain groups of people had betrayed Germany at the end of World War I, causing national humiliation, shame, and ruin. The deep and searing pain of this perception of wrongdoing triggered within him and those who believed him a powerful desire for revenge. The Cambridge University professor of history Brendan Simms states it this way: "It was not the war that made Hitler . . . but the peace."[3]

For seventeen years, from 1922 to the start of World War II in 1939, Hitler and his followers methodically nursed, multiplied, and magnified their grievances against the "November criminals of 1918" and others. They fantasized and meticulously planned their revenge, creating organizations and systematizing processes for pleasurable revenge delivery within Germany. They formed the Protective Squad, Storm Troopers, and the Gestapo to seek revenge against and eliminate internal "traitors" and resisters. Hitler and his followers also worked to seize and expand Germany's enormous military-industrial complex and develop some of the most powerful weapons in the history of the world to obtain pleasurable revenge against other "criminal" nations. To do all this, Hitler and his followers relentlessly inflamed grievances among the German people, driving the nation to experience searing collective trauma, humiliation, shame, and betrayal and to crave revenge against the perceived wrongdoers in unison.

Behavioral research shows that psychological rather than physical grievances are more likely to lead to violence.[4] I've conducted full-text computer searches of Hitler's major speeches to the German people from 1922 through 1945. My searches reveal that he used derivatives of the following terms *more than thirteen hundred times* in his public addresses: "betray," "treason," "traitor," "humiliation," "conspiracy," "plot," "manipulate," "deception," "blackmail," "criminals," "insult," "slander," "lies," "shame," "degradation," "disgrace," "mutiny," "mocking," "stabbed," "violation," "abused," "oppressed," "enslaved," "guilt," "ruin," "decay," "catastrophe," "revenge," "vengeance," "retribution," and "retaliation."[5] These are not the words of a statesman. They are the words of a revenge addict.

REVENGE AGAINST THE JEWS—AND THE WORLD

Historians have found little evidence of antisemitism in Hitler prior to the signing of the armistice in 1918.[6] To the contrary, the historical record shows that Hitler maintained friendships and cordial relations with Jews in his younger years. What turned him into a genocidal maniac? To answer this question, we must look deeper into his past and his susceptibility to revenge addiction.

Although born in Austria, Adolf Hitler enlisted in the Bavarian Army when he was twenty-five years old, soon after Germany declared war with France at the start of World War I. His enlistment itself was a personal retaliation of sorts. Hitler's desire as a young man had been to work as an artist, not a soldier. He twice applied to study at the Vienna Academy of Fine Arts and was twice rejected. He nevertheless remained in Vienna for five years, living on a dwindling inheritance while painting tourist scenes and trying to sell them. With few buyers and his money running out, he experienced differing states of poverty, sometimes sleeping in homeless shelters and relying upon charity for food.[7]

During this period, Hitler developed a deep resentment for cosmopolitan, multiethnic Vienna with its growing population of immigrants, artists, musicians, intellectuals, businessmen, and prosperous Jews who, he believed, had rejected his talents. He became increasingly drawn to the nationalistic and socialistic political movements seething in Vienna at the time calling for a greater Austria-Germany based on racial purity. As an Austrian, Hitler was obligated to serve in the army of his homeland. However, disaffected by his experiences in Vienna, he moved to Munich. When World War I broke out, he applied to serve in the Bavarian Army, deliberately depriving the Austria that had rejected him of his service. The young Hitler, it seems, was deeply aggrieved and vengeful.

In the German military, Hitler found the acceptance he craved and discovered something he was both good at and appreciated for doing. Given the entry-level rank of private, he was sent to the western front as a rifleman. At Ypres, he encountered death and danger on a wide scale. His first taste of combat came, surprisingly, not from enemy forces but from other German troops who, disoriented by a dense morning fog, mistook his regiment for British soldiers and opened fire. With Germans shooting Germans, an officer ordered Hitler and another private, Ernst Schmidt, to trek back through the deadly cross fire to their regimental command and plead for an order to stop shooting. Hitler and Schmidt somehow delivered the message without getting killed, and the shooting finally ended.[8]

When Hitler and Schmidt returned to their unit, they found their comrades under a withering British artillery attack. Their commanding officers and all but one sergeant lay wounded or dead. In a letter to an associate, Ernst Hepp, Hitler described running for his life across an open field with shells bursting all around him, uprooting trees and filling the air with a thick yellow haze. He spotted a trench and leaped in, landing unexpectedly on cushioned ground. Looking down, he realized he was standing on the bodies of dead and wounded British soldiers.[9] German artillery returned fire on the British. A shell shrieked past Hitler, exploding in a nearby trench. Hitler described British soldiers crawling up from the earth like insects and how he and his comrades attacked them, slaughtering those who refused to surrender and seizing the remainder as prisoners.

All this happened on Hitler's first day of battle.

Two days later, Hitler and Schmidt were remembered for getting the word through to German regimental headquarters and permanently assigned to be battlefield messengers. Hitler loved this job and performed it admirably, exhibiting bravery and cunning while traversing active battlefields. At one point, he even risked his own life to save the life of a lieutenant from British machine-gun fire. For these acts of courage, Hitler was awarded the Iron Cross, Second Class and given the rank of lance corporal. Upon receiving the medal, he wrote in a letter to his landlord in Munich, "It was the happiest day of my life."[10]

By the end of the war, 3,754 men in Hitler's regiment had been killed. Hitler had been hit by shrapnel and wounded seriously in the thigh. He was gassed and nearly blinded. Yet reflecting upon it years later in *Mein Kampf,* he described his experience of World War I as "the greatest and most unforgettable time of my earthly existence."[11]

Hitler believed that all this—the glorious victories and noble sacrifices—had been stolen from him and his comrades by the "November criminals of 1918." He was convinced, as were many Germans at the time, that Germany was defeated not by its enemies on the battlefield but by its own citizens working from within: politicians on the left and the right, communists, and Jews who allegedly betrayed Germany's soldiers. Unknown to Hitler and most of his fellow citizens, it was the German general field marshal Paul von

Hindenburg and the German general Erich Ludendorff—not the politicians or Jews—who had requested the 1918 armistice. They insisted that politicians sign the armistice rather than themselves, giving them the opportunity to avoid blame for the loss.[12]

Thus was born the great stab-in-the-back myth that worked all too well. In Lance Corporal Adolf Hitler's eyes, and in the eyes of many Germans, the politicians and the Jews were in fact traitors who had betrayed the German Army and people. From 1918 onward, Hitler saw himself and Germany as victims of the greatest form of national betrayal, shame, humiliation, and dishonor imaginable—and, therefore, entitled to seek revenge by all means available.

Hitler surely learned at some point that he and his countrymen had been duped. The stab-in-the-back myth was an outright lie. But by this point, he had also learned the most powerful lesson of all violent political movements: By repeating and embellishing grievances, one can enrage the masses and inflame their cravings for revenge, and the person who promises to gratify these cravings will be uplifted, worshipped, and, ultimately, given absolute power to gratify their lust for retribution.

This doesn't mean that Hitler didn't believe what he was saying. From his early rejection and humiliation as an artist in Vienna through his experiences during the war, Hitler was, like all mass killers, a collector of grievances imaginary and real. His belief that Jews had betrayed Germany was, by all accounts, genuinely held and unshakable despite undeniable evidence to the contrary. The science of revenge tells us that a false grievance, even one completely manufactured, is sufficient to trigger a genuine desire for revenge. The science also suggests that addicted people will search for and fabricate reasons to feel aggrieved to drive revenge craving and gratification in vicious cycles.

Hitler was thoroughly hooked on revenge and told us so. In *Mein Kampf*, he describes his enthusiasm for victory in war and the destruction of one's enemies as "an intoxication."[13] He also describes how, in mass gatherings of thousands, the desire for revenge can be converted "into the mighty effect of suggestive intoxication and enthusiasm."[14]

In these ways, Adolf Hitler, and all of us, manufacture the world's most dangerous drug inside our own brains, and inside the brains of others. Sometimes we do this with the assistance of vengeful tyrants; other times we become the vengeful tyrants of our own private worlds. We become perpetrators of suffering and violence by believing we've been the victims of suffering and violence. We may even invent these wrongs, or have them invented for us, or cling to them long after they've been disproven. Truth and objectivity have never been preconditions to murder. If anything, murder is the natural child of their absence. Beginning in 1922, Adolf Hitler went on a twenty-three-year binge of revenge seeking unparalleled in the history of the world, infecting and reinfecting millions of Germans with imagined grievances and indulging in greater, more satisfying frenzies of revenge intoxication. Hitler became both junkie and kingpin.

As Hitler's addiction deepened, he sought new and more potent ways of gratifying it. From June 30 to July 2, 1934, during an event known as the Night of the Long Knives, Hitler oversaw the ruthless execution of his close friend, former ally, and head of the Nazi Party's Storm Troopers, Ernst Röhm, and more than eighty others, for opposing his leadership, violating his orders, threatening his power, and alleged acts of treason—all events largely invented by Hitler's fellow Nazi leaders Hermann Göring and Heinrich Himmler. In a national speech explaining the executions afterward, Hitler—much like Olga Hepnarová after murdering eight people with a truck in Prague—described the courtroom inside his mind, grandiosely expanding it to national scale:

> If anyone reproaches me and asks why I did not resort to the regular courts of justice, then all I can say is this. In this hour I was responsible for the fate of the German

people, and thereby I became the supreme judge of the German people. I gave the order to shoot the ringleaders in this treason, and I further gave the order to cauterize down to the raw flesh the ulcers of this poisoning of the wells in our domestic life.[15]

With power now consolidated and sufficient warning having been given to all German civilian and military officials never to cross him, Hitler would target not only German Jews but also intellectuals, artists, dissidents, gypsies, homosexuals, and disabled people—anyone who he imagined might bring shame or humiliation upon his vision of a pure Aryan race.

Hitler expanded his revenge seeking outward through the doctrine of *Lebensraum* to the non-Aryan people of neighboring nations. In this way, he justified the use of force to seize territory in eastern Europe and Russia and to exterminate resisters as aggressors and enemies. He ordered the development of advanced new tactics, devices, and means of gratifying his revenge cravings and mopping up the aftermath of his binges, including death squads, death camps, and mechanized crematoria for destroying the bodies. He ordered the development of panzer tanks, mechanized artillery, blitzkriegs, U-boats, torpedoes, fighter aircraft, bombers, machine guns, flamethrowers, and ballistic missiles. Hitler's revenge addiction went on to consume the lives of approximately 24 million Soviet soldiers and civilians; 7 million Germans; 5.6 million Poles; 1 million Yugoslavians; 800,000 Romanians; 567,000 French; 500,000 Greeks; 580,000 Hungarians; 460,000 Italians; 450,000 British; 350,000 Lithuanians; 418,000 Americans; 300,000 Dutch; and many others—including nearly 6 million Jews.[16]

Adolf Hitler evolved from a homeless and harmless artist into a savage, dangerous revenge addict who, by a series of tragic events, near misses, and remarkable circumstances, seized control of a wounded nation and used its vast human, technological, and material resources to spread and gratify his insatiable addiction. To be sure, revenge gratification can explain only the brain-biological motivation that drove Hitler to kill. It cannot explain the delusional grievances and perceived victimizations that triggered the motivation, or the drive to expand it to cataclysmic scale. But by using the lens of the science of revenge, we're able to cut through the chaos and distraction inside Hitler's mind and see the conversion from perceived victim to glorified, gratified, and reviled mass murderer.

Cost of Hitler's revenge addiction: forty-two million lives. It matters.

JOSEPH STALIN

Like the führer, Stalin traded in the grievances of betrayal, humiliation, and conspiracy. The outcome of his revenge addiction was the same: mass violence, mass suffering, and masses of dead bodies. How do we know Stalin was a revenge addict? Like Hitler, because he told us so, and because his atrocities can only be explained as the result of compulsive revenge seeking on a massive scale.

In 1915, two years before the Russian Revolution and long before he ruled the Soviet Union, Stalin was serving a second forced exile in Siberia at the hands of the tsar. While dining with other exiled Bolsheviks, he was asked by one of them, Lev Kamenev, to share a personal secret: "What is your greatest pleasure in life?"

"My greatest pleasure," replied the thirty-six-year-old aspiring tyrant, "is to choose one's victim, prepare one's plans minutely, slake an implacable vengeance, and then go to bed. There's nothing sweeter in the world."[17]

There you have it. Joseph Stalin, future despot, describing his addiction to revenge with the precision of a psychiatrist. The Princeton historian Robert C. Tucker describes Stalin's vengefulness as "one of his distinctive characteristics."[18]

To understand how Stalin got so hooked, and how he went on to unleash thirty years of revenge-fueled slaughter, it is helpful to know something about his youth. The historian Simon Sebag Montefiore provides a detailed account in his captivating book *Young Stalin*.[19]

Born Josef Vissarionovich Djugashvili in 1878 in Gori, Georgia, he adopted the name Stalin (meaning, "steel") much later in adulthood as one of many aliases used throughout his life. Stalin's childhood in Georgia was brutal. His father, Vissarion "Beso" Djugashvili, was a cobbler and alcoholic who beat and terrorized his son from the age of four, seriously injuring him on multiple occasions. Beso also beat Josef's mother, Ekaterine (Keke), who in turn tried to protect her son but often beat him herself, perhaps as a proxy for the abuse inflicted by her husband.[20]

To her credit, Keke enrolled young Josef in a local church school. There, he became both a star pupil and, as is common among children who have been abused, a bully and hooligan.[21] The city of Gori was awash in violence and known for its street gangs. Georgia and the surrounding states of the Caucasus were also known for their long, infamous tradition of murderous blood feuds. Blood feuds are an ancient symptom of community-level revenge addiction in which clans offended by a wrongful act (for example, a killing, a rape, or even an insult) avenge the offense by killing the perpetrator or as many of their living male relatives as possible, sometimes unleashing cycles of retaliatory violence lasting decades.[22] We'll see in a moment how Stalin, as a dictator, elevated this practice to industrial scale by ordering the executions of thousands of suspected anticommunist traitors and their families.

But back to the boy Stalin. Josef's academic success at the church school failed to impress his father, who had separated himself from the family. One day the drunk old man kidnapped his son from the school and dragged him off to work as a cobbler.[23] With some assistance, Keke retrieved the boy and returned him to his studies. Josef continued to thrive in the classroom and among the street gangs, developing a reputation as a clever and fearless fighter. His teachers, however, were not pleased by his aggression or the delinquency he inspired in his classmates. To pacify the boys, they devised

an unusual plan. They would require them to attend the public hanging of three Georgian peasants accused of stealing a cow and murdering a policeman.[24]

The executions were carried out by Russian soldiers who occupied Gori under the simmering resentment of the Georgian popu-
lace. On the appointed day, Josef and his classmates arrived at the
garrison and climbed a tree to watch the spectacle amid a throng of
angry onlookers who considered the executions unjust. The three
condemned men were marched to the gallows in leg irons. A last-
minute reprieve freed one of them, but the other two were not so
fortunate. The hangman arranged them on stools and placed nooses
around their necks. The crowd grew restive and began throwing
stones, causing the Russian soldiers to tighten their ranks. With
fourteen-year-old Josef Djugashvili looking on surrounded by his
friends perched on tree branches, the hangman kicked away the
stools.

There followed some amount of cruel carnival: The rope broke
before strangling the first peasant, requiring the hangman to string
him up a second time. The other man dangled helplessly by his neck,
slowly suffocating. When the pair were finally dead, the hangman
cut them down, and the stunned crowd dispersed. Discussing the
spectacle afterward, the youthful but observant Josef demonstrated
a nuanced sense of justice, reasoning to his classmates that surely the
executed peasants wouldn't be cast into hell, because it would be
unfair of God to punish them twice.[25]

At his mother's request, Josef went on to attend a seminary in
Tiflis. Yes, Joseph Stalin attended a seminary! There he received the
classical and liturgical education that would prepare him, ironically,
to become one of the world's greatest atheists, communists, and
mass murderers. He continued to demonstrate academic talent and
displayed new gifts for writing poetry and singing in the choir. But
Stalin's interests lay elsewhere. He secretly read books forbidden by
the seminary, including the works of Karl Marx and Vladimir Lenin.
In the process, he became a believer in violent socialism as "a philo-

sophical system" based on the false promise, shared by all other forms of systematized revenge, that "many storms, many torrents of blood" will accompany "the struggle to end oppression."[26] Stalin snuck out of the seminary to meet workers in Tiflis who had become Marxists. Inside the seminary, he grew more belligerent. His studies suffered, and he found himself increasingly confined to the punishment cell. He was eventually expelled without graduating in 1899.

Eight years later, at the instruction of Vladimir Lenin, who was serving exile at the time in Finland, the young adult Stalin made headlines by becoming a bank robber and murderer. At the center of Tiflis—the very town where he had attended seminary and sung so beautifully in the choir—Stalin assembled a gang of twenty criminals known as the Outfit and armed them with rifles, handguns, and bombs. The plan, devised by Lenin and Stalin, was to rob a heavily guarded cortege of horse-drawn carriages of the State Bank bearing approximately 300,000 rubles. The money would be used to fund the Marxist revolution.[27]

At the designated moment, when the cortege had entered Yerevan Square, the gang members pulled the fuses on their bombs and tossed them beneath the carriages. Explosions shook Tiflis, unleashing chaos and a red rain of human and equine body parts. Gunfire erupted. When the smoke cleared, the money and Stalin were on their way to Lenin. Forty Cossack guards, police, and bystanders lay dead, but all members of the Outfit escaped with their lives. It was one of the greatest bank robberies of its time and established Stalin as a ruthless killer. And all for revenge. Stalin didn't keep the money for himself; he believed he had merely "expropriated" ill-gotten gains of the tsarist monarchy, giving the money to the more worthy Bolsheviks who, after "many torrents of blood," would use it to end oppression.[28] Stalin was showing the world his definition of communist justice.

That definition would expand. After seizing supreme power over the Soviet Union in 1929, Stalin supercharged his revenge addiction with bouts of homicidal mania. His "philosophical system" required all peasant farmers to surrender their privately held lands to state-owned farms. This included confiscation of their grain and animals. The peasants resisted collectivization by hiding their grain and slaughtering their livestock to prevent the communists from seizing their means of survival. Between 1928 and 1933, the population of horses, cattle, sheep, and pigs in the Soviet Union declined by nearly 66 percent.[29] Stalin retaliated by having peasants who hid their grain or killed their livestock shot, shipped to work camps, or deprived of food.[30]

It gets worse. Peasants with more than a few animals, acres, employees, or pieces of equipment were designated "bloodsucking kulaks." In Stalin's Soviet Union, these kulaks were the Jews of Hitler's Germany—alleged traitors scapegoated and blamed for the ills of the nation. Stalin proclaimed a "policy of eliminating the kulaks as a class."[31] This meant arresting and sentencing them to the Gulags, deporting them to remote areas, or, if they were willing to cooperate, merely taking their land and relocating them to collective farms.[32] About two million were sent to the Gulags or remote areas.[33]

That's the least bad part of the story. Destroying the agricultural system upon which much of the Soviet Union depended for food so Stalin could "slake an implacable vengeance" had an unsurprising effect: A famine broke out between 1932 and 1933. This famine starved to death between seven and ten million Soviets and Ukrainians, none of whom was named Joseph Stalin.[34] This man-made famine was in part the result of Stalin's use of "food as a weapon, and hunger as a punishment" against peasants and kulaks to force them to accept collectivization and support rapid Soviet industrialization.[35]

In December 1934, Stalin moved on from punishing traitorous peasants to punishing traitorous officials within his own government in what became known as the Great Purge. The purge began after the assassination of Sergei Kirov, a communist leader in Leningrad who was being groomed to succeed Stalin.[36] Stalin viewed Kirov's assassination as evidence of a vast conspiracy of counterrevolutionaries bent on restoring capitalism and led by Stalin's arch-enemy, Leon Trotsky. The collectivization and industrialization of the Soviet Union were failing miserably in the 1930s. Rather than acknowledge flaws in the communist system, Stalin convinced himself of deliberate sabotage from within. To address this, he took inspiration from Hitler's vengeance-fueled Night of the Long Knives that had unfolded about six months earlier. "Some fellow . . . that Hitler," Stalin remarked with baleful envy upon hearing news of Hitler's executions of Nazi officials. "Knows how to treat his political opponents."[37]

Stalin went on to outdo Hitler in political revenge. He ordered or approved the executions of between 700,000 and 1.2 million Communist Party members and associates for alleged treason and conspiracy and sent more than 1 million to the Gulags.[38] Those killed included most of Stalin's Bolshevik buddies and allies who had led the Russian Revolution. Believing the Red Army was plotting a coup against him, Stalin also directed the execution of more than 30,000 soldiers, including one-third of all Red Army officers. He ordered the execution of the head of the NKVD secret police, Genrikh Yagoda, for not being ruthless enough. Stalin replaced him with Nikolai Yezhov, who efficiently orchestrated more than 7 million arrests and nearly 1 million executions before Stalin had him executed and replaced by Lavrenty Beria.

Over time, the Great Purge expanded to include allegedly traitorous intellectuals, writers, artists, ethnic minorities, and peasants. This also included Leon Trotsky himself, who was living in exile in Mexico. In 1940, Stalin had Trotsky assassinated—with an ice pick.[39] Also, over time, several members of Trotsky's family. Under the Caucasian custom of the blood feud, revenge for Stalin often meant imprisoning or killing the offenders' relatives. Many people were shipped to the Gulags for no reason other than that a husband, father, or other relative had confessed to a crime he didn't commit.[40] In Simon Sebag Montefiore's prior book, *Stalin: The Court of the Red Tsar,* he reports that although Stalin rarely attended executions, he often asked for the proceedings to be recounted to him in detail so that he could enjoy the suffering and humiliation of his victims at the final moment—an example of his "greatest pleasure" before going off to sleep.[41]

Stalin wasn't a sociopath who killed for the sake of killing, however. The historical record is clear that he killed for revenge. The Great Purge depended upon elaborate efforts Stalin imposed upon the NKVD to gather evidence of crimes deserving of the ultimate punishment that could be established during hearings and trials.[42] Confessions were the gold standard, giving Stalin exactly what he needed to kill—proof of betrayal and treason justifying death.[43] That most confessions came only after endless hours of interrogation, threats, and torture—and that victims were told, or led to believe, that if they confessed their lives would be spared—made no difference. For Stalin, this only confirmed the guilt of the confessor and that extreme measures had been necessary to reach the truth—and that extreme punishment was required.

Projecting the courtroom of his mind into the public sphere, Stalin conducted show trials of the highest-ranking government officials to demonstrate that his killings were legitimate punishment for crimes perpetrated against the state rather than sadistic barbarity. The historian Robert C. Tucker describes Stalin's show trials this way: "Stalin was litigious. He became addicted to using the courtroom as a theater of revenge."[44]

The greatest betrayal for Stalin, and the one that launched his greatest act of revenge, was an act committed by none other than Adolf Hitler. On August 23, 1939, Stalin and Hitler entered into the Molotov-Ribbentrop nonaggression pact, agreeing not to attack each other for ten years and to divide Poland and other parts of eastern Europe between themselves. On September 1, 1939, Hitler invaded Poland. This was fine by Stalin; under the pact, the Soviet Union and Germany split Poland between themselves, east and west. In turn, Stalin conquered Estonia, Latvia, and Lithuania, which was fine by Hitler. Hitler defeated France. Still all good; the dictators were playing nice. But then, on June 22, 1941, less than two years after signing the pact, Hitler launched Operation Barbarossa and invaded the Soviet Union. In shock, Stalin descended into several days of despair, at one point lamenting, "Lenin left us a great inheritance and we, his heirs, have fucked it all up!"[45]

Having caught the Soviet Union by surprise, German forces surged through Russia on a tidal wave of blood, reaching the outskirts of Moscow by December 1941. That's when Stalin finally pulled himself together. He launched a counteroffensive that, over the next four years, would drive the Germans all the way back to their borders. Germany lost nearly four million soldiers battling the Soviet Union. The Soviet Union lost nearly nine million soldiers and eighteen million civilians battling Germany.

To achieve such an enormous sacrifice from his people, Stalin resorted to his usual tactic—launching revenge campaigns against those who allegedly betrayed the nation by refusing to fight and lay down their lives. He issued orders forbidding retreat or surrender, executing 158,000 Red Army soldiers for wavering, cowardice, or desertion.[46] But Stalin also offered a form of reward for those who fought all the way into east Germany. He permitted his soldiers to rape as many as two million German women in a literal orgy of revenge for Hitler's betrayal.[47] When questioned about this depravity, Stalin offered the following explanation:

> Do you see what a complicated thing is man's soul, man's psyche? Well, then, imagine a man who has fought from Stalingrad to Belgrade—over thousands of kilometers of his own devastated land, across the dead bodies of his comrades and dearest ones! How can such a man react normally? And what is so awful about his having fun with a woman, after such horrors?[48]

Alas, in the epic war between revenge kingpins, Hitler had the last laugh. He committed suicide inside his bunker in Berlin on

April 30, 1945, depriving Stalin of the opportunity to slake his most implacable vengeance. Disappointed on hearing the news, Stalin muttered, "So that's the end of the bastard. Pity he couldn't be taken alive."[49] Within six months, Stalin had a heart attack and a stroke. But still he lived on, executing many others for alleged betrayals and conspiracies until his death on March 5, 1953.

Cost of Stalin's revenge addiction: twenty million lives. It matters.

MAO ZEDONG

The Chinese communist dictator Mao Zedong doubled Stalin's death toll and nearly equaled Hitler's. Unlike his fellow revenge junkies, however, Mao tried—very, *very* unsuccessfully—to kick the habit. He even expressed occasional remorse for the destruction he wrought. But with forty million deaths on his hands, it's difficult to feel sorry for the Great Helmsman and butcher of China.

Many biographies have been written about Mao. Insights into his early affinity for revenge appear in at least two of them: *Mao Zedong: A Life*, by Jonathan Spence, and *Mao: The Unknown Story*, by Jung Chang and Jon Halliday.

Like the relationship between Stalin and his father, Mao's relationship with his father, Yi-chang, was framed by violence and brutality. The elder had been a soldier and was known for having a hot temper. He and Mao's mother—who, being a woman in Hunan, received no proper name—had seven children, only three of whom, all boys, survived infancy. Yi-chang considered his eldest son, Mao, an essential but unreliable implement on the small peasant farm from which the family eked out a living in rural Shaoshan. He required Mao to begin working in the fields from age six and did not hesitate to strike the boy when he failed to perform his duties.[50]

Yi-chang sent Mao to the local village school at age eight to learn enough math to help keep the family's accounts.[51] Like young Stalin, young Mao excelled academically, demonstrating a powerful memory and love for literature and history. Also, like young Stalin, young Mao possessed a deep streak of disobedience, leading to his flight or expulsion from three different schools and four different tutors by the age of thirteen. Hoping to impose discipline on the unruly boy, his father arranged for Mao's marriage at the age of four-teen to Luo Yixiu, a distant relative four years Mao's senior. The marriage lasted only three years, ending when Luo died at twenty-one years old without children. Mao detested the arrangement. He later wrote that arranged marriages are a form of "indirect rape" of children by their parents.[52]

Mao despised his father. The biographers Chang and Halliday recount an episode when, after his father accused him of laziness, Mao threatened to harm himself by leaping into a pond if the abuse didn't stop. Yi-chang backed down, which served only to lower Mao's respect for him. Mao's contempt deepened when, at age six-teen, during a local famine, he learned that Yi-chang was shipping his rice crop to more prosperous areas of Hunan where it would re-ceive a higher price, enriching himself at the expense of starving neighbors. Decades later, during the revenge-fueled bloodbath of the Cultural Revolution unleashed by Mao against his political en-emies, leaving more than one million tortured and murdered, Mao remarked that if his father were still alive, he would wish for him to be tortured in the same manner.[53]

Like Stalin, Mao was exposed to communal levels of retaliatory violence early in his life. When Mao was seventeen, a landlord won what was considered an unjust legal verdict against a group of Sha-oshan villagers. When the villagers protested, the landlord spread a false rumor that the group had sacrificed a child, resulting in one of them being caught and beheaded.[54] In nearby Changsha, the pro-vincial capital of Hunan, rioters were arrested and decapitated, after which their heads were hoisted on poles as a warning to others.[55] At the age of eighteen, while in Changsha, Mao came across the corpses of two young men he admired who had been killed for leading an uprising against the controlling Qing dynasty. As we will see, these traumatic experiences sharpened rather than discouraged Mao's appetite for revenge.

In 1912, Mao enrolled in a middle school in Changsha. There he studied the writings of the notorious Shang Yang, much despised minister of the ancient state of Qin and author of *The Book of Lord Shang*, written in the fourth to third centuries BCE. In this book, Lord Shang expounds a ruthless theory of governance, emphasizing that the best practice is to administer harsh punishments upon the people for minor offenses, enslave the poor and lazy, compel citizens to become either farmers or soldiers, and force neighbors and family members to denounce and punish each other for offenses against the state.[56] Mao wrote a school essay praising these laws of Lord Shang as "good laws." He would later enact versions of them to horrifying effect when he became ruler and lord of China.

During the next eight years, while continuing his studies, Mao was exposed to communist ideas flowing down the Yangtze River from Europe and Russia.[57] He emerged from this period as a teacher, publisher, and contributor to various journals and magazines. In these endeavors, he argued for the education of the peasant masses and, for a brief time, the nonviolent end of oppression and a revolution of pacifist communalism. Mao's interest in pacifist ideas did not last long, however. By 1921, he rejected the possibility of revolution without war and was being encouraged by Russian and Chinese operatives to attend the First Congress of the Chinese Communist Party in Shanghai to help in an uprising. At the conclusion of this congress, Mao received instructions to return to Hunan and recruit new members to the party. He happily complied, successfully organizing strikes and peasant revolts that led to his elevation in 1923 to the Communist Party's Central Executive Committee.

In 1927, Mao wrote an ecstatic report to party bosses boasting of his successes and reveling in the pleasures of witnessing the retaliatory violence he had unleashed among the people. With great delight he described scenes of peasants abducting their landlords and others against whom they had grievances and marching them through villages wearing tall pointy dunce caps in pageants of public humiliation and physical torture, beating some of them to death.[58] This would mark Mao's first direct experiment with Lord Shang's injunction to turn the people against themselves to subdue them. In the report, Mao exalted that the peasants "really have created terror in the countryside." Like a drug addict, he described the effect it had on him as "a kind of ecstasy never experienced before."[59]

Mao would destroy the lives of many to get more of this drug. In April 1927, Chiang Kai-shek, leader of the governing Guomindang (Nationalist Party), who vehemently opposed communism, launched a purge of communists in Shanghai, killing thousands and sparking the Chinese Civil War.[60] Mao's peasant Red Army fought back but was no match. Leaving behind his second wife, Yang Kaihui, and their small children, Mao fled with his comrades into the mountains of Jinggangshan. Chiang gave chase, driving Mao to Jiangxi. In 1930, the Guomindang executed Yang Kaihui when she refused to denounce her husband.

In 1934, facing his own likely capture and execution, Mao and his pregnant third wife, He Zizhen, joined more than eighty-five thousand communists in a great escape to the north of China known as the Long March. Carrying their belongings, weapons, and equipment on their backs, they fled Jiangxi, leaving behind Mao's infant child and sick younger brother, who was later executed by the Guomindang. The march lasted a year and covered more than six thousand miles. Along the way Mao and his comrades endured withering artillery barrages from Chiang Kai-shek's forces, attacks from local tribes, starvation, frigid temperatures, and disease. Fewer than eight thousand of the original eighty-five thousand reached their destination in Shaanxi in 1935. Mao and He Zizhen were among them.

Mao's many grievances against Chiang Kai-shek and the

Guomindang multiplied exponentially, meaning the revenge to come would be severe and sweet indeed. But more practical considerations intervened when, in 1937, Japanese forces invaded China across the Marco Polo Bridge in Beijing.[61] Mao and Chiang formed an unlikely alliance and combined their armies into a united front against the invaders. The Japanese made swift progress, forcing the Guomindang from their capital in Nanjing. What followed was the horrifying Rape of Nanjing, during which Japanese forces brutalized and slaughtered more than 200,000 Chinese civilians and prisoners.

The United Front continued battling the Japanese for eight more years. Only after the United States dropped nuclear weapons on Hiroshima and Nagasaki in 1945 did the Japanese finally end their assault on China.[62] This became the signal for Mao and Chiang Kaishek to turn on each other again. But Mao, now the undisputed leader of the Chinese Communist Party, had the upper hand due in significant part to the support of Soviet Russian troops and the capture of Japanese war matériel.

Mao was merciless in his revenge upon the Guomindang. He ordered his army to prioritize the slaughter of Guomindang fighters and the seizure of their weapons over the occupation of territory.[63] By the end of 1949, Chiang Kai-shek and the Guomindang had fled to Taiwan, leaving Mao and the Communist Party in control of mainland China. The death toll from the Chinese Civil War between the communists and the Guomindang was an appalling five million to seven million people. Yet this is a fraction of the revenge deaths Mao would go on to cause.

After he assumed power over the entire nation, Mao's first big step was to order a violent purge of real or suspected Guomindang sympathizers and "counterrevolutionaries" throughout China. Mao decreed that "killing counterrevolutionaries should be fast and thorough like blast rain. We must kill a huge numbers [sic] of them."[64]

During this same period, Mao also launched his Land Reform campaign, ordering the violent redistribution of agrarian lands from their rightful owners to peasant collectives.[65] A program to implement economic and political principles of landownership might not be thought to have anything to do with revenge, but in Maoist China its success depended on it. In his 2022 book, *Righteous Revolutionaries: Morality, Mobilization, and Violence in the Making of the Chinese State,* the Harvard social scientist and China expert Jeffrey Javed explains how, to motivate peasants to destroy the existing feudal system of landownership and institute communal ownership of property, Mao systematized his 1927 "ecstasy" of peasant revenge. To do this, he ordered the widespread denunciation and punishment of so-called landlords—which included any peasant deemed more well-off than others—in ritualized "struggle sessions."[66]

Similar to the Inquisition and witch trials of medieval Europe, struggle sessions were village revenge spectacles carefully orchestrated by Communist Party cadres to carry out Mao's vision of whipping peasants into frenzies of rage by encouraging them to recall, denounce, and punish real or imagined past abuses and moral transgressions of landlords for mostly minor things like acts of dishonesty, cheating, oppression, unjust beatings, withholding support, and demanding rents even in times of famine.[67] In an interview, Dr. Javed described to me how communist cadres "creat[ed] the conditions for essentially priming people before the struggle session happens. So, there's all this, usually weeks, if not months, of . . . going into villages. They will go to poor peasants' homes and stay up, you know, until the wee hours of the night, just talking with them about their grievances."

The effect was profound. Revenge killings turned into cyclones of violence that ravaged the Chinese countryside, with villagers attacking, torturing, and butchering each other over petty grievances.[68] Rather than using secret police and death squads to eliminate undesirable people, as Hitler and Stalin had done, Mao systematically stimulated grievances and violent revenge cravings among millions of peasants, causing them to do the work themselves. Following the teachings of Lord Shang, the people became their own secret police and death squads. Mao rationalized it this way: "To put it bluntly, it is necessary to create terror for a while in every rural area, or otherwise it would be impossible to suppress the activities of the counterrevolutionaries in the countryside or overthrow the authority of the gentry. Proper limits have to be exceeded in order to right a wrong, or else the wrong cannot be righted."[69] This is classic revenge rationalization. The death toll from Mao's counterrevolutionary and Land Reform campaign was between one million and three million peasants murdered between 1950 and 1952—most of them at the hands of their own neighbors.[70]

Mao took a breather after all this and even expressed a desire to cut back on his revenge habit. With his benignly named Hundred Flowers Campaign in 1957, he created his own revenge rehab program by encouraging Communist Party members to stage an intervention by criticizing his regime and proposing reforms.[71] However, when they took him up on his offer and unleashed a torrent of complaints, Mao became aggrieved again. He indulged his resulting revenge cravings by persecuting and purging 500,000 cadres, sending many of them to labor camps.

Mao's greatest death toll came between 1958 and 1962, during the horrific famine unleashed by Mao's Great Leap Forward (GLF) campaign. Normally, a widespread famine would have little to do with revenge, but in Maoist China revenge had everything to do with it. As the historian Zhou Xun observed, "Terror and violence were the foundation of the Great Leap Forward."[72]

The GLF was Mao's effort to transform China from backward, agrarian state into modern industrial superpower in less than ten years. His vision was based on a grandiose delusion that if small farms were converted into massive communes, fewer workers would be required to till less land that would yield more crops than ever produced—in fact, a surplus that would feed not only China but the poor of the earth.[73] Those freed from the fields could be used to produce steel in quantities that would rapidly exceed the output achieved by the richest capitalist nations.

To realize this vision, Mao issued a radical set of orders that would transform the Chinese economy and society. He did this, however, without first testing whether any of it would work, or whether it might lead to undesirable consequences. He drastically reduced the number of acres in China to be sown with grain, closed grain markets, ordered peasants to eat in communal mess halls, mandated that they begin smelting iron in backyard furnaces, sent millions of peasants from farms into the cities to work, and compelled tens of millions more to toil extreme hours building canals and other large public works projects by hand. He also imposed unrealistic quotas, exaggerated output, confiscated grain, and violently punished peasants when production quotas fell short.[74]

Word of famine in the countryside reached Mao in late 1958 and early 1959. To everyone's surprise, Mao's initial reaction was to accept blame and call for moderation in his own radical GLF policies. At a summer 1959 conference in Lushan among top Chinese Communist Party leaders, Mao continued to accept responsibility. As during his Hundred Flowers Campaign, he even invited others to point out his mistakes—provided they acknowledged that the benefits of the GLF far outweighed the costs.[75] Many top officials openly criticized Mao. However, the defense minister, Peng Dehuai, went further. He wrote Mao a personal letter stating his opinion that the costs of the GLF outweighed the benefits and that this had been caused by putting politics and fanaticism before economic laws. Following a now familiar pattern, Mao became enraged, and his revenge cravings roared back.

Mao distributed Peng's letter to attendees of the conference and forced them to choose between him and Peng under threat that if they abandoned him, he would return to the countryside, raise a new Red Army, and start a new civil war. Given Mao's demonstrated ability to carry out this threat, most of the assembly sided with him. He promptly had Peng and his supporters tried and found guilty of conspiracy and removed Peng from his political posts.[76] Like a vengeful teenager, Mao also attacked Peng with vile insults. "I fucked your mother for 40 days," he shouted at him.[77]

Mao then embarked upon an epic revenge binge rivaling the greatest in human history. Fully aware that his radical GLF policies were lethal and had already brought famine to the country in 1958, instead of moderating these policies as he promised, he reestablished and expanded them out of spite against Peng and his critics.[78] Mao ordered increased grain requisitions from the farms even though there was little grain left, forced peasants out of the fields where they could have produced food and into the cities to toil in new commune industries, expanded food-wasting mess halls and large, grain-consuming hog farms, and enforced these policies through a violent anti-rightest purge campaign against peasants and cadres who resisted.[79] The historian Zhou Xun describes how, during this period, violence "permeated every aspect of daily life" and "for some the practice of violence became habituated, or indeed for some an 'addiction.'"[80] Peasants were beaten, tortured, and starved into delivering their last stores of grain, and they were also beaten, tortured, and starved for having no grain left to give.

What followed was a revenge-made famine of biblical proportions. With no edible foodstuffs left, peasants were reduced to eating grass, bark, dirt, corncobs, and even human corpses.[81] Between late 1959 and 1962, *more than thirty million Chinese peasants*—the very people whom Mao had set out to free from capitalism and oppression—perished of starvation, of disease, or from being beaten, tortured, or gunned down by communist officials, police, and soldiers for allegedly hiding grain—and even for fleeing to save themselves.[82] The Great Leap Forward famine is considered the deadliest famine in human history. At its root, it was caused by Mao's desire for revenge.

When news of the deaths emerged, Mao, as he had done before, initially accepted responsibility, displayed remorse, and, at the Seven Thousand Cadres Conference held in 1962, invited officials to speak openly of what had gone wrong.[83] Liu Shaoqi, the first vice-chairman of the Chinese Communist Party, who had supported Mao at Lushan, now turned on him, insisting that the famine had been a man-made disaster caused primarily by political mistakes. "So many people have died of hunger!" he shrieked at Mao. "History will judge you and me, even cannibalism will go into the books!"[84]

Because he'd been humiliated and betrayed again, Mao's revenge cravings resurfaced with a vengeance. In 1965, Mao launched his final revenge campaign upon the people of China, affixing to it the deceptive title "Great Proletarian Cultural Revolution."[85]

Mao's stated goal for the Cultural Revolution was to purge moderates from the Communist Party; he wanted only radical followers now. To achieve this goal, he reprised his tried-and-true methods from the Land Reform campaign, causing the people themselves—this time students rather than peasants, whom Mao designated as Red Guards—to take revenge against Mao's enemies during ritualized struggle sessions.[86] Like the peasants, the student Red Guards performed their tasks with maximum violence and maximum glee, parading intellectuals, artists, politicians, and others through the streets wearing pointy dunce caps and berating, beating, torturing, executing, and, sometimes, butchering and eating them.[87] The death toll from the Cultural Revolution has been estimated to be between 500,000 and 2 million people.[88]

Mao designated two high-ranking officials for special punishment during the Cultural Revolution: Peng Dehuai and Liu Shaoqi—the two officials who had turned on him at Lushan and the Seven Thousand Cadres Conference.[89] Having nursed his grievances for several years, Mao enjoyed a slow ecstasy of revenge. He had Peng locked in solitary confinement for the next eight years, during which he was interrogated more than 250 times and subjected to dozens of public struggle sessions where he was mocked, kicked, and beaten with lengths of wood and had his ribs broken.[90] He ultimately died of cancer on November 29, 1974, but Mao kept news of Peng's death from the public until after his own death.

As for Liu Shaoqi, Mao ordered both him and his wife, Wang Guang-mei, subjected to a public struggle session during which they were accused, insulted, beaten, kicked, and trampled in front of their own children—with a film crew documenting the festivities.[91] Guang-mei was then sent to a maximum-security prison for twelve years during which she was rarely allowed to walk, destroying her ability to stand upright. Liu, aged seventy, was imprisoned inside his own home, where he was barely kept alive as he battled pneumonia, diabetes, and paralysis in one leg. In October 1968, while Liu was being drip fed through the nose, Mao finally removed him from his political posts and purged him from the Communist Party. Liu died on November 12, 1969. Mao kept his death from the public until after his own death as well.

The historian Frank Dikötter sums up Mao Zedong and the Cultural Revolution this way: Mao "was easily offended and resentful, with a long memory for grievances. Insensitive to human loss, he nonchalantly handed down killing quotas. . . . The Cultural Revolution, then, was also about an old man settling personal scores at the end of his life."[92]

The torture and deaths of Peng Dehuai and Liu Shaoqi cement compulsive revenge seeking as Mao's motive behind the mass killings during the Land Reform campaign, Great Leap Forward famine, and the Cultural Revolution (and many of the killings he ordered during the Chinese Civil War). Mao Zedong was truly one of the deadliest revenge addicts in human history. By persuading his countrymen to slaughter each other to avenge their grievances and his own, Mao might have addicted more people to revenge inside a single nation than any person in human history.

Cost of Mao's revenge addiction: forty million lives. It matters.

CHAPTER 7

THIS IS AMERICA ON REVENGE

W e've explored some deeply disturbing events in the past few chapters. Let's lighten things up a bit. Maybe enjoy a nice, heartwarming family film?

LIONS, DEER, DOGS, AND A MOUSE

According to *Forbes*, as of 2019 the top-earning entertainment franchise in box-office history was Disney's beloved *Lion King*. Released in 1994, it has earned a whopping $11.6 billion in worldwide ticket sales through its combined animation, live-action, and theatrical releases.[1]

What exactly did the world's children get in exchange for $11.6 billion in tickets to *The Lion King*? They got stirring music, realistic characters, stunning animation, clever dialogue, outstanding voice acting—and a powerful dose of revenge.

Recall that in the movie, the Pride Lands are ruled by the lion king Mufasa, whose brother, Scar, is next in line to the throne until the birth of Mufasa's son, Simba. That's Scar's grievance: He's being denied the crown by a puny little lion cub. What does Scar (whose name says everything) do with his revenge desires?

First, he plots to have Simba killed by hyenas, but Mufasa rescues him. Next, he plots to have both Mufasa and Simba killed by luring them into a gorge and having the hyenas whip a herd of wildebeests into a stampede to trample them to death. Mufasa again rescues his son, but he's left hanging perilously from a cliff with Scar sneering above him. Mufasa pleas for help, but Scar cruelly casts his brother down into the stampede, where he's trampled and killed before Simba's eyes. Then Scar convinces Simba that *he's* responsible for the stampede and his father's death and that he must leave the Pride Lands forever. Scar then tries but fails to kill him.

These are Simba's grievances: the traumatizing death of his father at the paws of his uncle, the shame of having caused it, being the subject of multiple murder attempts, and the loss of his family, home, and right to the throne. What does Simba do? Growing up in exile, he tries to get over it and live a carefree life, but his unhealed grievances nag him like a festering wound. His friends make things worse, telling him that he must return to honor the memory of his father and save the Pride Lands from Scar's tyrannical rule. Mufasa appears to him in a dream, telling him that he must "remember" the past and his noble heritage, implying that he must avenge what has happened. Simba finally relents and sets off to confront his uncle.

When he returns to the Pride Lands, Simba finds them in ruin and witnesses Scar striking his beloved mother, further inflaming his desire for revenge. Scar, threatened by Simba's return, declares before the pride that Simba murdered Mufasa and the penalty is death. He forces Simba to the edge of a cliff to finish him off. But before killing him, Scar admits with a malicious whisper that he's the one who murdered Mufasa. Enraged, Simba finds renewed strength, leaps at Scar, and chokes him into confessing the crime to the pride. Scar breaks free, but Simba corners him at the top of Pride Rock. Flames rage below them, touched off by a lightning strike.

Scar now pleads for his life, just as Mufasa had pleaded for his. Simba offers to let Scar live if he agrees to leave the Pride Lands forever. Scar pretends to accept the deal but suddenly wheels on Simba and attacks. Simba deftly responds by launching Scar off the cliff to his doom. Scar descends into the flames below, where he's surrounded by a pack of hyenas who pounce on him and maul him to death. In the final scene, we see Simba sitting high on Pride Rock, gazing out upon his domain with a new young son of his own who will succeed him, completing the circle of life.

The Lion King is an epic story with similarities to Shakespeare's very adult but more nuanced revenge tragedy *Hamlet*. Audiences have been enthralled by the Disney version. But we should be aware while watching it that we're being systematically traumatized by the filmmakers and having our darkest revenge desires stoked and gratified. We're wounded to our cores by the homicidal revenge addict, Scar, who callously murders Mufasa and terrorizes poor Simba and his mother to take the throne. Having so thoroughly incited our grievances, Disney could offer us some free popcorn to make us feel better—or, perhaps, some free theme park tickets. But Disney knows that's not what we really want. *We want that bastard Scar dead.* And we want him to suffer along the way. The filmmakers brilliantly activate the reward circuitry inside our brains, awakening the anterior insula ("pain network") to cue our nucleus accumbens and dorsal striatum (GO!) to crave revenge against Scar and silence our prefrontal cortex (STOP!). And the filmmakers deliver the goods. Scar is burned alive *and* torn to shreds for our dopamine viewing pleasure.

Bravo, Disney, for so vividly animating the science of revenge!

The lesson of the film for the world's children is that when somebody hurts you, hurt them back. Hard. Nurture your grudges from childhood into adulthood. Prepare yourself for war. Seek vengeance. Not only will you feel great, but you'll become king. But did Disney breach its sacred trust with parents by selling a product that traumatizes kids and gives them what might be their first hit of violent revenge just to make money off it?

We've known for a long time that there's something dodgy going on between revenge and entertainment. To explore this codependency, I asked Rich Ross, former chairman of Walt Disney Studios and former president of both the Disney Channel and the Discovery Channel, whether the entertainment industry is aware that when a storyteller victimizes an innocent protagonist on-screen, the audience feels victimized, and when the protagonist gets revenge, there's a payoff for the audience in the form of a release and a high?

"There's an awareness," Mr. Ross acknowledged.

"Why does this trope work?" I asked.

"Well, look, most things you find they work till they don't work, right? And this one has never not worked. . . . I think this is more a general societal issue; we all are angry about something and surrounded by others who are as angry as we are. . . . And I think the storytelling is the fodder or the protein of that experience. . . . So, when you say, you know, why does that work? Whether it's a fairy tale or a superhero or historical picture that's made, or TV show or drama or comedy for that matter—I mean, *Seinfeld* has tons of revenge stuff in it, because, you know, George always feels like there's people taking advantage of him. . . . This is the story that runs through everything."

"Do you think revenge plots are more bankable?"

"I would say it fits in a category very clearly to me of understandable risk, understandable reward. . . . So, I think when you're trying to sell a story to somebody to make it in any kind of genre, there's a little bit always of, 'Oh, I get that. Oh, I understand that. Oh, I see that. Oh, this is what happens.' I think what we know [about] that kind of vengeful storyline is that it's to be expected, always understood, relatively, by, like, a consumer viewer. . . . For the most part, the easier to understand, the broader the audience. . . . But in everything I've worked in, it's not that people are not aware of it. There's a line that people want to understand and how close they're getting. Because no one wants to be that company or that person who feels that they've seemingly let loose the dogs of war."

Ah, yes, the dogs of war. There's danger in playing with revenge as entertainment. It might go boom. Rich Ross isn't one of the mad bombers, however. *The Lion King* was made long before he was tapped to lead Walt Disney Studios, and he's one of the genuine good guys in an industry that too often crosses the line. "While I understand why [revenge] works," he explained to me, "it's not the goal I have to deliver entertainment that makes people feel good about feeling bad. To me, it's very counterproductive."

Back in the day, when Simba was but a gleam in his parents' eyes, *The Lion King* was pitched inside Disney as "*Bambi* in Africa."[2] Comparing *Bambi* and *The Lion King* through the lens of the science of revenge is illuminating. *Bambi* was released in 1942 and, like *The Lion King*, went on to become a huge financial success for Disney, earning $268 million worldwide.[3] Adjusting for inflation, one analysis puts the total box office for *Bambi* in today's dollars at about $8.9 billion.[4]

There are striking similarities between the two films, but revenge isn't one of them. Bambi's father rules the forest as the Great Prince and is raising Bambi to succeed him. Bambi's mother is killed, not his father, by an unseen hunter named Man. Bambi is devastated. Unlike Simba, however, he doesn't spend his childhood nursing a grudge or, in young adulthood, going on a revenge-fueled mission to run Man through with his antlers. Yet the little fawn thrives, rises to the throne, and replaces his father as Prince of the forest. The circle of life continues. Both pictures have the same happy ending, but *Bambi*'s uplifting and life-affirming message to children is far different from the malevolent catechism sold by *The Lion King*. Have courage, be resilient, persevere, *Bambi* says. You can overcome even the greatest tragedies that befall you. Leave the pain of the past where it belongs, in the past. Avoid revenge. Don't allow it to destroy the hope and joy of your present and future.

Bambi proves that *The Lion King* could have worked without the revenge plot. Would it have brought in $11.6 billion? Disney apparently didn't think so, or why would it have risked such a winning formula and exposed children to such a powerful dose of revenge? The bet paid off, financially. So much so that since *The Lion King*, and following Mr. Ross's departure from the studio, Disney has gone all in on revenge addiction and made a killing: *Avengers: Endgame* (2019, $2.788 billion); *Star Wars: The Force Awakens* (2015, $2.064 billion); *Avengers: Infinity War* (2018, $2.048 billion); *The Avengers* (2012, $1.515 billion); *Avengers: Age of Ultron* (2015, $1.395 billion); *Black Panther* (2018, $1.336 billion); *Star Wars: The Last Jedi* (2017, $1.331 billion); *Iron Man 3* (2013, $1.215 billion); *Captain America: Civil War* (2016, $1.151 billion); *Captain Marvel* (2019, $1.129 billion).[5] Disney's total take from these ten revenge films alone is *$15.972 billion.*

Mickey seems to be as hooked on revenge as his audiences. But Disney isn't the only American media company to have built a lucrative business by pushing sweet revenge on the masses.

THE FACE (BOOK) OF REVENGE

From 2019 to 2023, Facebook's parent, Meta Platforms, earned annual sales revenues ranging from $70.697 billion to $134.902 billion—thoroughly trouncing even the Wonderful World of Disney.[6] Most of Meta's revenue comes from selling advertising on its social networking platforms, in particular Facebook and Instagram, which are free to access for their billions of daily active users worldwide.[7] The key to all this advertising revenue is keeping all those users engaged and seeing ads on Meta's platforms.

How does Facebook do this? One way is by deploying an algorithm that rewards users for posting and spreading grievances on the platform, and then giving them an immediate way to get revenge on the platform by verbally and psychologically attacking those who harm them (or their proxies), creating new grievances and keeping the grievance-revenge party going, endlessly.

This is among the disturbing revelations to have emerged from a trove of internal Facebook documents given by the former Facebook employee and whistleblower Frances Haugen to *The Wall Street Journal* in 2021, becoming the foundation of the *Journal*'s investigative reporting called "The Facebook Files."[8] The documents reveal that the primary way users interact with and spend time on Facebook is through the News Feed, which is an always-updating scroll of news stories, advertisements, and popular postings from friends, followers, groups, and others, all controlled by Facebook's proprietary machine learning algorithm that ranks and "feeds" the information to users.[9]

According to *The Wall Street Journal*, in 2018 Facebook noticed that user engagement was declining, which Facebook considered a major threat to its business.[10] To reverse this trend—meaning, to enhance user sharing, posts, comments, reposts, and similar activity—Facebook changed its algorithm to award fewer points (and therefore less popularity, lower ranking, and fewer views) to posts reshared with Facebook's cheerful little thumbs-up "like" buttons and more points (and therefore greater popularity, higher ranking, and more views) to reshares using Facebook's grumpy, red-faced "angry" buttons. The algorithm also included points multipliers for posts with long threads of many people arguing and fighting over the content. In other words, Meta started using the science of revenge to prop up user engagement by promoting compulsive grievance and revenge activity across its platforms.

The algorithm change worked almost immediately, slowing the decline of user engagement and increasing the total number of daily active Facebook users. But divisiveness and rage across Facebook went super-viral. Facebook data scientists acknowledged in internal memos that "misinformation, toxicity, and violent content are inordinately prevalent among reshares."[11] News and political organizations around the world started complaining and shifting their Facebook strategies to more grievance-based content to get their messages heard. The algorithm change heralded a race to the bottom of human interaction. Experiments conducted by Facebook scientists and engineers found that "viral content favored conspiracy theories, hate speech and hoaxes." Yet when the scientists and engineers proposed ways of correcting this, documents viewed by the *Journal* show that the CEO, Mark Zuckerberg, refused to adopt them if it would risk reducing user engagement and platform growth.[12]

Jeffrey Javed, the Harvard social scientist and expert on Mao Zedong's strategy of provoking personal grievances among Chinese peasants in the 1950s, also happens to be an artificial intelligence and machine learning researcher who has worked for Facebook.[13] Comparing 1950s communist China to twenty-first-century America, he told me during an interview that he's concerned about the way social media algorithms automate personal grievances: "Social media is powered by machine learning algorithms that rank content that is most engaging for people at the top of their feeds. And, you know, you have to wonder, what is the algorithm learning about people's predispositions . . . ? If someone has a kind of latent psychological predisposition to being inflamed or incited by a grievance, there's no reason why we wouldn't assume that an algorithm would be able to figure that out. . . . The same algorithm that sends you an ad for a lamp that you love . . . is the same algorithm that can deliver inflammatory content to someone who's more predisposed to be angry or angered by that content."

This is particularly troubling when it's happening simultaneously to millions of users who have no idea what's going on. Dr. Javed is also concerned about the emphasis social media companies place on user engagement to generate ad revenue: "Social media is so driven by engagement. You want to maximize people's time on these platforms. You're essentially trying to maximize the amount of attention that you're getting from users. You want them to log on every day. You want them to spend a lot of time per session. It's hard to create an algorithm . . . that would somehow keep up engagement while also reducing bad engagement."

What exactly does "bad engagement" look like? Evidence of Facebook's role in the January 6, 2021, insurrection at the U.S. Capitol is damning. The science of revenge explains how the insurrection was a predictable act of violence in response to an imagined grievance of grave consequence: the false allegation by the then president, Donald Trump, that Democrats had stolen the presidential election. This is the fabricated Stop the Steal myth that mirrors in too many ways for comfort the fabricated stab-in-the-back myth used by Hitler and his followers to seize power in Germany and perpetrate the Holocaust by falsely claiming that Jews had conspired to undermine and destroy Germany in the aftermath of World War I. Photographs and video coverage from January 6 record the pain, victimization, and seething rage of the insurrectionists in the hours prior to the attack— whipped up for weeks by hyperbolic expressions of grievance from Trump and others. The photographs and video coverage also record the cathartic release, joy, and pleasure of breaching the Capitol, injuring police officers, and hunting down politicians to hang them.[14] The January 6 insurrection was a matter of brain biology.

Other documents leaked by Frances Haugen describe how Facebook unintentionally supercharged the Stop the Steal myth and was unable to stop it. Analysts at Facebook evaluating how this happened wrote in one of the documents, "Almost all of the fastest growing [Facebook] groups were Stop the Steal during their peak growth. . . . [The groups] were amplifying and normalizing misinformation and violent hate in a way that delegitimized a free and fair election."[15] An investigation by ProPublica and *The Washington Post* found 650,000 Facebook posts between Election Day and the insurrection that attacked the legitimacy of Joe Biden's victory, "with many calling for executions or political violence."[16]

Just how addictive could all this become? According to *The Wall Street Journal*, Facebook scientists know that 1 in 8 Facebook users report compulsive use of social media.[17] That's 12.5 percent, or 360 million of Facebook's 2.9 billion users. Facebook's engagement algorithm became both a super-spreader source of imagined victimization and grievance among millions of Americans—activating powerful revenge desires—*and* a means to enable revenge gratification by aiding aggrieved individuals in organizing, planning, and implementing violent and highly pleasurable acts of revenge at the U.S. Capitol. The January 6 insurrection, as well as Facebook's role in it, is a case of digital age mass-induced revenge addiction.

Social media engagement algorithms don't only pose a threat of revenge addiction to adults. In 2023, the U.S. surgeon general issued an advisory on the health risks of social media for children. The advisory reports that 95 percent of youth aged thirteen to seventeen use social media platforms, and many suffer serious health consequences, including symptoms of depression, anxiety, low self-esteem, self-harm, cutting, cyberbullying, harassment, exposure to hate-based content, and increased risk of suicide. The surgeon general also noted studies showing that "social media exposure can *overstimulate the reward center in the brain* and, when the stimulation becomes excessive, can trigger pathways comparable to *addiction*" (emphasis added).[18]

Social media engagement algorithms hit users with a double whammy: social media addiction plus revenge addiction. We now know these algorithms exploit reward circuitry vulnerabilities in human brain biology and, in the process, cause serious mental illness and incite civil unrest, violence, and death. It's obvious what must be done. We must restrict or ban the use of these algorithms just as we restrict or ban the use of carcinogens and other substances that exploit vulnerabilities in human biology and cause serious illness and death. The harms caused by these algorithms are beginning to resemble the harms caused by the promotion and sale of tobacco products and opioids even after the companies knew the risks. The "safe harbor" protections of Section 230 of the Communications Decency Act relied upon by social media companies to avoid legal liability for dangerous user postings on their platforms would not apply: The algorithms are created and deployed *by the social media companies themselves*, not users.

A recent study by researchers from more than fifteen different universities worldwide—with Meta's cooperation—demonstrated that replacing Facebook's engagement algorithm with a simple chronological feed of information "dramatically reduced the amount of time users spend on the platform, reduced how much users engaged with content when they were on the platform, and altered the mix of content they were served." Users received more moderate content (although with an increase from less trustworthy sources) and content that was less "uncivil"—defined by the researchers as less mean-spirited, disparaging, name-calling, pejorative, or laced with vulgarity, profanity, and slur words.[19] The study didn't include assessments of user mental health, grievances, revenge desires, or addictive behavior, but we would expect improvements in these areas based on the findings of reduced grievance-inducing content.

THE BLUE BIRD AND BLACK LETTER OF REVENGE

The microblogging platform X (formerly known as Twitter) has far fewer users than Facebook but punches above its weight in contributing to revenge addiction in America and around the world. This may be due to the inherent nature of the platform, which is ideal for compulsively posting 280-character rants about things we perceive to be unfair and quickly striking back.

Researchers have found that X is among the top choices for recruitment and radicalization by revenge terror groups, including al-Shabaab, Boko Haram, ISIS, and neo-Nazi, militia, neo-Confederate, KKK, QAnon, and other far-right organizations.[20] Posting shared grievances and victimization and the desire for revenge is the primary entry point for winning converts to extremism and violence—both as part of a group and among lone actors.[21] X's own 2021 Transparency Report concedes that more than a third of the 3.8 million posts it removed from the platform for content violations in the six months leading up to the January 6 insurrection were marked as hateful or violent.[22] Researchers testifying before Congress about the causes of the insurrection estimate that before those posts were removed by X, they received a minimum of *295 million views.*[23]

Other researchers have found that X posts promoting fear, violence, and divisiveness (grievances) in the aftermath of traumatic community events, such as officer-involved shootings, spread more widely than posts promoting peace.[24] The phenomenon of digital posts remaining for long periods of time (or forever) on social media platforms like X, and the anonymity offered by alias accounts and the platform's always-on, 24/7 availability, appear to increase grievance rumination and make revenge seem more attractive and less risky.[25] This creates perfect conditions for developing an addiction to revenge.

Unfortunately, X has only gotten worse since the acquisition of the platform for $44 billion by Elon Musk. Violence researchers at the RAND Corporation recently found that "[X] remains a popular target platform for violent extremists, particularly following Elon Musk's takeover of the company in 2022."[26] Another team of researchers performed an audit of Musk's impact on hate speech at X and concluded that toxic hate speech (defined as speech employing words used by hate groups and so rude or disrespectful as to cause people to leave a discussion) "increased dramatically upon Musk's purchasing [X]."[27]

Why would the new owner of X permit all this on his platform? One possibility is that Musk himself may be addicted to revenge. Although I've never met him and have no way of knowing his inner thoughts and motivations, his public behavior bears the hallmarks of compulsive grievance nurturing and revenge gratification.

For example, like Facebook, X depends on selling advertising for most of its revenue. In July 2023, nine months after Musk acquired the company, he reported that ad revenues had plunged by half, seriously threatening the business.[28] Four months later, in November 2023, he posted to his 160 million followers his personal endorsement—as "actual truth"—of an antisemitic conspiracy theory claiming that Jews espouse "hatred against whites."[29] In reaction, some advertisers, including Disney, began pausing their advertising on X, further threatening its viability.[30] Musk tried to walk back his post, but the advertisers weren't having it.

Weeks later, at a conference sponsored by *The New York Times* to which both Musk and Disney's CEO, Bob Iger, were invited as speakers, Musk acknowledged to the assembled audience that "what this advertising boycott is going to do is it's going to kill the company." Yet, slitting the company's throat with advertisers and Iger personally, Musk went dark avenger and made this self-destructive statement to the audience: "If somebody is going to try to blackmail me with advertising, blackmail with money, go fuck yourself. Go-fuck-yourself. Is that clear? I hope it is."[31] About a week later, Musk doubled down, posting to his followers that Iger "should be fired immediately" from Disney.[32]

This looks to me like compulsive revenge seeking for pleasure despite the negative consequences. As a recovering revenge addict myself, I get it. Musk could be facing the loss of a $44 billion investment. The pain and humiliation of that must be enormous.

I discovered while doing research for this book that Elon Musk and I share a few experiences from our childhoods that might have led us to be attracted to revenge. Among other things, we were both bullied as kids, and somebody shot and killed our dogs. Walter Isaacson, Musk's biographer, writes of Musk being beaten and bullied as a child at a wilderness survival camp in South Africa known as a *veldskool* and, in high school, being attacked from behind by a group of bullies who beat him, kicked him in the head, and knocked him down a set of steps.[33] He had to be hospitalized and lost a week of school. Isaacson also writes of Musk recounting an incident when he was six and his favorite dog, a German shepherd, bit him in the back, resulting in a trip to the emergency room. Musk begged his parents not to punish the dog, and they agreed. Isaacson writes of Musk telling the story, "Musk pauses and stares vacantly for a very long time. 'Then they damn well shot the dog dead.'"[34]

Believe me, that's a grievance that can last a lifetime.

Musk and I also had strained relationships with our fathers, who expected us to take care of our business with bullies, and from whom we later became estranged.[35] As I said earlier, victims of bullying and trauma are at risk of becoming bullies and victimizing others.[36] I became a litigator with a reputation as a bully; Musk became the world's richest man with a reputation as a bully.[37] Maybe we should team up to found Revenge Anonymous? That's not entirely in jest. If humans are going to live together on another planet, as Musk envisions, we'd have a better chance of survival if we solved our revenge addiction problem.

REVENGE ADDICTION IN THE WHITE HOUSE

On December 12, 2020, I published an article in *Politico* titled "What the Science of Addiction Tells Us About Trump."[38] In that article, I warned the American public that the then president was displaying dangerous signs of revenge addiction arising from his grievances over losing the 2020 presidential election. As with other people in the throes of addiction, I explained that the addiction is likely to get worse before it gets better and that the nation needs to protect itself from harm, but that the president needs our help and compassion to overcome it. My article was a matter of science, not partisanship. The science turned out to be correct.

On January 6, 2021—twenty-five days after my article—the aggrieved president, using the Facebook and X/Twitter social media platforms discussed above, called upon his equally aggrieved supporters, including violent extremist and militia groups, to avenge his loss of the election by laying siege to the U.S. Capitol and installing him as president by force. Attempts to assassinate Vice President Mike Pence and Speaker of the House Nancy Pelosi were thwarted only by evacuating them to safe locations and the heroism of badly outnumbered law enforcement officers. At least five people died because of the attack, including one police officer, and at least 140 officers were injured.[39] More than eleven hundred people were arrested, and over six hundred received criminal sentences.[40] It is a national tragedy.

Yet even after all this Trump has continued to nurture his unhealed grievances and his desire for revenge. Making the case for his third campaign for president, he told his supporters during a March 4, 2023, speech at the annual Conservative Political Action Conference, "In 2016, I declared I am your voice. Today I add: I am your warrior. I am your justice, and for those who have been wronged and betrayed, *I am your retribution*" (emphasis added).[41] On November 5, 2024, Trump was re-elected to the presidency, suggesting that a majority of the American people have voted for a national government based on revenge.

The renowned Yale and Harvard–trained psychiatrist Bandy Lee, MD, author of a textbook on violence, collaborated with thirty-six other psychiatrists and mental health experts to write the best-selling book *The Dangerous Case of Donald Trump*, arguing that Trump presents a clear and present danger to the nation and individual well-being.[42] Dr. Lee agrees with my theory of revenge addiction and its applicability to Trump:

> I think your substance addiction model [of revenge] is incredibly important because whether the addictive substance is a chemical, or whether it is an action . . . is almost immaterial. The seeking of that gratification of that psychological need and physical need and physiological need will be seen in both, as you have discovered. And that's a remarkably important discovery that explains a lot and illumines pathways we could use to confront this issue.

I asked Dr. Lee if she sees evidence of Trump as a revenge addict—compulsive, constantly wanting to retaliate for his grievances despite the negative consequences. Her response: "Oh, yes. Absolutely." She went on to explain:

In the book that I edited, *The Dangerous Case of Donald Trump*, in 2017, what we were most afraid of was Donald Trump as a public health threat because, well, the psychological dangers he brought were not unusual. In fact, I've treated at least probably about a thousand individuals with his psychological structure through my work over the last quarter century of specializing in treating violent offenders. And so, yes, he fits the profile entirely. The only difference with him that he would become a large public health threat is because of the position that was granted him and the influence and exposure that he would have to the public, and therefore [he] would spread his violence proneness, his grievances, his paranoid ideas, as well as his fixed false beliefs. . . . And pathological symptoms are far more contagious than rational ideas or persuasion. . . . So, do I see him as a griever? Yes, very much so. I've actually called it more of a victim complex, but yes.

Again, this is a matter of science, not partisanship. Revenge addiction knows no political boundaries. For example, according to the Council on Foreign Relations, the former president Barack Obama, a Democrat, ordered more than five hundred targeted drone strikes in the Middle East during his two terms in office, killing 3,797 people, including 324 civilians.[43] Obama is reported to have remarked wistfully to his aides in 2011, "Turns out I'm really good at killing people. Didn't know that was gonna be a strong suit of mine."[44]

Like Trump, Obama appears to have struggled with revenge addiction—his born of the searing trauma and national grievances of the 9/11 terror attacks. To be fair, some of these drone deaths could be argued to have been perpetrated as a matter of national self-defense. However, the line between self-defense to avoid an imminent threat and revenge for past acts is thin, malleable, and too often depends on who's pulling the trigger. The point is that anyone can be a revenge addict. My goal is to bring scientific light to the malady, not to politicize or stigmatize it. Revenge addicts need help and compassion, not derision and scorn—or retaliation, which only fuels the disease.

JUSTICE FOR ALL

In 2023, Trump told his supporters, "I am your justice." What, exactly, does "justice" mean in twenty-first-century America? The answer isn't as obvious as it might seem. Justice in America has developed a split personality, one benign and the other malignant. Dictionaries and thesauri tell us justice means equity and fairness, with synonyms like "egalitarianism," "honor," "uprightness," "decency," "integrity," "righteousness," "morality," "virtue," "propriety," "trustworthiness," and "incorruptibility." That's the virtuous, Dr. Jekyll side of justice—the one we think of when we advocate for social justice and revere luminaries like Martin Luther King Jr., Mahatma Gandhi, Jesus of Nazareth, the Buddha, and Lao-tzu.

But justice has a much darker side, a Mr. Hyde. This meaning of justice is the polite, politically correct term we use when we really mean revenge, as in the refrain after the September 11, 2001, terrorist attacks on America: "Justice will be done!" We all know what this form of justice means, and it's not equity, decency, virtue, or morality. After the al-Qaeda leader and 9/11 mastermind, Osama bin Laden, was killed by U.S. Special Forces on May 1, 2011, American leaders proclaimed that he had been "brought to justice."[45] This did not mean that bin Laden had been treated virtuously, decently, or honorably. He was shot multiple times in the head. Unarmed. Without a trial. America had finally gotten revenge.

Justice is to revenge as OxyContin is to heroin: consumer branding of a highly dangerous, addictive substance.

President George W. Bush, who launched America's quest for "justice" after 9/11, was particularly fond of using the term "justice" when he meant revenge. Speaking to a joint session of Congress less than three weeks after the 9/11 attacks, he famously said, "Whether we bring our enemies to justice, or bring justice to our enemies, justice will be done."[46] A little more than a year later, during his January 28, 2003, State of the Union address, Bush coined a new term for this darker form of justice—"American justice." "We have the terrorists on the run," he bragged to the American people. "We're keeping them on the run. One by one, the terrorists are learning the meaning of American justice."[47] A month later, he invoked the term again during a speech at the American Enterprise Institute: "We have arrested, or otherwise dealt with, many key commanders of al Qaeda. Across the world, we are hunting down the killers one by one. We are winning. And we're showing them the definition of American justice."[48]

Yes, the terrorists, and the rest of us, have learned the definition of American justice. It's revenge. Why do we say justice when we really mean revenge? Because when it's called justice, all manner of torture and atrocities are instantly sanitized and sanctified. By calling it justice, bin Laden persuaded aggrieved Muslim extremists to fly passenger jets into occupied office towers and slaughter three thousand people. By calling it justice, Bush persuaded aggrieved Americans to wage wars in the Middle East that lasted nearly twenty years and, according to Brown University's Watson Institute for International and Public Affairs, have resulted in more than 940,000 total direct deaths due to war violence, including the deaths of more than 15,000 U.S. service members and contractors and 432,000 civilians, at a cost to American taxpayers of nearly $8 trillion.[49] Bush knew that if he had spoken the truth—if he had said, "Whether we bring our enemies to *revenge,* or bring *revenge* to our enemies, *revenge* will be done"—the American people would have revolted. We are a good and decent people. We don't want to think of ourselves as bloodthirsty. He knew we wouldn't have given our consent, or sacrificed so much, for such an unworthy enterprise, no matter how badly and understandably we craved revenge for 9/11.

President Obama, who was in office when bin Laden was killed by American forces, contributed to this national fiction and deepened our revenge addiction. Informing the American people on live television that bin Laden had been killed, he explained what happened: "I determined that we had enough intelligence to take action, and authorized an operation to get Osama bin Laden and *bring him to justice*" (emphasis added).[50] With swelling pride, Obama continued, "We can say to those families who have lost loved ones to al Qaeda's terror: *Justice has been done*" (emphasis added). Echoing the science of revenge, he described the reward and pleasure of killing bin Laden: "The countless intelligence and counterterrorism professionals who've worked tirelessly to achieve this outcome . . . *feel the satisfaction of their work and the result of their pursuit of justice*" (emphasis added). Then Obama concluded his remarks with a crowning bait and switch: "Let us remember that we can do these things not just because of wealth or power, but because of who we are: one nation, under God, indivisible, with liberty *and justice for all*" (emphasis added).

That was a nice touch at the end, quoting from the Pledge of Allegiance. But exactly what form of "justice for all" does the pledge promise to the American people? Is it the justice that President Obama had just explained had been done to Osama bin Laden's skull with an assault rifle? Presumably not. The pledge must be referring to the opposite form of justice—the equity, decency, virtue, and morality form of justice. Obama didn't explain the distinction for good reason. Doing so would have shattered the illusion of plausible deniability that we had been seeking revenge all along.

And that's the black magic of it. Invoking the Jekyll and Hyde word "justice" without specifying which one we mean is how good, decent people throughout history have become killers. It's how we Americans become killers—not only of bin Laden and the many hundreds of thousands of other people in the Middle East who died during the wars in Afghanistan and Iraq, but of our own family members, classmates, neighbors, co-workers, lovers, friends, and fellow citizens. When we incant the word "justice," our last line of defense against the searing brain-biological craving for revenge hijacking our brains when we have a grievance is obliterated by a duplicitous, linguistic fraud.

Justice has cast a dark spell on America. We have become a revenge-addicted nation. Justice in the form of revenge was the basis of the deadly insurrection at the U.S. Capitol. Justice in the form of revenge is the unifier and sanctifier of racism, antisemitism, misogyny, Islamophobia, homophobia, xenophobia, group and gang conflict, and all other causes that convert grievances into repression and violence. "Justice" is the go word that has unleashed murder, war, genocide, and terror throughout human history. It's also the word that American lawyers plaster on billboards and bellow in commercials, stimulating revenge cravings to entice and berate us into hiring them to get "justice" against the people who harm us. The American criminal "justice" system exacts societal revenge against approximately 5.5 million people (1 in 48) in U.S. prisons and jails and on probation and parole, often deepening their revenge addiction rather than correcting it.[51] Because revenge addiction works so reliably and predictably, it's exploited everywhere, from liberal and conservative news organizations hoping to attract viewers and sell advertising to religious institutions hoping to attract followers and generate collections by convincing people that God is an all-powerful revenge addict who, in implementing divine justice, deputizes his followers to punish sinners and infidels and promises to torture them in the afterlife for all eternity.

If civil war comes again to America, it will be waged by both sides in the name of justice, and people on both sides will happily spill their own and other people's blood in the belief that the sacrifice is noble and patriotic. The science of revenge shows us this is folly. Justice in the form of revenge isn't noble or patriotic. It's primal and biologic. Revenge addiction infects, distorts, murders, and destroys without regard to party affiliation, geography, nationality, class, race, religion, sex, age, or any other distinction that we might imagine exists between ourselves and other human beings. If we're going to confront America's rage and violence epidemic and the waves of violent extremism threatening our society, we'll have to confront, and speak honestly about, our addiction to justice in the form of revenge.

CHAPTER 8

THIS IS HUMANITY ON REVENGE

How could it be?

You might be thinking that this has got to be all wrong. If revenge addiction is so widespread and so terrible, and so similar to substance addiction, why hasn't anyone ever heard of it before or done anything about it? It just seems so . . . implausible.

There have been similar implausible situations in human history when science unexpectedly revealed truths hiding in plain sight and saved millions of lives. For example, the bubonic plague, also known as the Black Death, raged on and off for about fourteen hundred years—from 541 CE into the 1950s—and is estimated to have killed more than 200 million people. The plague took lives cruelly and efficiently, with high fever, headaches, and severe pain in the limbs and abdomen rapidly progressing to the swelling of lymph nodes (buboes) that hemorrhaged, leading to necrosis, sepsis, and death.[1] The terror and widespread devastation caused by the plague were unparalleled. So was ignorance about its cause. Throughout the centuries, as millions died painful deaths, people blamed the bubonic plague on all sorts of things that seem backward and foolish today but mirror current beliefs about the causes of violence. Things like evil, sin, divine judgment, demonic forces, and fate.[2]

It wasn't until 1894, during an outbreak of the plague in Hong Kong, that the physicians Alexandre Yersin and Shibasaburo Kitasato looked more closely and discovered that the Black Death was caused not by demonic forces but by an invisible bacterium hiding in plain sight, now named *Yersinia pestis* in Yersin's honor.[3] Four years later, the physician Paul-Louis Simond discovered that fleas from infected rats spread the bacteria to humans. Armed at last with the "implausible" truth about the real cause and manner of transmission of the Black Death—*an invisible bacterium*—scientists developed sulfonamides and antibiotics in the 1930s and 1940s that yielded a cure and finally brought the disease under control.

Is it possible that the cause and manner of transmission of human rage and violence—*an invisible addiction*—has been misunderstood for thousands of years? Read on and see how revenge addiction has been hiding in plain sight throughout recorded human history.

IN THE BEGINNING . . .

Let's begin at the beginning because that's where humanity's revenge addiction starts. According to the fossil record, the first hominin murder occurred approximately 430,000 years ago in northern Spain.[4] One of our ancient ancestors used a crude weapon, perhaps a wooden spear or a stone ax, to smash two holes through their neighbor's skull. Using modern forensic techniques, researchers theorize that the killing happened during a face-to-face confrontation and was an act of interpersonal violence. In a cold case for the ages, the police still don't know the identity of the perpetrator or the motive. But there's reason to suspect it was a revenge killing: The murder occurred in the middle of the Pleistocene epoch when scientists believe human revenge evolved.[5]

Mythically speaking, the first human murder occurred more

recently, when Cain killed his brother Abel. We know the motive for this one. According to both the book of Genesis of the Hebrew Bible and the Surah Al-Ma'idah in the Quran, Cain and Abel were the sons of the first two humans on earth, Adam and Eve (Gen. 4; Quran 5).[6] Cain was a sharecropper and Abel a shepherd. On a certain day, Cain offered some of his crops to God as a tribute, and Abel offered a sacrificed lamb. According to the story, God is a carnivore because the Bible says, "And the Lord had respect unto Abel and to his offering: But unto Cain and to his offering he had not respect" (Gen. 4:4–5).

So, basically, Cain got upstaged by his brother and dissed by God. That's Cain's grievance, and he was thoroughly *pissed*.

God speaks to Cain and tries to calm him down: "Why art thou wroth? And why is thy countenance fallen? If thou doest well, shalt thou not be accepted? And if thou doest not well, sin lieth at the door. And unto thee shall be his desire, and thou shalt rule over him" (Gen. 4:6–7). John Steinbeck's masterpiece, *East of Eden*, is devoted to the idea that this passage gave to Cain, and all humanity, a choice: conquer your desire for revenge or be conquered by it. In Hebrew, *timshel*, "thou mayest."

Unfortunately, Cain is conquered by it. He finds Abel in a field and murders him. The Quran explains what was happening inside Cain's head: "So the *Nafs* (self) of the latter one [Cain] encouraged him and made fair-seeming to him the murder of his brother" (Quran 5:30–31). This passage could have been written by an addiction scientist.

Of course, it's revenge by proxy, vicarious retribution.[7] God is the one who rejected Cain's offering, not Abel. But Cain could hardly have murdered God, so he did the next best thing and tried to hurt God by killing Abel. Mission accomplished. Now God has a grievance and craves revenge. "What hast thou done?" God rages at Cain. "The voice of thy brother's blood crieth unto me from the ground" (Gen. 4:10). In retaliation, God prevents the land from producing any more crops for Cain and condemns him to wander the earth for the rest of his life as a fugitive. Yet God also uses the threat of revenge to protect Cain from those who might want to harm him. "Whosoever slayeth Cain," God says, "vengeance shall be taken on him sevenfold" (Gen. 4:15).

The story of Cain and Abel is more than the story of the first murder. It's the story of the first addiction.

The Bible tells us revenge addiction passes genetically from generation to generation. Cain has a son, Enoch, who has a son, Irad, who has a son, Mehujael, who has a son, Methusael, who has a son Lamech. One day, Lamech announces to his wives, "I have slain a man to my wounding, and a young man to my hurt. If Cain shall be avenged sevenfold, truly Lamech seventy and sevenfold" (Gen. 4:23–24). In other words, I killed two people because they wronged me, and if anybody tries to retaliate against me, they'll pay a higher price than the one God put on anyone retaliating against Cain.

The next killing in the Bible is the most horrific and deadly act of revenge ever recounted. It's perpetrated by God on a revenge bender. After humans began multiplying across the planet, "God saw that the wickedness of man was great in the earth, and that every imagination of the thoughts of his heart was only evil continually" (Gen. 6:5). And "the earth is filled with violence through them" (Gen. 6:13). "And indeed they have led many astray" (Quran 71:24).

That was God's grievance.

This was God's revenge: "And the Lord said, I will destroy man whom I have created from the face of the earth; both man, and beast, and the creeping thing, and the fowls of the air; for it repenteth me that I have made them" (Gen. 6:7).

God wasted no time in carrying out his death sentence. For forty days and forty nights, the rains fell, flooding the earth and slaughtering every human being and every living creature on land except Noah and his family and the pairs of animals on the ark. Yet even God couldn't escape the negative consequences of revenge. Seeing that all creation had been destroyed when the waters receded, God was filled with shame and remorse and promised to quit revenge cold turkey: "I will never again curse the ground for man's sake, although the imagination of man's heart is evil from his youth; nor will I again destroy every living thing as I have done" (Gen. 8:21). To help stay sober, God strung rainbows from the clouds as a reminder.

THE GOOD BOOK (OF REVENGE ADDICTION)

Although God kicked the revenge habit (at least insofar as flooding the earth is concerned), humans have clung to it with a vengeance. The Old Testament is a terrifying early account of humanity's revenge addiction. I'm going to compress all six hundred pages into about two. Ready? Let's go:

Pharaoh enslaves the Hebrews in Egypt in revenge for conspiring with Egypt's enemies, then orders the drowning of all their newborn sons. A Hebrew infant, Moses, survives with the help of Pharaoh's daughter, who raises him into an Egyptian prince. After seeing an Egyptian beating a Hebrew, Moses gets revenge by murdering the Egyptian (Exod. 2:11–12).

Moses leads the Hebrews out of Egypt to Mount Sinai, where he receives from God the Ten Commandments and an order to seek revenge against those who disobey: "Thou shalt give life for life, Eye for eye, tooth for tooth, hand for hand, foot for foot, Burning for burning, wound for wound, stripe for stripe" (Exod. 21:23–25). Moses takes God at God's word and transforms himself into a revenge addict par excellence.

Upon returning from the mountain and finding the people worshipping false idols in violation of the first two commandments, he orders the sons of Levi to slay them en masse (Exod. 32:27–28). He leads the remaining Israelites onward. When they encounter resistance from the Amorites and the people of Bashan, he orders the

Israelites to exterminate them. When they encounter resistance from the Midianites, his soldiers slaughter every adult male. But that's not enough revenge gratification for Moses. He orders them to "kill every male among the little ones, and kill every woman that hath known man by lying with him. But all the women children, that have not known a man by lying with him, keep alive for yourselves" (Num. 31:17–18).

The addiction passes to Joshua, who begins the Israelite conquest of Canaan by leveling Jericho when it refuses to yield. With the exception of Rahab the harlot and her family, "they utterly destroyed all that was in the city, both man and woman, young and old, and ox, and sheep, and ass, with the edge of the sword" (Josh. 6:21). Joshua does the same to the other cities of Canaan: "The spoil of these cities, and the cattle, the children of Israel took for prey unto themselves; but every man they smote with the edge of the sword, until they had destroyed them, neither left they any to breathe" (Josh. 11:14).

David rivals Moses for revenge addiction. He wants to marry King Saul's daughter, but Saul tells him that he'll first have to deliver a dowry of one hundred foreskins of Philistines. Eager to impress, David delivers two hundred foreskins. Even Saul is alarmed by this and begins to fear David and plot against him. David continues his rise, defeating the Philistines in a huge battle. The Philistines retaliate by waging war against Saul, killing three of his sons and wounding Saul. Saul takes his own life, and the Philistines celebrate by decapitating him and hanging his body on the wall of Bethshan. In retaliation, David goes on a rampage against the Philistines and others until he reigns over all of Israel, where he "executed judgment and justice unto all his people" (2 Sam. 8:15).

In 63 BCE, the Romans seize Jerusalem from the Jews. About thirty years later, Herod the Great, a Jew appointed by Rome to be the king of Judaea, orders the murder of all children in Bethlehem in response to a prophecy that a new King of the Jews has been born

(Matt. 2:16–18). An infant named Jesus of Nazareth narrowly escapes. As an adult, he goes on to preach against revenge, telling people that Moses was wrong: "Ye have heard that it hath been said, An eye for an eye, and a tooth for a tooth: But I say unto you, That ye resist not evil: but whosoever shall smite thee on the right cheek, turn to him the other also" (Matt. 5:38–39). Jesus might have been the world's first addiction counselor. However, his message enraged the rabbis and leaders who dedicated their lives to upholding the Mosaic law. In revenge, they persuaded Pontius Pilate, Roman procurator of Israel, to crucify Jesus for treason and blasphemy (Mark 14:53–65; Matt. 27:1–2, 11–26).

Total number of people murdered in the Bible: about 1.6 million (of which perhaps 300,000 are historically plausible).[8]

ROMAN REVENGE ADDICTION

Now let's look at the Romans. The Roman emperors might have been the first to turn revenge into entertainment for the masses. They staged what today would be considered live-action snuff films for revenge-hooked audiences in local Roman arenas.

The primary sentences for serious crimes in the Roman Empire were forced labor and execution. Most executions were for crimes such as treachery, murder, treason, arson, incest, slave revolts, being captured as a prisoner of war, or, sometimes, being a Christian and refusing to make sacrifices to Roman gods. Executions were public revenge spectacles. Methods included feeding prisoners and slaves to wild beasts, forcing them to train as gladiators and fight each other to the death, crucifixion, burning alive, burying alive, throwing from cliffs, beheading and scourging, pouring molten gold or lead down throats, forced suicide, and sewing them inside sacks with live dogs, snakes, monkeys, or chickens and dropping them into bodies of water to drown.

The wide variety and hideous nature of these forms of capital punishment, combined with performances before cheering throngs, reveal a purpose far beyond maintaining law and order. The fact that those being executed were convicted of crimes rather than randomly chosen indicates that mass sadism wasn't the motive either. These were primarily revenge orgies in which grievances against prisoners and slaves were inflamed among the crowds to provoke powerful revenge cravings to be indulged in the most pleasurable ways imaginable. Roman leaders used these spectacles to gain popularity and competed to outdo each other in staging the most extravagant shows. Julius Caesar produced 320 pairs of gladiator fights and epic reenactments of famous battles—with real weapons, real bloodshed, and real deaths. Caligula and Commodus participated directly in the fighting and killing to prove their mettle and maximize their pleasure. Claudius enjoyed having the helmets of dying gladiators removed so he and the audience could enjoy the final moments of suffering. His nucleus accumbens must have been in overdrive.

Total executions in the Roman Empire: about 3.5 million.[9]

REVENGE OF THE CHRISTIANS

Despite the founder of Christianity imploring his followers to avoid revenge, it has proven too enticing and become a featured part of Christian theology and practice in many sects. This started early.

The Crusades

After Christianity replaced paganism in the Roman Empire in the fourth century and made its way across Europe, Christians found themselves being persecuted by the believers of a newer religion, Islam, in Palestine. In the eleventh century, Muslims destroyed the Church of the Holy Sepulchre and seized Jerusalem, and the Turks began conquering Byzantium. In response, Pope Urban II called upon the monarchs and knights of Europe to take up a revenge crusade to smite the infidels and free the Holy Land.

As the Christian crusaders assembled, they perfected their killing techniques on what they considered local populations of infidels—Jews. Across central and eastern Europe, they slaughtered thousands.[10] When they set out for Byzantium, they found the Turks fiercer than expected. Thousands of crusaders were killed. In retaliation, a second group of crusaders was dispatched. This group routed the Turks, slaying thousands before pushing on to Antioch. The crusaders slaughtered twenty thousand Saracens at Ma'arra[11] and conquered Jerusalem in 1099, killing seventy thousand Muslims and Jews.[12] Saladin, a Kurd, recaptured Jerusalem for the Muslims in the twelfth century. Richard the Lionheart, king of England, responded in part by beheading three thousand Saracens outside the gates of Acre.[13]

There were a total of eight large Crusades between the eleventh and the thirteenth centuries. All were fueled by revenge.

Total killed during the Crusades: one million to three million.[14]

The Inquisition

While all this was happening in the Middle East, European Christians got busy rooting out and punishing nonbelievers at home, staging revenge spectacles that rivaled Roman arenas if not in numbers killed then in cruelty inflicted.

The Inquisition orchestrated by the Catholic Church began in the twelfth century and lasted hundreds of years. Pope Lucius III in 1184, and Pope Gregory IX in 1231, ordered bishops and friars to eradicate heretics from southern France, northern Italy, and Germany. Heresy was punishable by death throughout most of Europe. Inquisitors descended upon towns and villages, accused a small number of inhabitants of heresy based on the suspicions of local priests and congregants, and then offered plea deals of lighter forms of punishment (such as fasting and forced pilgrimages) if these unfortunate souls confessed their sins and accused others. Those who refused to play along were tortured. If they continued to refuse, they were executed.

Torture methods during the Inquisition included the strappado (tying victims' wrists to pulley systems that would lift them from the ground, causing their arms to snap from their shoulder sockets), the *toca* (slow drowning), the rack (attaching victims' wrists and ankles to chains and pulling their bodies apart), the wheel (attaching victims to wagon wheels and bludgeoning them), searing flesh with heated metal pincers, and crushing fingers with thumbscrews.

Public auto-da-fé executions were staged as village revenge festivals. Those found guilty of heresy were paraded through town squares before their sentences were publicly announced. The favorite means of execution was burning at the stake. In 1278, more than two hundred Cathar "heretics" were burned on a single pyre. Joan of Arc was burned at the stake for heresy in 1431.

The Spanish Inquisition, which began in 1478, was perhaps the most Romanesque of all. King Ferdinand II and Queen Isabella believed wealthy Jews known as conversos were converting to Christianity to avoid expulsion from the country while practicing Judaism in secret. They pressured Pope Sixtus IV to launch an inquisition to root them out and permit the monarchy to seize their wealth. The pope appointed the Dominican friar Tomás de Torquemada to be the grand inquisitor of Spain. A revenge addict extraordinaire, Torquemada expanded the role of the Inquisition beyond heresy to include prosecution of sorcery, blasphemy, sodomy, bigamy, and even economic crimes. He's believed to have condemned two thousand people to burning at the stake.

Total executions during the Inquisition: about thirty-two thousand.[15]

The Witch Hunts

Twice that number were killed during the witch hunts conducted by Catholics and Protestants throughout Europe from 1400 to 1800

CE. The witch hunts were revenge spectacles of a slightly different sort, targeting those who supposedly practiced sorcery rather than merely holding different religious beliefs. They followed the Inquisition playbook of prosecutors and judges swooping into villages, making accusations, offering plea deals, and compelling the naming of other "witches." Inquisitors used torture to obtain confessions and publicly executed those who refused. To gin up grievances among the people and maintain enthusiasm for the trials and executions, witches were blamed for all sorts of things that made life miserable in the Middle Ages, including unexplained deaths, illnesses (like the bubonic plague), and natural disasters.

One of the greatest revenge addicts of the witch hunts was a German Catholic priest named Heinrich Kramer. Kramer (and possibly his associate Jacob Sprenger) penned a medieval best seller called *The Hammer of Witches*. Among the first books to be published on Gutenberg's new movable-type printing press, *Hammer* became the definitive treatise on sorcery and what to do about its practitioners: namely, find, torture, and burn them. The majority, but by no means all, of those burned during the witch hunts were women— often betrayed by other women but tried, tortured, and executed by men.[16] Kramer was a deadly misogynist. He devoted a key portion of *Hammer* to accusing women as a group of immorality and dishonesty, uncontrollable carnal lust, the frequent practice of sorcery, introducing evil into the world, and the destruction of kingdoms and the downfall of men.[17] Frankly, women have reason to be aggrieved.

Total executions during the witch hunts: about sixty thousand.[18]

MULTICIDES AND REVENGE ADDICTION

Let's pause here for a quick summary. So far, we've uncovered evidence of revenge addiction dating as far back as the first mythical murder in human history and, potentially, the first murder in the fossil record. From there, we've found evidence of revenge addiction causing massive numbers of deaths throughout the ancient Middle East, the Roman Empire, and the Europe and Middle East of antiquity. Total deaths: 6.6 million to 9.6 million. Unfortunately, this is only the frost on the tip of the revenge iceberg.

In *Atrocities: The 100 Deadliest Episodes in Human History*, the multicide researcher Matthew White ranks the largest mass slaughters that occurred between 480 BCE and 2011—a span of 2,491 years. White's book contains detailed accounts of each multicide and is prefaced with a laudatory forward by the Harvard violence researcher and professor Steven Pinker. As mentioned in chapter 1, White calculates the combined death toll from the top hundred atrocities in human history at a staggering *455 million people killed*.[19] The smallest number killed during any single atrocity is 300,000. The largest is 66 million killed during World War II.

Using White's accounts and other historical sources for atrocities covered elsewhere in this book, in the chart below I've analyzed the aggressors' primary motive for *deliberate killing* (not the causes or circumstances of the underlying conflicts, upheavals, or events) during the twenty largest atrocities in human history identified by White. These twenty atrocities represent a jaw-dropping 80 percent of the total number killed in White's entire top one hundred—363 million people. As the chart indicates, with the lone exception of the British India famines (27 million dead), the primary motive for killing in the twenty largest atrocities in human history was compulsive revenge seeking. ***This yields a revenge addiction death toll of 336 million people.***

PRIMARY MOTIVE FOR TOP 20 ATROCITIES IN HUMAN HISTORY (BY NUMBERS KILLED)

MULTICIDE	DATE	TOTAL DEATHS[20]	
1. World War II	1939–45	66 million	
2. Genghis Khan	1206–27	40 million	

AGGRESSORS' PRIMARY MOTIVE FOR KILLING	NOTES
Compulsive revenge seeking by Hitler and the Nazis against the Allies and Jews for oppressive terms in the Treaty of Versailles ending World War I, economic and social collapse, and other alleged betrayals and transgressions; revenge by Japan against the West for oppression, embargoes, and colonialism; revenge by Japan against the Chinese for resistance to Japanese colonization; revenge by the Allies, Chinese, and others against Germany and Japan for invasions and other atrocities.	See chapter 6 for lifetime evidence of Hitler's revenge addiction. Partial body count: 24 million deliberately killed by the Germans, including systematic revenge killings of Jews, other minorities, hostages, political adversaries, and prisoners; 11 million deliberately killed by the Japanese; 4 million by the Soviets, 2 million by the British, 1 million by the Americans, 0.6 million by the Chinese. Other civilian deaths: 46 million.
Compulsive revenge seeking by Khan against almost every person, leader, village, city, and state in Mongolia, China, and central Asia that opposed him or refused to give him what he wanted, and for committing alleged atrocities against him.	Tartars murdered Khan's father when Khan was 9 years old. He retaliated when he grew older by forming an army and killing almost every male Tartar older than a small child. In 1211, Khan and his band invaded northern China to conquer the Jin dynasty. When Khan's efforts to subjugate the sultan of Khwarazm and the governor of the city of Utrar were rebuffed, Khan retaliated with an army of more than 100,000, unleashing massive destruction. They slaughtered 160,000 of the sultan's forces, leveling Utrar, capturing the governor and pouring molten silver in his eyes and ears, slaughtering the inhabitants of the city of Balkh, raping and slaughtering the inhabitants of the city of Bukhara, sacking the city of Gurganj leaving 1.2 million dead, killing more than 1 million at Nishapur, and slaughtering another 1.3 million at Merv.

MULTICIDE	DATE	TOTAL DEATHS[20]	
3. Mao Zedong	1949–76	40 million	
4. British India famines	1700s–1900s	27 million	
5. Collapse of the Ming dynasty	1635–62	25 million	
6. Taiping Rebellion	1850–64	20 million	

AGGRESSORS' PRIMARY MOTIVE FOR KILLING	NOTES
Compulsive revenge seeking by Mao and Chinese communists against Nationalists, capitalists, right-wing opportunists, counterrevolutionaries, landowners, business owners, intellectuals, and peasants for opposing them or hindering the conversion of China to communism, and for committing atrocities against them.	See chapter 6 for lifetime evidence of Mao's revenge addiction. Partial body count: 1–3 million executed during political purges; 3–4 million killed during the Cultural Revolution; 30 million killed during the Great Leap Forward famine that Mao knowingly unleashed in retaliation against critics and resisters; 3 million killed in massacres, executions, prisons, and death camps.
Greed, exploitation, and indifference by the British to Indian starvation and suffering resulting from drought and crop failure, combined with retaliation against Indians for their poverty and overpopulation.	Although not the primary motive for the deaths, revenge played a role in Britain's willingness to allow millions of Indians to starve despite controlling the means and power to save them.
Compulsive revenge seeking by competing rebels Li Zicheng and Zhang Xianzhong to destroy the Ming dynasty and split China between themselves, and for committing atrocities against each other.	Partial body count: The population of China dropped by 25 million people during the wars of Li and Zhang, resulting from direct killing and war-related famine and disease.
Compulsive revenge seeking by Hong Xiuquan, self-proclaimed messiah of the Taiping, for resistance by the Manchu Qing dynasty in the conversion of the Chinese people to Taiping beliefs, and for committing atrocities against him. Compulsive revenge seeking by the Manchu Qing to punish Hong and the Taiping for their atrocities and attempts to destroy the dynasty.	Partial body count: 40,000 Manchus massacred in Nanjing and 70,000 Taiping massacred in retaliation; slaughter of an opposing messiah and his clan; beheading of an ally king; beheading of 32,000 Taiping by the Qing; 100,000 Taiping massacred by the Qing in Nanjing.

MULTICIDE	DATE	TOTAL DEATHS[20]	
7. Joseph Stalin	1928–53	20 million	
8. Middle East slave trade	800–1800s	18.5 million	
9. Timur	1370–1405	17 million	

AGGRESSORS' PRIMARY MOTIVE FOR KILLING	NOTES
Compulsive revenge seeking by Stalin and Soviet communists against non-communists, capitalists, kulaks, peasants, saboteurs, conspirators, counterrevolutionaries, Cossacks, Chechens, dissidents, soldiers, officers, intellectuals, minorities, Ukrainians, Poles, and others for opposing them or hindering the conversion of the Soviet Union to communism, and for committing atrocities against them. Compulsive revenge seeking by Stalin and the Soviet Union for Hitler's betrayal and Germany's invasion and for committing atrocities.	See chapter 6 for lifetime evidence of Stalin's revenge addiction. Partial body count: 7–10 million killed by forced starvation of kulaks and Ukrainians for resisting communization and Soviet control; 3 million executed during the Great Purge; 1–2 million Gulag deaths; 43,000 Soviet army officers executed for disloyalty; 22,000 Polish officers and civilians slaughtered; 55,000 Baltic state civilians slaughtered; 158,000 Soviet soldiers executed for desertion and refusal to obey orders; 231,000 Chechen and Caucasian prisoners murdered; and 650,000 prisoners of war murdered.
Compulsive revenge seeking by slave hunters, traders, transporters, and owners against Africans, people of other lands, and those trying to help them, for resisting capture and enslavement and attempting to escape.	The deaths of slaves meant economic losses to slave hunters, traders, transporters, and owners—negative consequences. Deliberate killing was in revenge for resisting. Many others died of abuse, mistreatment, and overwork, much of which was also in retaliation for resistance. Racial grievances inflamed retaliation, and dehumanization reduced moral controls. Partial body count: Three slaves died for every 2 who survived; or "18 million deaths to produce 12 million slaves."[21]
Compulsive revenge seeking by Timur against almost every person, leader, village, city, and state in Persia, India, the Levant, and surrounding lands that opposed him or refused to give him what he wanted, and for committing atrocities against him. (If this sounds like Genghis Khan, that's because Timur sought to continue Khan's legacy by restoring and expanding Khan's empire using Khan's bloody tactics.)	Partial body count: 28 towers of 1,500 severed heads each in Isfahan; 20,000 severed heads at Aleppo; 120 towers of 750 severed heads each in Baghdad; 150,000 slaughtered in Delhi; 120 miles of blood and bodies after the Battle of Kunduzcha.

MULTICIDE	DATE	TOTAL DEATHS[20]	
10. Atlantic slave trade	1452–1807	16 million	
11. European conquest of the Americas	1492–?	15 million	

AGGRESSORS' PRIMARY MOTIVE FOR KILLING	NOTES
Compulsive revenge seeking by slave hunters, traders, transporters, and owners against Africans, African Americans, and those trying to help them for resisting capture and enslavement and attempting to escape.	The deaths of slaves meant economic losses to slave hunters, traders, transporters, and owners—negative consequences. Deliberate killing was in revenge for resisting. Many others died of abuse, mistreatment, and overwork, much of which was also in retaliation for resistance. Racial grievances inflamed retaliation, and dehumanization reduced moral controls. Partial body count: 50% of captured slaves died before they reached a ship, 10%–15% died during transport, 33% died during "breaking and seasoning" to live out their lives as slaves.
Compulsive revenge seeking by Europeans against Native Americans for resisting colonization and seizure of lands and resources, and for committing retaliatory atrocities. Diseases carried by Europeans to which Native people had no resistance killed vast numbers of Native peoples. Native peoples killed Europeans in both self-defense and revenge for colonization and committing atrocities.	Deliberate killing was in retaliation for resistance. Racial grievances inflamed retaliation, and dehumanization reduced moral controls. Partial body count: 57,000 Taino dead; 200,000 Aztecs slaughtered (not counting those who died of smallpox); 8,000 Incas killed; 200 Chiskiack killed; 600 Pequots killed; 3,000 natives killed at Metacom; 500 Creek killed; 4,000–8,000 Cherokee killed; 38 natives hanged in a single mass execution; 250 Shoshoni slaughtered; 163 Cheyenne murdered; 173 Blackfeet murdered; 128–300 Sioux gunned down; collapse of the Native population of Brazil by 800,000.

MULTICIDE	DATE	TOTAL DEATHS[20]	
12. World War I	1914–18	15 million	
13. An Lushan Rebellion	755–63 CE	13 million	
14. Xin dynasty	9–24 CE	10 million	

AGGRESSORS' PRIMARY MOTIVE FOR KILLING	NOTES
Compulsive revenge seeking by many: Austria against Serbia for the assassination of Franz Ferdinand; Russia against Austria for Austria's declaration of war against Serbia; Germany against Russia for Russia's declaration of war against Austria; Germany against France for refusing to assure it would stay out of its war against Russia; the United States against Germany for attacks on commercial shipping and trying to forge an alliance with Mexico; Muslim Turks against Christian Armenians for alleged treason; and revenge by most of these parties between each other for committing atrocities.	Trench warfare and artillery barrages were the primary means of getting revenge at scale. Partial body count by battle: Gallipoli, 125,000; Somme, 306,000; Verdun, 305,000; Passchendaele, 150,000; 1,200 passengers on the *Lusitania*; 970,000 Armenians.
Compulsive revenge seeking by An Lushan against the emperor and officials of the Tang dynasty for threatening his life in response to alleged disloyalty and for committing atrocities against him.	Partial body count: Records from more than a millennia ago are sparse, but Chinese census data from the period show a loss of 36 million people between 754 and 764, and a loss of between 4 and 5 million households. The total deaths from the rebellion are conservatively estimated.
Compulsive revenge seeking by usurper emperor Wang Mang against members and supporters of the Han dynasty for opposing his attempts to replace them with a new Xin dynasty and to impose strict Confucian law, and for committing atrocities. Revenge by members and supporters of the Han dynasty against Wang for usurpation and committing atrocities.	Partial body count: Conservative estimates place the Chinese population loss during the period at about 10 million. Civil wars, executions, and human-caused floods and famines followed, with the eventual defeat of Wang and restoration of the Han dynasty.

MULTICIDE	DATE	TOTAL DEATHS[20]	
15. Congo Free State	1885–1908	10 million	
16. Russian Civil War	1918–20	9 million	
17. Thirty Years' War	1618–48	7.5 million	

AGGRESSORS' PRIMARY MOTIVE FOR KILLING	NOTES
Compulsive revenge seeking by King Leopold II and his security forces against the native population of Congo for resisting enslavement, the forced construction of infrastructure, and the forced collection of rubber for sale in Europe.	Deliberate killing was in retaliation for resistance. Racial grievances inflamed retaliation, and dehumanization reduced moral controls. Leopold's security forces had killing quotas and were required to produce severed hands as proof. Bags of severed hands of native men, women, and children punished for failing to meet rubber quotas also proliferated. Diseases and illnesses caused by abuse and overwork killed the highest numbers.
Compulsive revenge seeking by and between communists, anticommunists, Cossacks, Czechs, Poles, Ukrainians, peoples of other eastern European nations, people of the Caucasus, and other groups for resisting conflicting demands for control over Russia and/or desire for independence from Russia, and for committing atrocities. Also revenge by many of these groups against Jews for alleged disloyalties, betrayals, and conspiracies.	Partial body count: execution of 60,000–150,000 Jews; execution of 50,000–200,000 counterrevolutionaries; execution of 12,000 Cossacks; execution of Tsar Nicholas II and his family and servants; deaths of 304 American troops in subarctic ports, coup d'état by Admiral Kolchak and his subsequent execution. Millions of civilians died from disease, malnutrition, and starvation caused by grain confiscation, disruptions in farm production, famine, and economic collapse.
Compulsive revenge seeking between the Catholic-Austrian Hapsburgs (and their allies) and Protestant-German nobles (and their allies) for resisting each other's attempts to impose, respectively, Catholic or Protestant monarchies, rule, and religion across much of western Europe, and for committing atrocities.	Partial body count: 350,000 soldiers killed. The remaining deaths were civilian and resulted from starvation, exposure, and plague as armies raped, pillaged, confiscated crops and livestock, and destroyed homes and villages.

MULTICIDE	DATE	TOTAL DEATHS[20]	
18. Fall of Yuan dynasty	1340–70	7.5 million	
19. Fall of the Roman Empire	395–455 CE	7 million	
20. Chinese Civil War	1927–37 1945–49	7 million	

AGGRESSORS' PRIMARY MOTIVE FOR KILLING	NOTES
Compulsive revenge seeking by the Mongol Yuan dynasty (ruled by Genghis Khan's successors) and between and among competing would-be Chinese emperors seeking to expel the Mongols and replace the Yuan with either the Ming or the Han dynasty, for resisting each other's claims to the Chinese throne, and for committing atrocities.	Partial body count: 60,000 sailors killed in one of the largest naval battles in world history, on Lake Poyang and the Yangtze River. During this period, the population of China plummeted by about 30 million people. White estimates that 7.5 million of these deaths resulted from warfare and violence.
Compulsive revenge seeking by and between Romans and various tribes of Visigoths, Vandals, Huns, Franks, Burgundians, Saxons, Britons, Angles, Scots, and other barbarians, for resisting each other's claims to control the lands and riches of western Europe and North Africa, and for committing atrocities.	Partial body count: Generals assassinated emperors; usurpers emerged and were executed; imperial families were kidnapped, ransomed, and slaughtered; and barbarians marauded, rampaged, and plundered villages and cities with Roman armies chasing them and, too often, being defeated by them because of their advantage in using cavalry over infantry. Rome was sacked. Attila the Hun butchered his way from north to south. Population loss and mass deaths resulted from human-caused disease and famines.
Compulsive revenge seeking by Nationalists against communists, warlords, and the invading Japanese, and by communists against Nationalists, warlords, and the invading Japanese, for resisting each other's competing claims and demands to rule China, and specific territories within China, and for committing atrocities.	Partial body count: White estimates more than 2 million communist and Nationalist soldiers were killed fighting each other; about 2.2 million Japanese, communist, and Nationalist soldiers were killed fighting each other; and the remaining deaths were civilians. The totals include 300,000 civilians killed by communists in Changchun; 260,000 civilians and soldiers slaughtered by the Japanese in Nanjing; 250,000 Nationalist soldiers and 40,000 Japanese soldiers killed or wounded fighting between Beijing and Shanghai; and more than 50,000 communists died during the Long March.

ZEROING IN ON REVENGE ADDICTION

As you can see, we have overwhelming historical evidence of pathological revenge seeking by human beings worldwide and from ancient to modern times. Revenge addiction is an ongoing pandemic that has lasted thousands of years and been the source of incalculable tragedy and suffering. Entire civilizations have been destroyed and hundreds of millions of people have been killed by it.

Now let's discuss what we can do about it.

CHAPTER 9

THIS IS YOUR BRAIN ON FORGIVENESS

The central question in this book has been why we want to hurt people who hurt us. The science of revenge tells us we do this to make ourselves feel better. Our brains seek to maintain balance between pleasure and pain. In response to the pain of a real or imagined grievance, evolution appears to have wired our brains to seek temporary pleasure through the infliction of pain upon the person who hurt us (or their proxies). This might have been adaptive in prehistoric times, but it's become an increasingly maladaptive death sentence in modern times, leading to the violence, murder, and mayhem we've seen in the preceding chapters.

Although balancing pain with a fleeting dose of pleasure has a certain logic, it's destined to fail like all addictive pleasures because the pain is still there—it's not healed—and new pains emerge. Is there a way to reduce or eliminate the pain of remembered grievances, and thereby reduce or eliminate the desire for revenge, rather than just trying to cover it up? Wouldn't that be a less risky, more satisfying, more permanent fix?

Recent advances in neuroscience reveal that this is the role of forgiveness inside our brains—to reduce or eliminate the pain of remembered grievances, reduce or eliminate revenge desires, and restore control over retaliatory urges that lead to negative consequences. In this sense, forgiveness appears to be a potent antidote for revenge addiction. To understand this, we're going to take a close look at the neuroscience of forgiveness. But before doing that, we need to clear up a couple of misconceptions.

First, forgiveness, like revenge, is a matter of brain biology, not philosophy or religion. This doesn't mean that philosophy and religion haven't played important roles throughout history in educating people about the benefits of forgiveness.[1] Among the most valuable teachings of many of the world's philosophies and religions has been that to achieve personal peace and security and preserve relationships with each other, it's better to forgive than avenge. On this score, philosophers, theologians, poets, prophets, and playwrights have been far ahead of science. Yet we know that atheists, agnostics, and even the unenlightened all can and do forgive without subscribing to any specific philosophy, religious tradition, or belief system. Science is finally catching up, helping to reveal the biology behind ancient forgiveness teachings and practices. Evolutionary psychologists now theorize that forgiveness evolved as a means for humans to avoid the high risks and costs of revenge seeking and preserve valuable relationships—exactly what many philosophies and religions have been saying all along.[2]

The second misconception we need to dispel is that forgiveness means "giving" something to the person who hurt you. It doesn't. As we're about to see, forgiveness is part of *your* brain's biological pain management and revenge control system. The person who receives the benefit from forgiving is *you*, the person who was hurt, not the person who did the hurting. To achieve the brain-biological benefits of pain and revenge craving reduction that come from forgiving, the person who harmed you is irrelevant. They don't need to seek, beg, or accept your forgiveness—or even be informed about it. And you're not required to overlook or condone their behavior.[3] The remembered grievance, the pain, and the desire for revenge are all inside *your* brain—the courtroom of the mind where you try, convict, sentence, and imagine punishing the people who hurt you. That's where the remedy of forgiveness is applied, directly where it's needed. Refusing to forgive—under the belief that you're somehow denying a gift to the person who hurt you (perhaps hoping to exact a measure of revenge?)—achieves little more than denying yourself the healing you need. That's a self-inflicted tragedy. Within the biology of the human brain, the person who receives the greatest gift from forgiving is *you,* the forgiver. And it's a valuable gift indeed, as we'll see in a moment.

THE SCIENCE OF FORGIVENESS

Let's look at the science of forgiveness by comparing it with the science of revenge. Remember that in chapters 2 and 3 we saw how experiencing a grievance activates the "pain network" inside our brains—specifically, a structure called the anterior insula. The brain seeks to maintain balance, or homeostasis, between pleasure and pain. Revenge feels good—*for a while.* The brain wants pleasure to counteract the pain. The reward and pleasure (GO!) circuitry—specifically the nucleus accumbens and the dorsal striatum—activates in response to the painful grievance. Dopamine surges in these brain regions in anticipation of revenge pleasure and then, scientists believe, crashes, producing the craving or desire for revenge that spurs us to go out and get it.

The brain also knows that revenge comes with negative consequences. The executive function and control (STOP!) circuitry in the prefrontal cortex spools up to consider whether getting revenge really is a good idea. When working properly, it usually decides it's not and slams on the brakes. Sometimes the prefrontal cortex is inhibited, weakened, or makes mistakes, and with revenge addiction it may be hijacked or overridden by the reward circuitry. And even when it hits the brakes, the pain is still there lurking, ready to trigger revenge cravings at a time when the prefrontal cortex may be less able to control it. Result: We indulge our craving for revenge and hurt not only the people who hurt us but ourselves and innocent bystanders. That's the science of revenge.

Now let's look at the science of forgiveness.

The neuroscientists Golnaz Tabibnia, Ajay Satpute, and Matthew Lieberman at the University of California, Los Angeles, are among the first to have used fMRI brain scans to illuminate the brain biology of forgiveness.[4] As is often the case with science, they didn't set out to do this. They merely wanted to know how our brains respond to fair and unfair treatment. To investigate that, they arranged for twelve undergraduates to play the "ultimatum game" inside a brain scanner. In this game, the students were each paired with a fictitious partner who proposed to split a sum of $23 in different combinations (for example, the student gets to keep $5 and the fictitious partner gets to keep $18, or the student gets $10 and the partner keeps $13). If the student accepts the offer, they and the partner each get to keep the amount of money proposed. If the student rejects the offer, neither the student nor the partner gets to keep any money. Therefore, it's always in the student's financial interest to accept any amount offered rather than reject the offer and get nothing at all. But . . . if the offer seems unfair, the student is allowed to retaliate against their partner by denying the partner any of the money—at the cost of denying themselves as well. In other words, it's a game set up so that revenge comes with high negative consequences. What would the students do?

The students received a total of twenty-eight offers each, and the researchers manipulated the offers made by the fictitious partners within a range of between 50 percent of the total $23 stake (that is, the student and the partner each keep half, or $11.50—a very fair offer) and about 10 percent of the stake (that is, the student receives only $2.30, and the partner keeps $20.70—a very unfair offer). Although it was always in the students' financial interest to accept even unfair offers rather than reject the offers and get nothing, the students accepted only 56.3 percent of the total offers, meaning that 43.7 percent of the time they chose to punish their partners for unfair offers and pay for the pleasure of doing that. However, of the offers the students *accepted,* they ranked 49 percent of them as being unfair, meaning that the students suppressed their desire to retaliate in those cases and forgave their partners. The researchers were interested in what was happening inside the brains of the students when they forgave.

On the brain scans, as expected, the researchers found that unfair offers spurred increased activity in the anterior insula—part of the brain's pain network. Unfairness and injustice are classic grievances that cause emotional pain. The science of revenge tells us that when this happens, we should expect the GO! reward circuitry of the nucleus accumbens and dorsal striatum to activate in anticipation of counteracting the pain of unfairness with the pleasure of retaliation. But when the students decided to forgive (by accepting the unfair offers rather than retaliating), *the researchers found that the STOP! circuitry of the ventrolateral prefrontal cortex activated and the GO! circuitry remained quiet—reducing the desire for revenge.* On top of this, *activity in the anterior insula began to decrease, suggesting that the emotional pain of the grievance was decreasing.* Tabibnia and colleagues concluded, "The ability to swallow one's pride, overcome the insult, and take an unfair offer may involve active down-regulation of emotional response to unfair treatment."[5]

This study provides what may be the earliest brain-biological evidence that forgiving rather than retaliating reduces revenge-seeking behavior by (a) activating the brain's STOP! circuitry, (b) inhibiting the GO! circuitry, and (c) reducing the emotional pain of the grievance. This makes forgiveness a powerful brain-biological process for addressing revenge addiction—if we use it.

Other researchers have reported similar results. The neuroscientists Alan Sanfey, James Rilling, Jessica Aronson, Leigh Nystrom, and Jonathan Cohen at Princeton University and the University of

Pittsburgh also found decreased anterior insula (pain) activation among study participants who accepted (forgave) unfair ultimatum game offers.[6] Unfortunately, these researchers did not report the effects of forgiveness on the STOP! or GO! circuitry. However, the neuroscientists Martin Brüne, Georg Junkel, and Björn Enzi at Ruhr University in Germany observed increased activation of the STOP! circuitry (dorsolateral prefrontal cortex) and no activation in the GO! circuitry (nucleus accumbens) among study participants who received unfair offers from partners in ultimatum games but chose to forgive rather than retaliate during follow-up dictator games.[7] These researchers didn't report the effects of forgiveness on the anterior insula. Combining the Sanfey and Brüne studies supports the findings of the Tabibnia study.

A recent meta-analysis of fifteen different brain imaging studies on forgiveness performed by researchers around the world found consistent activation of the prefrontal cortex (STOP!) circuitry during forgiveness and silence in other brain regions such as the reward and pleasure (GO!) circuitry, further supporting the proposition that forgiveness reduces revenge cravings at the brain-biological level.[8] Reviewing this and related studies, the researchers Joseph Billingsley and Elizabeth Losin at the University of Miami have argued that the dorsolateral and ventrolateral prefrontal cortex, and the dorsal anterior cingulate cortex, "may act as part of a network downregulating negative affective responses of the [anterior insula] to unfairness and other social harms, while also inhibiting the punitive motivations generated by the striatal reward centers of the brain."[9] In other words, forgiveness appears to reduce the pain of grievances and the desire for revenge rather than just covering it up.

Forgiveness might be a wonder drug that works wonders. In addition to decreasing emotional pain and reducing revenge cravings, forgiveness has been shown to provide significant psychological and physical health benefits. My friend and collaborator Loren Toussaint at Luther College is a leading researcher in identifying the health benefits of forgiveness. Across multiple studies while collaborating with scientists from around the world, Dr. Toussaint has found that forgiveness reduces stress, anxiety, anger, regret, rumination, depression, cognitive impairment, and symptoms of post-traumatic stress—and improves cognitive resilience and overall sense of well-being.[10] Forgiveness is also associated with lower blood pressure; reduced rates of cardiovascular disease, mortality, and physical pain; and improved sleep, cardiovascular response to stress, immune system function, and even life satisfaction and health outcomes among people living with HIV infection.[11] That's a lot of bang for your buck. It seems there's almost nothing forgiveness can't do. And did I mention that forgiveness is free, available without a prescription, and can be manufactured and delivered inside your own brain 24/7, 365 days a year?

Psychologists distinguish between two forms of forgiveness: "decisional forgiveness" (deciding to forgive and control unpleasant emotions and revenge desires) and "emotional forgiveness" (moving beyond the wrongs of the past by letting go of negative emotions, resentment, and bitterness and replacing them with more positive emotions).[12] Achieving these forms of forgiveness requires the use of three different types of psychological strategies: *cognitive control* (controlling thoughts and behavior); *perspective taking* (understanding and reframing the circumstances, motivations, intentions, and emotional state of the person who caused the harm); and *social valuation* (assessing the severity of the harm, risk of repetition, nature of any apology, and value of the relationship).[13] The better you are at each of these psychological strategies, the more quickly and easily forgiveness occurs.

Neuroscientists are identifying the brain structures involved in each of these three strategies. We've already discussed *cognitive control,* which involves activation of the STOP! circuitry of the ventrolateral and dorsolateral prefrontal cortex and dorsal anterior cingulate cortex to hit the brakes on revenge desires. By contrast, *perspective taking* requires us to activate a network composed of an entirely different set of brain structures: the medial prefrontal cortex (front-middle of the brain), the temporoparietal junction and posterior superior temporal sulcus (rear-middle of the brain), and the precuneus and posterior cingulate cortex (rear and middle-rear-center of the brain). This all boils down to one amazing and essential human trick: the ability to imagine and interpret the thoughts, feelings, mental states, and behaviors of *other people*—known in psychology as the ability to develop a "theory of mind."[14]

The third psychological strategy involved in forgiveness, *social valuation,* requires us to activate our ventromedial prefrontal cortex to engage in social reasoning and weigh the costs, benefits, and values of different options, behaviors, and outcomes.[15] Being able to control our thoughts, understand the behaviors and intentions of the people who hurt us, and accurately assess the value, costs, and benefits of revenge and forgiveness play a major role in healing from emotional wounds, moving on from past trauma, and overcoming dangerous revenge cravings.

To learn how all this works, the neuroscientists Emiliano Ricciardi, Giuseppina Rota, Lorenzo Sani, Claudio Gentili, Anna Gaglianese, Mario Guazzelli, and Pietro Pietrini at the University of Pisa and Pisa University Hospital used fMRI to scan the brains of ten adult volunteers while they read grievance scenarios in which they were asked to imagine being emotionally harmed and then instructed to forgive the grievance or remain resentful and plot revenge.[16] One of the scenarios, for example, asked the volunteers to imagine being an employee attending a company meeting with other employees when the boss unexpectedly demeans, insults, and fires you for poor work. They were also asked to imagine knowing that they didn't give their best effort to the company.

On the brain scans, while the volunteers read the scenarios, the researchers observed activation of the dorsolateral prefrontal cortex during forgiveness. That's the brain structure that researchers believe helps downregulate negative emotions and silence the anterior insula (pain network).[17] Consistent with this activation, volunteers in the study reported that forgiveness was accompanied by a feeling of "subjective relief."[18] Ricciardi and colleagues theorized that this sense of relief from forgiveness occurs because the dorsolateral prefrontal cortex initiates a process of cognitive reappraisal in which the negative event (the insults and firing) and the offender's motivations (presumably malicious) are reinterpreted by the victim in more benign ways.

Supporting this theory, the researchers found activation of the precuneus and the inferior parietal lobule—brain structures involved in perspective taking and imagining the mental states and motivations of others (theory of mind), leading to feelings of empathy, positive emotions, and relief.[19] Being told to imagine that they really didn't do their best for the company might have cued this process, helping study participants reframe their suppositions about why the boss behaved in such a hurtful manner. This suggests that in the same way grievances can be imagined and lead to real revenge desires, the circumstances and motivations of the wrongdoer can be imagined and lead to real forgiveness.

So, there you have it: a scientific snapshot of your brain on forgiveness from nearly thirty neuroscientists and research psychologists around the world. And one lawyer. It's a much kinder, gentler, healthier picture than your brain on revenge. Which leads to the question: If forgiveness is a superior response to grievances, and yields such abundant mental and physical health benefits, why don't we do it more often? The answer appears to be that revenge is so pleasurable, and revenge cravings so powerful, that they often seem impossible to resist. Of course, that's the same reason people with substance addictions give for not quitting, even when they know it's destroying them. Which is why it's so important that we begin to understand and treat compulsive revenge seeking as an addiction and a brain disease.

The iron grip of revenge addiction is so strong, in fact, that forgiveness sometimes seems almost miraculous when we see it—something that only rare, special people like Jesus, Gandhi, and

Martin Luther King Jr. could do. But that's not true. Neuroscience shows us that evolution has equipped all of us with the brain biology necessary to forgive and set ourselves free from wrongs of the past. We're going to learn more about *how* to overcome revenge addiction using forgiveness and other addiction-informed techniques in the next two chapters. But, first, let me tell you the story of someone I met recently, an ordinary man, not a saint, who forgave something that most people would consider unforgivable and performed what looks like a miracle.

THE FATHER OF JONATHAN LEWIS JR.

Jonathan Lewis Jr., a tall, slender, seventeen-year-old boy with long blond hair, full lips, and sensitive eyes, died on November 7, 2023, of multiple blunt-force injuries. An autopsy report issued by the Coroner's Office of Clark County, Nevada, states that Jonathan Jr.'s internal injuries included a brain hemorrhage, aneurysm of an artery in his neck, cardiac arrest, and respiratory failure.[20] These injuries are consistent with a pedestrian being struck by a vehicle, but police investigators determined that they were inflicted upon Jonathan by ten of his own high school classmates who viciously beat, kicked, and stomped him to death before a crowd of jeering students in broad daylight in an alley just outside his school in North Las Vegas.[21] Investigators believe that Jonathan had come to the aid of his smaller friend in a fight over the alleged theft of a vape pen and pair of headphones.[22] The attack was captured on video that went viral across social networking platforms, resulting in calls for harsh punishment for the perpetrators. As of this writing, four of Jonathan Jr.'s classmates, aged thirteen to fifteen, have confessed to charges of voluntary manslaughter. Four others, aged sixteen to eighteen, have been indicted on charges of second-degree murder and pleaded not guilty. Yet Jonathan Jr.'s father, Jonathan Lewis Sr., who has the same sensitive eyes as his son, has forgiven all of them.

I first met Jonathan Sr. on the set of the *Dr. Phil* television show in January 2024—less than three months after the killing. He had been invited as a guest on the show to talk about his son, and I was asked to appear as an expert on revenge addiction and youth violence. Afterward, Jonathan and I got to know each other, and he agreed to speak with me for this book.

During our discussions, I discovered that Jonathan Sr. has been through nearly as many traumatic experiences in his life as Chris Buckley, the former soldier and KKK Imperial Nighthawk I discussed in chapter 4, but somehow those experiences led Jonathan Sr. in a different direction—away from revenge addiction and extremism and toward forgiveness. Jonathan Sr. taught me that forgiveness isn't about morality, religion, or giving anything to the people who hurt you. It's about realizing that it's the only cure on offer for deep emotional pain, and you take that cure when you can't stand the pain any longer and you're tired of making it worse.

Jonathan Sr. was raised in Salinas, California—the fertile green valley and town that John Steinbeck envisioned as the land to the east of Eden where good and evil, and revenge and forgiveness, wage their battle for the human soul. When Jonathan lived there during his childhood in the 1990s, this battle was waged between rival members of the Norteños and the Sureños street gangs, who turned Salinas and surrounding Monterey County into the youth murder capital of California with a gun homicide rate more than seven times the national average.[23] Together with his parents and four brothers, Jonathan lived two houses down from a small children's park in Salinas that served as the dividing line between the Norteños and the Sureños. From the age of six to eleven, while playing in this park with his friends, Jonathan witnessed men beating each other to death with baseball bats and waging gunfights that, he said, left "murdered dead bodies on the ground."

Jonathan escaped the gang violence when his family moved to a better neighborhood, but he couldn't escape the physical and psychological abuse meted out to him by one of his relatives and the leaders of his church and school. The Lewis family belonged to a strict church that, in cultlike style, was led by a charismatic preacher who isolated families from the surrounding community, prohibited them from owning televisions, required wives to submit to their husbands, and encouraged parents to use a "spare the rod, spoil the child" approach to discipline. The church also operated a school, and this is where Jonathan and his brothers received their education. According to Jonathan, discipline at the school included molestation and beatings: "They would make you take your pants down to your naked ass to spank you in the priest's and principal's office, and they did that to all the children." Jonathan doesn't believe his parents were aware of this at the time. His only solace was his dog and family trips into the mountains, parks, and beaches of California, where he felt safe among the trees and nature.

The family moved to Las Vegas when Jonathan was eleven, by which point his oldest brother (eight years his senior) had enlisted in the Marine Corps. In Las Vegas, Jonathan enrolled for the first time in a public school and became exposed to popular culture and television, signaling a brief turn toward normalcy. Within about a year, however, his mother left his father. Until she could establish a new home and find work, she placed Jonathan's youngest brother with her own mother and left Jonathan and his two other brothers, one older and one younger, with their father. This proved to be a fateful decision. Relations between the brothers and their father rapidly deteriorated. Jonathan's mind began filling with anxiety, despair, and suicidal thoughts.

Time passed. One night, Jonathan and his brothers had a vicious confrontation with their father. Living with him was no longer tenable. By this point, their oldest brother had completed his tour of duty with the Marines and was living with a friend in Southern California. He drove to Las Vegas, deposited the younger brother with their mother, and took Jonathan and the older brother back with him to California. The three Lewis brothers lived together for several months, doing odd jobs while their mother secured a small apartment. She then asked Jonathan to return home to answer truancy charges and attend school or risk being taken from her. Jonathan boarded a bus back to Las Vegas. Due to a miscommunication, however, he went straight to the truancy court without his mother.

Alarmed by the appearance of a child with no parent or guardian, the judge remanded Jonathan into the custody of child protective services and a juvenile detention center until foster care could be arranged. He was thirteen at the time and deeply traumatized. While he was being questioned by two detention center guards, one of the guards accused him of using drugs and lying about his background and grabbed him aggressively. Jonathan reacted by trying to break free. The guards responded by striking him and spraying him with Mace to subdue him. Then they dragged him to a holding cell, rinsed his face, and left him lying on the floor for several hours. He was eventually permitted to call his mother, who, overwrought by what had happened, contacted his oldest brother, who drove back from Southern California with the other brother, appeared at the detention center, and demanded custody of Jonathan. The guards granted his request, and all the Lewis brothers moved into their mother's apartment, reunited at last.

Things temporarily stabilized for Jonathan. His older brothers eventually found jobs and other places to live. Jonathan remained in school until the eighth grade, at which time he dropped out to work in construction with his brothers. During this time, he experimented with psilocybin, which, he says, "profoundly changed my life" by giving him peace and dispelling his suicidal thoughts. However, like Chris Buckley, as he approached the age of eighteen, news of the terror attacks of September 11, 2001, drew him to service in the army.

Just before Jonathan enlisted, one of his brothers was killed while a passenger in a drunk driving accident. The loss devastated Jonathan and fueled his desire to deploy quickly to Iraq or Afghanistan. But Jonathan's military career ended abruptly before he was sent overseas. During basic training, he experienced serious side effects from the mandatory anthrax vaccine administered to soldiers deploying to the Middle East at the time. Soon after he received the first shot, painful nodules and sores sprouted across his neck and back, leading to multiple surgeries.[24] It was all too much for him. He became suicidal again and, he says, "ended up with an M16 in my mouth." He was discharged from the army, leaving him humiliated and without VA benefits to seek care for his physical and mental wounds.

Jonathan returned to Las Vegas, where he soon met the woman who would become the mother of his son, Jonathan Jr. She got pregnant quickly. Jonathan married her, found an apartment, and took on two jobs to support his new family. However, he was in no condition to sustain any of this. He hadn't received mental health support, his suicidal thoughts were surging, the side effects from the anthrax vaccine weren't resolving, and he and his new wife were not getting along. He was eventually admitted into a psychiatric hospital with symptoms of severe PTSD and anxiety. The hospital placed him on medications that caused him to become psychotic and then released him. He wandered around Las Vegas delusional and sick, and broke into a store, resulting in police subduing him with a stun gun and arresting him. Fortunately, his case was heard before a mental health veterans court, which arranged for him to receive proper treatment and dismissed the charges against him. Jonathan and his wife divorced about a year later. She obtained custody of their son, limiting Jonathan's interactions with him.

Jonathan paid child support and eventually moved to Austin, Texas, to work as an electrician while establishing a start-up software company. For Jonathan Jr.'s twelfth birthday, he gave him a cell phone. From that day on, father and son had regular, almost daily contact. Jonathan Jr. planned to move to Austin to live with his dad when he graduated from high school. The last text message exchange they shared before Jonathan Jr. was killed by his classmates is poignant and heartbreaking:

JONATHAN SR.: You got it all if you have good people and love in your life and for yourself.

JONATHAN JR.: That's all you really need, I've been learning that more and more. Everything else follows that love.

JONATHAN SR.: Especially that you love who you are. So grateful to be connected son have a blessed night.

JONATHAN JR.: You too dad, get some good rest too I know you've been working hard.

The story of Jonathan Lewis Sr. is one of continuous suffering and victimization from childhood through adulthood. Yet instead of succumbing to revenge, he developed a strategy of quickly forgiving his persecutors. He has forgiven the Salinas gang members who terrorized his neighborhood; the relative, church, and school that abused him; the guards at the detention center who beat him and sprayed him with Mace; the drunk driver who killed his brother; the military that injured and discarded him; the police who shot him with a stun gun; the hospital that mistreated him; the wife who made things difficult for him—and now the group of ten students at Rancho High School in Las Vegas who killed his son.

How and why did he do this? I'll let him tell you in his own words. As you read them, see if you can find signs of the neuroscience of forgiveness at work.

JONATHAN: I think that when I experienced the gang wars in my childhood, you know, when I experienced that people have committed violence on each other, I just saw the torture and torment around on every side. Everybody's families would be hurting. When my friends next door, their cousin got assassinated by a gang when he turned eighteen years old, it was a tragedy for the whole community. Everybody was suffering. And when you see men beat each other to death with a baseball bat and they're on the ground, when you see these things when you're a child . . . I, I don't know why I'm different.

It's not justice for me to hurt people. It's justice for people to learn and begin not to hurt so bad that they want to hurt other people. Because I've received so much healing. I know how bad these kids [who killed my son] are hurting. People have to be hurting so bad to hurt somebody like that. They have to be so lost and so damaged inside. And I just think about these kids, and they're like thirteen, fourteen, seventeen years old, they're so damaged inside.

ME: You're talking about the kids who killed your son?

JONATHAN: Yeah. You know, it's only hurt people that hurt other people.

ME: How did you come to that realization?

JONATHAN: Well, I've just witnessed it over and over and over and over again. And I've seen it, you know, and then I've seen people that don't hurt people. And also myself not hurting other people. I know that the energy that I embody is what will reciprocate back into my life. I've lived that, and I'm a living example of that. But these kids don't know that, because they don't have examples of that in their life. You know in the ghetto that's not how it is.

One of my deepest desires for life is the breaking of the cycle of all the things that led to the things that I went through. I don't want anybody to go through those things. And so I know that if I'm vengeful and have the desire for revenge in any way, shape, or form, embodied inside of my being, then I am just reciprocating the cycle. And I want my children, I want all people, to live in a world where that doesn't happen and that the cycle gets broken. Because I believe in a world where there doesn't have to be violence.

ME: So, have you forgiven the teens who killed your son?

JONATHAN: Forgiveness is something that I don't think people understand the way I understand it. I see the best version of these kids. As the highest version of themselves, I know they regret so deeply what they did. And I know if their highest version of themselves came to me, they would ask for forgiveness and they would weep with me. They would weep at the loss of their humanity and the loss and enslavement of their minds that led them to become so violent. And they would weep for my loss and grieve with me. And of course I forgive that version of themselves.

I taught my son to be loving, and that if you love people, as a man, you have everything. And if you love yourself, and if you have other people that love you, you have everything I can show you. I don't think those kids had that in their lives. And now my son, who stuck up for his friend and defended him against these kids, is seen now as a hero and this brave young man. And these kids are now seen as monsters. And I feel like, you know, there should have been more love there.

I know that people hate me for this. They're like, "I don't know how you could forgive somebody like that. They just beat your son to death." But I'm like, *they* didn't beat my son to death. *Rage* beat my son to death. *Hate* beat my son to death. People don't understand that, but that's how I see it. I've experienced so much torture and torment in my life and so much pain in ways that people can't even imagine. But then I've experienced the most divine beauty and love. And I think that most people just don't get to have that. These kids definitely didn't get to have that. And I know that they must be placed into a cage, if you can't behave correctly and you harm others. But that's not justice. That's just stopping one little group of people from committing these acts.

. . .

When I forgave all those people who have harmed me, I was liberated, man. I was. I've never felt freer. I just don't think people understand that. I didn't understand it either. I never understood it. But that's what happened.

CHAPTER 10

THIS IS HOW TO KICK THE REVENGE HABIT

I've presented neuroscientific, psychological, sociological, historical, and other evidence demonstrating that compulsive revenge seeking is a deadly behavioral addiction. It *should* follow that kicking the revenge habit—and preventing the human suffering and violence it produces—can be achieved by using common and widely available substance and behavioral addiction recovery approaches that target imbalances and dysfunction in the brain's reward circuitry (GO!) and executive function circuitry (STOP!).

I emphasize that it "should" follow because the strategies and approaches for preventing and treating substance and other behavioral addictions have not yet been studied specifically for revenge addiction. We therefore need to proceed with caution in using them for this purpose, and you should do so only under the supervision of a doctor or other appropriately licensed and trained professional. (If your doctor hasn't heard of revenge addiction and is reluctant to treat you, you might want to give them a copy of this book, or consider consulting a different doctor.) This is particularly important because revenge cravings too often are gratified through acts of violence. Individuals overwhelmed by revenge desires who present an imminent threat of serious physical harm to others or themselves require immediate emergency medical attention and/or law enforcement involvement to save lives. However, there is good reason to believe that revenge addiction will respond like other addictions to professional and self-help interventions, giving us hope that existing addiction recovery strategies will yield effective public health violence prevention and treatment dividends.

As we discussed in the previous chapter, unlike other forms of addiction, evolution has equipped our brains with a powerful neurobiological system designed specifically for reducing the psychological pain of past grievances and controlling revenge desires. It's called forgiveness. Forgiveness has probably been around for nearly as long as revenge, which is to say many thousands of years. Its safety and efficacy are well-known, and it's been highly recommended and practiced by many wisdom traditions, philosophies, and individuals throughout much of recorded human history. Although forgiveness has traditionally been considered within the domain of philosophy and religion, we saw in the previous chapter that interest among doctors and scientists in the biological and psychological mechanisms, and medical benefits of, forgiveness is growing. Some psychologists have even developed forgiveness interventions for use in psychotherapeutic and psychoeducational contexts.[1]

This means we have *two* solid options for kicking the revenge habit: addiction interventions and forgiveness. Over the past twenty years, I've focused my research and practice on uniting aspects of these two options inside the courtroom of the mind that I've been talking about throughout this book. My combined approach for controlling revenge addiction is called The Nonjustice System. Many people have benefited from it, and I'm going to devote most of this chapter and the next to it, including giving you an opportunity within these pages to experience it directly for yourself. But, first, I need to set the stage by discussing addiction interventions in a bit more detail.

ADDICTION INTERVENTIONS FOR COMPULSIVE REVENGE SEEKING

If you're trying to recover from any type of addiction—substance or behavioral—I can think of no better place to start than the Stanford University addiction physician and scientist Anna Lembke's superb book, *Dopamine Nation*. You'll need to read the book for yourself to take advantage of its abundance of science and wisdom, but to give you a flavor of her approach, Dr. Lembke recommends an initial four-week period of "dopamine fasting" to restore the natural balance between pleasure and pain inside your brain, regardless of the type of addiction you're facing.[2] This means abstaining from the addictive substance or behavior to reset your brain's reward circuitry.

In the case of revenge addiction (or "revenge use disorder"), that would mean no revenge seeking of any kind for thirty days. If you're struggling with revenge desires and the pleasure you get from retaliation, even a brief period of abstinence might seem nearly impossible. But let's be honest: You can stop doing almost anything that isn't necessary for your survival for thirty days. And the benefits of abstaining from revenge seeking will be life-changing. Do you want to feel better and live a more secure, peaceful, and enjoyable life? Do you want to reduce the risk of being victimized by people who retaliate against you for your revenge seeking? Do you want to stop being the source of other people's (and your own) pain and suffering? Going a month without retaliating against those who wrong you is a small price to pay for all this. And that doesn't mean going a month of being a victim without defending yourself against real and present threats of harm. It only means not punishing people for harms that happened *in the past*—whether that's ten minutes or ten years ago.

To help patients make it through their four-week dopamine fast, and to help them maintain control over their addiction afterward, Dr. Lembke has developed a framework in which she recommends engaging in aspects of the following seven self-help activities that I'm only summarizing here: (1) reflect upon the *objectives or reasons why* you engage in the addictive behavior; (2) identify the *problems* that engaging in the behavior are causing you; (3) *become mindful of* and allow yourself to feel the painful emotions that cue your addictive cravings rather than running from them; (4) *identify the benefits* of abstaining from the behavior; (5) develop next steps for maintaining your hard-won pleasure-pain reward circuitry reset (either through continued abstinence, or, at minimum, moderation); (6) engage in *self-binding*, meaning placing distance, obstacles, and limits between you and the addictive behavior; and (7) practice *radical honesty* about your addiction with yourself and others, which creates pathways to empathy, support, and empowerment.[3] These seven self-help activities "should" work with revenge addiction too. Try to remember them, because I'm going to return to them in a moment.

Other interventions shown to be effective for controlling substance and behavioral addictions should also work for revenge addiction. These include cognitive behavioral therapy, motivational interviewing, peer support, psychosocial approaches, and possibly anti-craving medications like naltrexone and nalmefene.[4] On the horizon, new classes of pharmaceuticals are being evaluated that might one day prove useful for revenge addiction. For example, GLP-1 semaglutide drugs like Ozempic, Wegovy, and Mounjaro—used to treat type 2 diabetes and obesity by reducing the desire for food—are being studied for their effect on addictive desires and behaviors.[5] New ultrasound devices that target and neuromodulate the brain's reward circuitry have shown early promise in reducing cravings in substance use disorders.[6] Even psychedelic drugs such as psilocybin, MDMA, ketamine, and ibogaine are being investigated for their potential value in addiction treatment.[7] Obviously, none of these interventions should be attempted for revenge addiction without the supervision of a physician or other properly trained and licensed professional.

Switching for a moment from treatment to prevention, public health experts have long used mass media campaigns to educate people about the dangers of addictive substances and behaviors like tobacco, alcohol, opioid use, and compulsive gambling.[8] Similar public health campaigns should be developed to educate the public about the dangers of, and to reduce the prevalence of, compulsive revenge seeking. For children and youth, this should include school programs and curricula that address the risks of and how to manage grievances, revenge desires, and revenge addiction as a young person and throughout the life-span. The CDC's Community Preventive Services Task Force has found that universal, school-based violence prevention programs are effective at preventing violence among school-age children and youth.[9] Adding revenge addiction education would undoubtedly help.

The point here is that a wide variety of existing substance and behavioral addiction interventions are available for repurposing into revenge addiction and violence prevention and treatment strategies. This is the windfall in violence reduction dividends that awaits us by using science to understand compulsive revenge seeking as the root cause of human violence.

THE NONJUSTICE SYSTEM FOR REVENGE ADDICTION

One of the most promising opportunities for overcoming revenge addiction and preventing and treating human violence is by combining addiction recovery principles with activation of our neurobiological forgiveness circuitry inside the courtroom of the mind where we try, convict, sentence, and imagine punishing the people who harm us. It's inside our minds, not in the physical world, where grievances reside as painful memories of the past and where revenge stirs to sabotage the future. Grievances and revenge desires are thought formations. We must meet them where they reside.

"Nonjustice" is a term I coined in my first book, Suing for Peace. Unlike injustice, which means unfairness, nonjustice, like nonviolence, means "to abstain from the pursuit of justice in the form of revenge."[10] I identified several principles of nonjustice in Suing for Peace:

1. The desire for justice in the form of revenge is the cause of human suffering, not the cure.

2. Seeking justice in the form of revenge can become an addiction.

3. The most important trial of your life is the trial of your enemies because *your* freedom is at stake, not theirs.

4. The most important reason to forgive your enemies is to heal yourself from the wrongs of the past and restore your own happiness, not theirs.

5. Even if you are unable or unwilling to forgive your enemies, you can still win the most important trial of your life by practicing nonjustice and not seeking revenge.

6. To overcome revenge addiction and win the most important trial of your life, you must learn to place your enemies on trial inside your mind in a way that allows you to safely release your revenge desires and gives you the opportunity to judge what is best for *you*, not what is worst for your enemies.[11]

To achieve these goals, I created The Nonjustice System, or NJS—a courtroom of the mind organized around the healing principles of nonjustice and forgiveness rather than the destructive principles of justice in the form of revenge.[12] The NJS is a virtual courtroom in which you play all the roles during the trial of the person who harmed you. In the NJS, you're the victim, prosecutor, defendant/perpetrator, judge and jury, warden, and judge of your own life.[13] Following a simple script, the trials proceed through the three phases of a traditional criminal trial: the Prosecution, the Defense, and the Verdict and Sentence. Two additional phases are added: the Punishment and the Final Judgment.

Because NJS trials unfold inside your mind and you play all the roles, they can take place anytime, anywhere, without the need for the real defendant, witnesses, a courthouse, or a lawyer. You control everything. You give and hear the testimony, render a verdict, hand down a sentence, imagine administering the punishment, and decide whether to set yourself free from the pain of the past. You can retry the same person for the same thing as often as you like and reach different verdicts. You can conduct NJS trials by yourself using the script, or with a trained facilitator, or in group settings. I've even developed a free online audio app version of the NJS called the Miracle Court app that guides you through the trial (www.miraclecourt.com). An NJS trial takes less than an hour to complete and, after you've done one or two, can be over in a matter of minutes or even seconds as you quickly jump to the resolution you know is right for you.

Sound strange? As we've seen throughout this book, we're already daily and hourly conducting trials of the people who harm us inside the courtrooms of our minds and playing all the roles in our imaginations. The NJS is designed to boot the kangaroos out of these kangaroo courts, allowing you to safely gratify and release your revenge desires and reframe the trials to reveal that the revenge you crave will only harm you, not resolve the pain of your grievances.

The renowned trauma expert and psychiatrist Bessel van der Kolk, MD, author of the best-selling book *The Body Keeps the Score: Brain, Mind, and Body in the Healing of Trauma*,[14] explains that the great psychological hurt experienced by victims of mistreatment, injustice, and trauma is from not the event itself "but the fact that nobody . . . says 'That's just terrible,' and nobody gives you justice."[15] A meta-analysis of thirty-three studies of crime victims reflects the need to be acknowledged and heard.[16] The NJS meets these needs by allowing you as the victim to be heard, believed, and validated, and to hold the perpetrator accountable inside your mind, releasing your revenge cravings without harming yourself, the perpetrator, or others. How can an imaginary trial inside your head be expected to help you heal real-life trauma and release real-life revenge desires? Because traumatic memories, psychological pain, and the desire for revenge all reside inside your head. It only makes sense to conduct the trial of the person who wronged you there. The better question to ask is how a trial inside a courthouse built of stone, steel, wood, and glass, and conducted by people who are not you, can possibly be expected to heal the traumatic memories, psychological pain, and revenge desires inside your mind? The answer is that it can't.

THE COURTROOM OF THE MIND, REIMAGINED

There's a growing body of evidence to support The Nonjustice System. Remember the neuroscience of forgiveness from the previous chapter and the three psychological strategies to activate it: cognitive control, perspective taking, and social valuation? And remember Dr. Lembke's seven self-help activities above for recovering from addiction? They're built into the NJS:

Reflect upon the *objectives or reasons why* you want to engage in revenge and *become mindful of the painful emotions* that cue your cravings: That's the NJS Prosecution phase, where you testify as the victim and tell the court what happened. It's also the Verdict and Sentencing phase, where you, as the judge, decide guilt or innocence and hand down an appropriate punishment.

Identify the *problems* that engaging in revenge seeking are causing you, the *benefits* of abstaining, and the *social value* of your relationship with the person who harmed you: That's the NJS Punishment and Final Judgment phases, where you imagine getting the revenge you seek and decide whether it benefits or harms you.

Engage in *perspective taking* and *radical honesty* about your addiction: That's the NJS Defense, Punishment, and Final Judgment phases, where you develop insight and empathy by playing the defendant and engaging in radical honesty about your revenge addiction, its costs, and what it's doing to your life.

Exercise *cognitive control* and *take next steps:* That's the NJS Final Judgment phase, where you decide whether to set yourself free from the pain and wrongs of the past by practicing nonjustice and forgiveness.

The NJS even includes aspects of addiction interventions such as motivational interviewing and cognitive behavioral therapy, which seek to help people become active participants in their own recovery by uncovering the implications of changing or not changing their behaviors, exploring their motivations, and testing maladaptive thoughts, assumptions, and behavioral patterns.[17]

Remember Billy the dog killer from chapter 3? In the study that my Yale colleagues and I conducted, we found that revenge desires among adult participants toward Billy decreased dramatically after using the NJS in one-on-one sessions with a trained facilitator, and that feelings of benevolence toward Billy increased significantly, as measured by the Transgression-Related Interpersonal Motivations Inventory.[18] Revenge desires remained low in follow-up assessments two weeks later. Study participants also reported a greater awareness of self and others, "thinking things through," and a sense of empowerment and control.

These are robust results, but they're not conclusive. This was only a single, small pilot study, without a control group, without using the participants' real-world grievances, and without fMRI brain imaging. Further indirect evidence of NJS effectiveness was suggested by the study I discussed in chapter 2 showing that jail inmates in the Pennsylvania forensic peer support community reentry program that Dr. Nulton and I created, which incorporated the NJS, experienced a nearly 50 percent reduction in reincarceration rate compared with the rate of inmates in the overall U.S. jail and prison population.[19]

Remember Michael Stokes from chapter 4, the navy cook who murdered the woman he believed had betrayed him and the man he mistakenly believed she was having an affair with? He asked me if he could use the NJS to deal with some grievances he had in prison. He told me afterward that the NJS helped him "let it all go" and forgive the person he believed had wronged him. He shared the NJS

with fifteen other inmates. Eleven of them felt the NJS was helpful to them too. Of the remaining four, only one reacted nega-
tively, insisting that people who do wrong should get what they
deserve and that there's little value in nonjustice or forgiveness. In a
maximum-security prison filled with violent offenders, it's surpris-
ing that more inmates did not share this view—and hopeful that so
many rejected it.

Chris Buckley, the former soldier and KKK Nighthawk who now
helps others escape from violent extremism, is also among the NJS
users and supporters. He put the male relative who sexually assaulted
him as a child on trial in the NJS. It was emotionally difficult for
Chris to do this because it caused him to confront the painful memories and rage that had been plaguing him all his life. The results
weren't immediate; he didn't just forgive instantly. But Chris explained that in the months after he used the NJS, "the subliminal
conversation that my mind would have" began to change and "soften"
him. He started repairing relationships with other family members.
Soon he realized he had become willing not only to forgive the relative who sexually assaulted him but to forgive himself. He had an
"aha moment" where he understood that "maybe I'm not forgiving
them for them. Maybe I'm ready to move on and just stop carrying
this weight around." He went on: "My life has gotten a lot better and
I'm more effective at the [deradicalization] work I try to do now
because of being able to let that go and being able to move on from
the past and realize that I'm not convicting that person. I'm not
doing any harm to that person. The only person suffering harm in
this whole cycle [has been] me."

Just before the COVID-19 pandemic, my Yale colleagues and I
launched a second study of the NJS with a group of ten military
veterans and ten civilians—some homeless and living in poverty—
who self-disclosed experiencing significant grievances and recent
intrusive, strong revenge urges. Instead of using the Billy story, the
participants put the actual people who had wronged them on trial in
the NJS. Our study protocol also included a control group and pro-

vided for a "booster" administration of the NJS. Unfortunately, the pandemic ended the study about halfway through, so we were unable to complete quantitative data collection or submit the results for peer review. Still, the partial qualitative data that we collected were encouraging. The chart below summarizes the types of grievances presented during the twelve NJS trials we were able to complete, the outcomes of the trials, and the emotional reactions of study participants during the different phases of the trials. Many of the cases were intense, and the outcomes were often inspiring.[20]

NONJUSTICE SYSTEM—YALE PRCH STUDY 2
QUALITATIVE SUMMARY

GRIEVANCE (STUDY PARTICIPANT'S REAL-LIFE GRIEVANCE)	NJS TRIAL OUTCOME (HOW PARTICIPANT FEELS AFTER TRIAL IS OVER)
Participant 1: Two years ago, my young daughter was sexually assaulted and raped by the boyfriend of her mother (my ex-girlfriend). The guy got charged and did time for it but I'm angry and can't get over it.	I'm still upset and angry but I'm more peaceful now. I feel better getting this off my chest. For the first time I think I'm able to move on from this.
Participant 2: I was riding a bicycle, and a guy in a car deliberately swerved into me, causing me to crash. He kept on going. He almost ran me over. I could have been seriously hurt or killed. I'm still upset.	I feel better about it now. It's not something I need to care about. I'm doing good.
Participant 3: My brother is dating my ex-girlfriend, who is also the mother of my child. I'm angry with him and can't get over it.	I feel a little better now. I know I need to let this go to feel better, but I'm still stuck between doing that and wanting justice. I know I will let it go eventually, with time.
Participant 4: My neighbor destroyed my property, disturbs the peace, is a rude jerk, makes loud noises all night, and refuses to leash his dog. I'm angry and can't stop thinking about it.	I still want justice against him, but I'm aware now that getting it will only make me feel worse.
Participant 5: My ex-wife got custody of my daughter. She won't let me see her, yet she still takes my money for child support. It makes me furious.	I feel less angry about this now. I feel happier.
Participant 6: My ex-wife's boyfriend and his buddies robbed me of money and drugs, beat me up, and left me with serious injuries. Because it was a drug deal, I couldn't call the cops. I want justice.	I feel better, lighter now. I feel some release from this. My anger isn't gone but I know now that it would be better for me if I don't seek justice against them.
Participant 7: I worked hard for a guy for years. I was injured on the job. The insurer denied the claim. The guy won't help me with my bills or make any changes to my job so I can keep working. It's unfair.	I'm confused and not sure what to do. Trying to get justice might help but it might make things worse. I just want things fixed so I can work again and get my bills paid.

EMOTIONS AND THOUGHTS EXPERIENCED (BY NJS STEP, ALL PARTICIPANTS COMBINED)

Step 1—The Prosecution (participants testifying as victim against the defendant) I feel: validated, heard, hopeful, good, pleasure, anger, sorrow, frustration, sadness, distrust, introspection, insight, self-awareness, self-judgment, empathy, revenge, forgiveness, understanding, betrayal, disgust, grievance/pain, calmness, resignation, relief.

Step 2—The Defense (participants pretending to be the defendant) I feel: anger, hurt, betrayal, desire for revenge, accountability, lack of accountability, harassed, threatened, remorse, lack of remorse, empathy, powerlessness, resignation, understanding, embarrassed, selfish.

Step 3—Verdict and Sentence (participants pretending to be judge and jury) I feel: power, prestige, anger, justice, retribution, guilty for bringing the person into court, fairness, reconciliation, compassion, empathy, teaching defendant a lesson, pleasure of revenge, vindicated, relief, happy.

Step 4—The Punishment (participants pretending to witness administration of the sentence) I feel: vindication, sadness, weariness, anger, rage, pleasure followed by feeling worse, hopeful, futility, revenge, remorse, empathy, reconciliation.

GRIEVANCE (STUDY PARTICIPANT'S REAL-LIFE GRIEVANCE)	NJS TRIAL OUTCOME (HOW PARTICIPANT FEELS AFTER TRIAL IS OVER)	
Participant 8: My former friend asked me to drive him around in his vehicle and encouraged me to violate some traffic laws. When we got pulled over, my friend didn't have insurance or registration for the vehicle. The cop ticketed me as the driver. My former friend refuses to pay the fine even though it was his fault. It's outrageous.	I can move on now. It's over, and I can even laugh about it. I'm not as angry. I was able to voice my opinion without arguing with the guy.	
Participant 9: I took care of my boyfriend when he had nothing and was using drugs. Then I caught him in bed with somebody else in my apartment. We're now split up. I'm angry and hurt.	I'm able to move on from this now. I can understand and accept what he did.	
Participant 10: I was standing in line waiting for food and a guy with obvious mental illness assaulted me for no reason. I wasn't hurt too bad, but it wasn't right and he should pay.	I feel better. I'm comfortable now. The anger went away. I can move on.	
Participant 11: My ex-wife stole my money and won't let me see my kids. It's not right.	I'm still angry because I'm homeless and on drugs and heading into detox.	
Participant 12: I took care of a friend when we were both homeless, struggling, and using drugs and he didn't have any money and needed to get high. When he came into some money, he refused to return the favor and share any of it with me.	I still want justice against him but I'm aware now that it will hurt me to get it. I'm able to move on and feel a little relieved.	

EMOTIONS EXPRESSED (BY NJS STEP, ALL PARTICIPANTS COMBINED)
Step 5—The Final Judgment (participants considering nonjustice and forgiveness while pretending to be judge of self) *At first I feel:* futility, frustration, anger, resentment, self-judgment, guilt, depression, vengeful, fear, self-punishment, embarrassed, trapped, conflict. *But then I feel:* relief, less angry, astonishment, surprise, bearing witness, validation, freedom, release, compassion, moving on, closure, peace, happiness.

Additional NJS studies are under way. I'm collaborating with the researcher Loren Toussaint at Luther College, and some of his students, on studies of the online Miracle Court app version of the NJS. Preliminary, unreported results of an initial small pilot study among undergraduates using the Billy story without a control group show that the online app delivers the same robust effect in reducing revenge desires as the in-person NJS we used in the first Yale study. We're now moving on to a study of the online app with a control group and a larger number of participants where they place the people who actually wronged them on trial for real-life grievances. In a separate effort, the researchers Kendell Coker at Connecticut College, Evan Harrington at the Chicago School, Jeffrey Treistman at the University of New Haven, and I are starting a comparison study with a control group between the in-person NJS and the Miracle Court app using the Billy story.

Much more research is needed into the efficacy of the NJS and other addiction interventions in reducing revenge cravings and controlling revenge addiction. Scientists at universities around the world are ready and waiting to do the work. Because the discovery of revenge addiction is so recent, government agencies, foundations, and philanthropists have been slow to provide funding. That needs to change if we want to save lives.

USING THE NONJUSTICE SYSTEM TO PREVENT GUN VIOLENCE

In 2019, the former ABC News and current *Politico* health and science reporter Erin Schumaker published an article about the use of The Nonjustice System by the Connecticut Violence Intervention Program (CTVIP) in New Haven.[21] New Haven is a medium-sized city that is home to Yale University and has a significant level of urban gun violence. CTVIP employs trained violence prevention professionals to work with youth aged thirteen to twenty-four who are active or at high risk of being active in street and gang violence.[22] The goal of the program is to interrupt and prevent revenge killings. That means sending violence prevention specialists to hospital emergency rooms to meet with shooting victims' families and friends to prevent next-round violence, de-escalating and mediating interpersonal and gang conflicts, and facilitating the return to the community of individuals after serving prison sentences for violent crimes. With CTVIP working to reduce deadly revenge addiction at city scale, I offered to train the executive director, Leonard Jahad, and his staff in using The Nonjustice System.

Many of CTVIP's violence prevention professionals themselves have histories of perpetrating revenge-fueled violent crimes and turning their lives around by becoming credible messengers and mentors in the community. Among those who received the NJS training is William Outlaw III. William, or "Juneboy," as he is known on the streets, is a former drug gang kingpin who was convicted and sentenced in his early twenties to eighty-five years in prison for homicide and armed assault. He was released after twenty years when his sentence was reduced on appeal. Following his return to the community, he dedicated his life to combating the type of violence he inflicted on his city. He's become CTVIP's lead violence prevention professional and the subject of the gripping and inspiring biography *Citizen Outlaw: One Man's Journey from Gangleader to Peacekeeper* by Charles Barber.[23]

Another one of CTVIP's violence prevention professionals who received the NJS training is a street-savvy guy named Doug, who came to CTVIP not as a former perpetrator of gun violence but as a victim: His son was shot and murdered about a decade earlier, and the killer escaped punishment. Doug has devoted his life to preventing other parents from seeing their children in caskets. Still not over his personal loss or the anger, he decided during the NJS training to put his son's killer on trial. While playing the role of judge, Doug found the man guilty and sentenced him to twenty-five years in prison. Erin Schumaker attended the training and reports in her article what Doug said when the trial was over: "It feels good. I'm elated. They found justice for my person being done wrong."[24]

Schumaker returned to New Haven a few months after the training to watch the executive director, Jahad, lead a man named Lamont Battle, a high school security officer, through a Nonjustice System trial. When Battle was five years old, his father was shot and murdered. Battle still wasn't over it. He had many questions but learned recently that the murderer had been killed during a police shoot-out. Since even dead people can be tried in The Nonjustice System, he decided to put the man on trial. While playing the judge, Battle sentenced the man to life in prison with an unusual stipulation: The only visitor he can have is Battle himself. Battle then imagines thirty years passing, during which he and his father's killer have been meeting inside the prison. Something remarkable has happened, though: They've become best friends. "You took my dad," Battle imagines saying to the man. "Now I'm your son." Battle explains to Schumaker afterward, "He told me he's sorry, finally. That helped a whole lot."[25]

All this, from revenge to forgiveness and redemption, takes place inside the courtroom of the mind.

Leonard Jahad is intimately familiar with that courtroom. He's a big, powerfully built man with a gentle face and an enormous heart. He played football in high school, got a scholarship to play ball in college, then lost it after getting in a fight. He went on to become a corrections officer and an adult probation officer before leading CTVIP. When he was seventeen, his older sister, who helped raise him while his parents worked, was stabbed thirteen times by her boyfriend and left for dead when she tried to break up with him. The boyfriend had been like a big brother to Jahad, and his parents liked him too. They were stunned, confused, devastated. And they wanted revenge. Jahad's father took him into the garage and showed him a pistol he kept hidden there. "If you do something to him," he said to Jahad, "just do it and don't tell anyone. Don't even tell me."

Jahad got the message. He rounded up his teenage cousins, and together they drove to the hospital to see his sister. The doctor told them it was bad, she might not survive. Distraught and looking for blood, they went back to the house to get the gun, but his father had reconsidered and hid it in a different location so Jahad wouldn't find it. Jahad obtained a different handgun from a friend, and one of his cousins armed himself with a sawed-off shotgun. The posse tore through the town kicking down doors trying to find the boyfriend. They threatened to shoot up a nightclub if the owner didn't tell them where he was hiding.

Empty-handed, Jahad and his cousins returned to the hospital for an update on his sister. A cop was there waiting and took Jahad aside. He told him the doctor said the knife punctured his sister's lung, but she was going to make it. Jahad was relieved. Then the cop asked, "Where's the gun?"

Jahad tried to evade the question.

"Did you use it?" the cop asked.

"No."

"Okay," the cop said. "Go put it under the wheel well of my car on the third floor of the hospital parking garage and walk away. The guy's upstairs: He tried to kill himself. He's under police guard. He's going to be charged with attempted murder. Don't change places with this guy."

Jahad's cousins urged him not to trust the cop, but Jahad recognized a once-in-a-lifetime opportunity. He put the gun in the wheel well of the police cruiser and walked away. He never looked back, and he never heard anything again about the gun.

Who better to lead an organization dedicated to stopping revenge killings?

Jahad tells me that when he and Juneboy use The Nonjustice System with their CTVIP clients, things are so heated and moving so fast that they "always go to the last step"—the Final Judgment, where you pretend to be the judge of your own life and consider nonjustice and forgiveness. "When you think about your life and you look back at things," he said, "the things that you may have done and the things you're going through right now, you think about the grand scheme of everything you do. What could be your response [to this act of violence], or what would you change?"

According to CTVIP's website, the organization has helped reduce the number of shootings with victims in New Haven by 33 percent—while using only eight violence prevention professionals.[26] Imagine if there were as many violence prevention professionals as there are police officers who respond to acts of violence after the fact.

USING THE NONJUSTICE SYSTEM TO PREVENT BULLYING AND SCHOOL VIOLENCE

As I explained previously, children as young as toddlers experience revenge desires when they're wronged.[27] Researchers have found that grievance-triggered retaliation is a primary motivator of youth violence and bullying and that bullies identify "revenge" as their primary reason for bullying.[28] What if we made The Nonjustice System available in schools as an anti-bullying and victim support program?

That's the question I posed to leaders of the renowned Clifford Beers Clinic in New Haven. Founded in 1913, Clifford Beers is the first outpatient mental health clinic in the United States. It has since evolved into a nationally recognized system of trauma-informed mental health care for children, adolescents, adults, families, and schools. The answer I received was a qualified "maybe."

With funding from a federal Victims of Crime Act grant, a group of clinicians and staff from Clifford Beers and its sister organization Mid-Fairfield Community Care Center collaborated with some Yale colleagues and me—and a group of bright students from local schools—to adapt the NJS for kids.

The team helped me create what I call the School Nonjustice System (SNJS). Rather than an adult criminal trial held in a courtroom, I modeled the SNJS on the phases of a school disciplinary hearing held in a school conference room to make it more familiar and less intimidating for kids. The five steps of the SNJS hearing include: "What Happened," with the student victim describing how they were harmed; "The Other Side of the Story," with the student victim playing the role of the person who hurt them; "What Should Be Done," with the student victim playing the school principal deciding fault and what the punishment should be; "How It Feels," with the student victim imagining how it feels to administer the punishment; and "You Have the Power," with the student victim playing a wise teacher guiding themselves in how to move on from the grievance by experimenting with nonjustice and forgiveness.

The team also helped me create two new artificial grievance scenarios based on the Billy story but more appropriate for children aged twelve to fourteen and fifteen to eighteen. The characters in the stories are kids rather than adults, and the dog is only injured rather than killed (kids found the dog's death too upsetting). The scenarios allow the SNJS to be used in classroom/group settings for bullying and violence prevention and education. Then SNJS can also be used in one-on-one settings with a school counselor or teacher to address a student's specific grievances and victimization.

After refining the SNJS and scenarios using student focus groups and developing a companion user manual, we conducted a small pilot evaluation among children in the Mid-Fairfield program and at a local school. Although the results have not yet been fully analyzed and submitted for peer review, our preliminary analysis indicates that the SNJS can be successfully adapted for youth, and that it decreased the desire by victims to avoid interacting with the imaginary perpetrator who mistreated the pet. A full study of the SNJS with a control group will be needed to assess the efficacy of the SNJS in reducing revenge desires and bullying among kids. In the meantime, the neuroeducation specialist Karen Grites, MS, in Palo Alto, California, has been so encouraged by the promise of the SNJS that she recently published an illustrated children's book based on it called *Step Back or Get Back?*[29]

USING THE NONJUSTICE SYSTEM TO PREVENT MASS SHOOTINGS

In 2015, I launched the first website to prevent mass murders by making resources about revenge addiction, including The Nonjustice System, available to people thinking of killing *before they strike*. Based on suicide prevention websites, it's called SavingCain.org.[30]

In mid-2016, I received an unexpected email from a young man named Robert (not his real name). Robert had visited SavingCain .org and told me he had no friends, had been mistreated by his parents and shunned by his community, owned multiple firearms and lots of ammunition, and had almost gone on a shooting spree murdering his parents and many other people several years earlier. He wanted to thank me for creating SavingCain.org and seeing him as a person, not as an evil monster. He did not reveal his true identity or where he lived.

I replied that I was relieved to learn that he had not acted on his revenge desires, and I encouraged him to use The Nonjustice System if he ever felt revenge urges returning. I also encouraged him to seek and maintain qualified clinical care, which he said he was doing. Robert and I communicated several more times in 2016, and then his emails stopped.

About six months later, in mid-2017, Robert emailed me again. He wrote that he was experiencing strong revenge desires and that he was considering a mass shooting soon and couldn't stop thinking about it. He made veiled references to a specific city and target. Alarmed, I replied that he might be experiencing a revenge attack. I wrote back urging him to treat what was happening to him as a medical emergency, just as he would a heart attack, and call 911 or the National Suicide & Crisis Lifeline (988)—or give me his real name and location so I could call for him. I also urged him to use The Nonjustice System. In the interim, I contacted police in the city he had referenced. The detective I spoke with emailed Robert in an attempt to establish contact and dissuade him from acting and began alerting businesses in the area. On the advice of Michael Norko, the Yale forensic psychiatrist who had invited me to speak at the American Psychiatric Association convention, I urged Robert to seek out his clinicians for support.

Robert stopped communicating with me. A couple of days passed. I didn't know what was happening and became increasingly worried. Then he finally emailed. To my great relief, he said he was feeling better, had made an appointment to see his doctor, and was no longer in danger of committing an act of violence. He explained that he tried The Nonjustice System and put *himself* on trial as the defendant. This is not uncommon; we can carry grievances and want revenge against ourselves, which can become a motive for suicide. Robert explained that by going through the trial and playing the different roles, he was able to release his revenge cravings against himself and others without anyone being harmed. He was also able to see clearly that harming people because of his grievances is not what he really wanted. He just wanted the pain to stop, and he said that it finally did. A day later, Robert emailed me again. He wrote, "Today is my birthday and you have given me the greatest gift . . . a way to move forward with my life and past this trauma. . . . Now I can convict these people under my jurisdiction. Something I have wanted to do for so long. Now . . . I can [safely] gratify my need for justice. . . . I am more grateful than you know."

Robert and I continued communicating on and off over the next couple of years. To my knowledge, he has been living a peaceful, productive, violence-free life. Regardless of the role The Nonjustice

System might have played in that, perhaps the most important takeaway from this experience is that listening to other people when they're in crisis, offering support, knowing the signs to look for, and being willing to act even when they're not—including by contacting the police—is critical in saving lives.

THE WARNING SIGNS OF A REVENGE ATTACK

Among the materials I include on the SavingCain.org website are "Warning Signs of a Revenge Attack." I took inspiration for doing this from well-known public health campaigns designed to educate the public about the warning signs of a heart attack and what to do.[31] I used active shooter research conducted by the FBI and U.S. Secret Service to develop the warning signs.[32]

We all know that heart attacks are life-threatening medical emergencies and that we should immediately dial 911 (in the United States) when we see the symptoms. Likewise, we should all know that revenge attacks are life-threatening medical emergencies and that we should immediately dial 911 or 988 (the Suicide & Crisis Lifeline) when we see the symptoms. The stakes are even higher for revenge attacks. Unlike a heart attack, which has a single direct victim, when a revenge attack strikes, the life of the person experiencing the attack is in danger but so are the lives of the target(s) of the revenge, innocent bystanders, and law enforcement officers. Tragedy can be avoided if people experiencing revenge attacks receive help and intervention before violence occurs.

I want to conclude this chapter with the warning signs of a revenge attack and what to do if you or someone you know experiences them:

THE WARNING SIGNS OF A REVENGE ATTACK

- Preoccupation or obsession with a grievance or injustice (real or imagined)

- Expressions of anger or rage over a grievance or injustice that get worse or do not go away

- Talking or writing about getting revenge or payback

- Threats to hurt or kill others, especially the perceived source of the grievance or injustice but also their proxies

- Acquiring or seeking access to weapons

- Identifying targets to hurt or kill, especially the source of the grievance or injustice or their proxies (targets may include individuals, groups, or types of people, such as by race, religion, nationality, gender, sexual orientation, families/friends, co-workers, customers, worshippers, groups, and gangs)

- Preparations to hurt or kill (training/practicing with weapons; acquiring or stockpiling ammunition, body armor, tactical gear; conducting surveillance of targets or locations)

- Planning to hurt or kill, especially the perceived source of the grievance or injustice or their proxies, including date, time, location, transportation, and site access

WHAT YOU SHOULD DO IF YOU OR SOMEONE ELSE MAY BE EXPERIENCING A REVENGE ATTACK

- Act quickly; do not hesitate. Fast action saves lives. Treat the warning signs of a revenge attack as a life-threatening medical emergency.

- Call for help—in the United States, dial 911 for emergency services or 988 (the Suicide & Crisis Lifeline); if that is not possible, go to the nearest hospital emergency room or police station.

- Remove access to weapons if safe to do so.

- Go to a safe location if you may be the target of a revenge attack; if others may be at risk, warn them to seek safe shelter.

- If safe to do so, attempt to dissuade the individual and encourage nonviolent alternatives, such as seeking clinical counseling, considering nonjustice and forgiveness, visiting SavingCain.org, and using The Nonjustice System.

CHAPTER 11

THIS IS THE NONJUSTICE SYSTEM FOR SETTING YOURSELF FREE

Mahatma Gandhi once observed, "There is a higher court than courts of justice, and that is the court of conscience. It supersedes all other courts."[1] This is the court that The Nonjustice System helps you access.

To show you how it works, I'm going to guide you through a trial in the NJS of someone who has hurt you. That someone is Billy, the man from the fictional grievance scenario in chapter 3 who betrayed your trust and cruelly killed your beloved dog, Harley.

Although the story of Billy involves only an imaginary grievance and an imaginary perpetrator, most people who read it and put Billy on trial in the NJS find the experience powerful and illuminating. Not everyone does, however. Some people aren't as readily able to imagine themselves in the scenario or to visualize the courtroom and the trial. Some struggle with changing roles. The abuse and loss of Harley hits some harder than others. And the NJS doesn't "work" for everyone—or doesn't work immediately, every time, for every situation. For example, you might feel that the NJS wasn't helpful at first and then, like Chris Buckley, gradually find yourself softening and your inner dialogue changing toward nonjustice and forgiveness over time.

This is common among addiction recovery strategies and explains why there are so many of them, and no magic bullets. From 12-step programs like AA/NA—in which people may participate for decades—to rehabs, short- and long-term counseling and therapy, and short- and long-term prescriptions for anti-addiction medications, some approaches take longer than others, some require repeated attempts, and some require different dosages or combinations.

To give yourself the best chance of success with the NJS, you must complete all five steps of the trial and do your best to play each of the different roles. The last step—the Final Judgment—is of critical importance. The more you invest in making the trial feel real, the more likely you are to experience the positive impact you're seeking. You may also want to consider using the NJS more than once, particularly if you find intrusive revenge desires returning. And allow yourself time to process the experience. You may be surprised weeks or months later by how you have begun thinking differently about grievances, revenge, justice, and the role of nonjustice and forgiveness in recovering from victimization and trauma.

THE STORY OF BILLY, REVISITED

Before you put Billy on trial in the NJS, I need to remind you of what he did to you. Recall from chapter 3 that in the fictional scenario you own a sweet dog named Harley and a gentle cat named Lucy. You got them from an animal shelter. They had been abused, and you nursed them back to health. You love them very much, and they've become important members of your family.

You have a neighbor named Billy who owns a vicious dog named King. One day, Billy said he had to leave town unexpectedly and asked you to watch King for him. King had attacked Harley before and you wanted to steer clear of him, but Billy begged you to help him, and you agreed. You took good care of King while Billy was away and learned that King could be a sweet dog when you got to know him.

About a month later, you had to leave town unexpectedly and asked Billy to return the favor and watch Harley and Lucy for you. Billy agreed, but when you returned, Harley was missing. Billy explained that Harley had run away while on a walk. You searched frantically for Harley but couldn't find him. Out of the blue, a guy named Sean called you. He sounded intoxiciated and said that he and Billy loved dogfighting, and that Billy recently put a bait dog in a ring with King and he killed it. Sean said that Billy told him you got the bait dog for him from an animal shelter. Sean asked if you could get him a bait dog too. You were shocked and confronted Billy, accusing him of harming Harley. Billy denied it, but you continued pressing him. Billy finally admitted that he put Harley in the ring and provoked King to kill him. Billy said he threw Harley's dead body in a dumpster, and he wasn't sorry about any of it.

Those are your grievances. Billy's conduct was cruel and outrageous. He betrayed your kindness and trust, tortured Harley, tore apart your family, and wounded you to your core. You're furious. The pain is intense. You want to make Billy pay. You can't stop thinking about it. How do you manage this? How can you ever get over it?

It's time to put Billy on trial inside the courtroom of your mind. The bailiff stands as the judge enters. "All rise!"

THE NONJUSTICE SYSTEM

Before You Begin

Consult your doctor before using The Nonjustice System with real-life grievances or revenge desires to confirm that it is safe and appropriate for you.

You may only use The Nonjustice System with real-life grievances or desires if you first review and accept the terms and conditions of the Limited License, Disclaimer, Assumption of Risk, and Release of Liability in the Appendix of this book ("the Terms and Conditions"). If you use The Nonjustice System with real-life grievances or revenge desires, you agree that you have reviewed and accepted the Terms and Conditions prior to use.

If you experience distress or believe you may harm yourself or others while using the NJS or afterward, dial 911 or 988 (in the United States) for emergency medical services or the Suicide & Crisis Lifeline (988lifeline.org), consult your doctor, and/or go to your nearest hospital emergency department or police department.

Do not harm yourself or others.

Introduction

When you've been mistreated or victimized, you might want justice in the form of revenge against the person who did it. But becoming preoccupied with justice and retaliation can stop you from healing and moving on, and sometimes lead to actions that harm yourself and others.

The Nonjustice System is a virtual court that empowers you to take control of this process and win the most important trial of your life. What is that trial? It's the trial of the people who wrong you.

During a *Nonjustice System* trial, you play all the roles: prosecutor, victim, defendant, judge, warden, and judge of your own life. Since you play all the roles, you're in control of the courtroom. Nonjustice System trials are faster, easier, less costly, and more convenient than trials in traditional courts. You don't need witnesses, a judge, or a lawyer. The trials can take place anywhere, in less than an hour. You can conduct Nonjustice System trials by yourself or with a partner guiding you. Everything you need is in the script that follows. Just read it and follow the prompts.

INSTRUCTIONS

- Find a quiet, private location

- If using a partner, pick someone willing to stick to the script and not be judgmental

- Speaking and testifying out loud, even if only to yourself, is recommended and will help the trial come alive; spoken testimony is a powerful part of all trials

- Testify honestly (use The Nonjustice System in a location where you cannot be overheard if you have confidentiality concerns)

- There are no wrong answers to the questions; go with whatever is true for you

- Each step of the trial is important; *be sure to complete all five steps*

THE FIVE STEPS OF A NONJUSTICE SYSTEM TRIAL

Step 1: The Prosecution

Step 2: The Defense

Step 3: The Verdict and Sentence

Step 4: The Punishment

Step 5: The Final Judgment

Beginning the Nonjustice System Trial

Close your eyes or do what you can to picture clearly in your mind what's about to unfold.

Imagine that the person who hurt you is the Defendant being put on trial for the wrongs committed against you.

You're in the courtroom. Notice the judge's bench, witness stand, and jury box. See the lawyers' tables and the gallery. Notice all the sights, sounds, and smells of the courtroom.

The case begins . . .

STEP 1: THE PROSECUTION

Imagine that the Prosecutor calls you to the witness stand to testify. You're placed under oath. You look out at the courtroom. You see the Defendant and the Defendant's lawyer, the Judge, and the Prosecutor. The Prosecutor approaches you at the witness box and begins asking you the following questions:

- First, as the Victim, please tell the court what happened that brought you here today. Tell the court what the Defendant did and how you were hurt by it. Take your time and give all the details.

- Next, tell the court the specific wrongs you're charging the Defendant with committing. They don't have to be violations of actual laws, and you can include charges that wouldn't be allowed in a traditional court.

- Now tell the court how you've been harmed by the Defendant. What specific injuries have you suffered? How has it impacted your life? Take your time and be specific.

- Last, have you thought about retaliating or getting even with the Defendant? How? How often have you thought about it? How does it make you feel? Take your time and be specific.

The Prosecutor's questioning is now over.

Before moving on to the next step of the trial, think about how it felt as the Victim to testify and tell the court what happened. How did it make you feel? Take your time and be specific.

STEP 2: THE DEFENSE

This is step 2, the Defense. Close your eyes or do what you can to picture clearly in your mind what's about to unfold.

Imagine now that you're no longer you. *You're now the Defendant who hurt you.*

Imagine that as the Defendant you are called by your lawyer to testify in your own defense. You're placed under oath. Your lawyer begins asking you the following questions:

- First, as the Defendant, please tell the court your side of the story. Take your time and be specific. Tell the court what happened the way you remember it as the Defendant.

- Now, as the Defendant, do you plead guilty or innocent to the charges against you?

- Is there anything you'd like to say in your defense?

- As the Defendant, what's it like to be accused and put on trial? Think about it. How does it make you feel?

The questioning by the defense lawyer is now over.

Before moving on to step 3, *switch roles from the Defendant back to being yourself, the Victim, again.* As the Victim, what was it like for you to hear the Defendant testify? Think about it. How did it make you feel? Take your time and be specific.

STEP 3: THE VERDICT AND SENTENCE

This is step 3, the Verdict and Sentence. Close your eyes again or do what you can to picture clearly in your mind what's about to unfold.

Imagine now that you're no longer you. *Now you're the Judge who decides the case.*

- As the Judge, after hearing all the testimony, are there reasons for finding the Defendant *innocent*? What are they?

- Are there reasons for finding the Defendant *guilty*? What are they?

- As the Judge, what's your decision? Do you find the Defendant *innocent* or *guilty*?

- If you've found the Defendant *innocent*, skip ahead to step 5—the Final Judgment.

- If you've found the Defendant *guilty*, continue with this step.

- If you found the Defendant guilty, you must now sentence the Defendant for the wrongs committed. As the Judge, what is the *harshest* sentence or punishment you believe the Defendant should receive? The sentence can be anything you want, not only what a traditional court would impose.

- As the Judge, what's the *lightest* (least harsh) sentence or punishment the Defendant should receive? The sentence can be anything you want, not only what a traditional court would impose.

- Now it's time to decide. As the Judge, what sentence or punishment do you give the Defendant?

- What has it been like for you to be a Judge and have the power to convict and sentence the Defendant? Think about it. How does it feel to have that kind of power and responsibility?

You're now finished being the Judge.

Before we move on to step 4, *switch roles back to being yourself (the Victim) again.* You've just heard the verdict and sentence handed down by the Judge against the Defendant. As the Victim, what was that like for you? Think about it. How did it make you feel? Take your time and be specific.

STEP 4: THE PUNISHMENT

This is step 4, the Punishment. Close your eyes again or do what you can to picture clearly in your mind what's about to unfold.

Imagine now that you're no longer you. *Now you're the Warden carrying out the Judge's sentence.* Because you are the Warden, it's your job to impose the sentence on the Defendant. Imagine that you're there, at the time and place where the punishment must begin. The Defendant's there, waiting.

- First, where are you? What does it look, sound, and smell like? Who else is there?

- As the Warden, what do you say and do when you begin carrying out the sentence? What does the Defendant say and do?

- How long does the sentence go on? What happens? As the Warden, what do you say and do? What does the Defendant say and do? What does it look and sound like?

- What happens when the sentence is finished? As the Warden, what do you say and do? What does the Defendant say and do?

- As the Warden, what's it like for you to punish the Defendant? How does it make you feel? What effect does it have on you? What effect does it seem to have on the Defendant? Take your time and be specific.

You're now finished being the Warden.

Before we move on to the final step of the trial, *switch roles back to being yourself (the Victim) again.* You've just seen and heard the sentence being carried out on the Defendant. As the Victim, what was that like for you? How did you feel during it? How do you feel now that it's over? Take your time and be specific.

STEP 5: THE FINAL JUDGMENT

This is the last step, the Final Judgment. Close your eyes or do what you can to picture clearly in your mind what's about to unfold.

Imagine now that you're in a much larger and grander courtroom than where the trial of the Defendant just took place. The ceiling in this new courtroom soars high above you, many stories tall. There's an enormous judge's bench that goes almost to the ceiling so that you can't even see the Judge.

Imagine that you're all alone in the courtroom. It's quiet. You're standing in front of the judge's bench, staring up at it in wonder.

Suddenly you hear a voice from high above you. The Judge begins asking you the following questions:

- Is the Defendant here in the courtroom with you? Think about it. If you're all alone, is the Defendant here?

- Are the things the Defendant did to you happening in this courtroom right here and now? Think about it. Can events that happened in the past be happening in the present?

- Do the things the Defendant did to you in the past exist anywhere other than as memories inside your mind? Think about it. Can you see, hear, taste, touch, or smell anything that happened in the past other than as a memory?

- Do your feelings of anger or rage against the Defendant exist anywhere other than inside your mind? Think about it.

Is your desire for justice against the Defendant anything other than a thought or feeling inside your mind?

- Did putting the Defendant on trial make you remember and reexperience the pain of what the Defendant did to you?

- Imagine that you decide to practice nonjustice, which means to abstain from seeking justice against the Defendant. You don't forgive the Defendant, but you decide to stop trying so hard to punish the Defendant. Think about it. How would you feel if you did this?

- Now imagine that you decide to forgive the Defendant. *Just imagine what it would be like.* You don't have to condone or excuse what happened, but for a moment imagine that it all happened in a distant past that no longer exists, like a wave crashing on a beach that can no longer be found. Think about it. You don't do this as a gift to the person who hurt you. You do it as a gift to yourself. How would you feel if you did this?

Now switch roles from the person standing in front of the bench to being the Judge on the bench sitting high above, looking down at yourself.

From high on the judge's bench, you can see yourself far below, standing all alone. You can see how unhappy you are and how much you've been suffering. You can see now that the trial of the Defendant has always really been about *you.* It's *your* peace, happiness, and freedom that are at stake, not theirs.

As the Judge, what is your Final Judgment about *you*? Do you sentence yourself to keep suffering? Or do you choose mercy and set yourself free?

YOU HAVE THE POWER

Your case against the person who hurt you is over. You can see now that it's really you who's been on trial. *Your* freedom, peace, and happiness are at stake, not theirs.

This is why the trial of your enemies is the most important trial of your life. This is also why the courtroom inside your mind is the most powerful courtroom in the world. And why the greatest judge and lawyer in the world is *you*.

You alone have the power to heal yourself from the pain of the past.

You alone have the power to restore your peace and happiness.

You alone have the power to give yourself mercy and set yourself free.

You alone have the power to win the most important trial of your life.

What is your verdict about you?

Thank you for using The Nonjustice System.
Go in peace.

A REVENGE RECOVERY STORY

I intended to end this book with an inspiring true story about someone who suffered from revenge addiction for many years and recovered to lead a life of peace. Such individuals exist, and they're not as difficult to find as might be imagined. In fact, I've told the stories of several of them in this book. But instead of singling out one more for special treatment, I'd like to tell an astonishing and inspirational true story of many millions of them.

Following Adolf Hitler's suicide in his bunker that marked the end of European fighting during World War II, the leaders of the three major powers that defeated Germany—the United States, Great Britain, and the Soviet Union—met at Potsdam to establish the terms of Germany's surrender. Here the world had arrived full circle at the fateful circumstances of the punitive Treaty of Versailles that concluded World War I and went on to become Hitler's precipitating grievance for launching the revenge-fueled cataclysm of World War II. The conquering parties were in position yet again to impose their will upon a defeated German nation—and this time one deserving of even more ferocious punishment for having greatly exceeded in destruction, horror, and loss of life the Germany that had waged the previous war.

A prior conference among Allied leaders had already taken place at Yalta in February 1945. That conference was attended by the Soviet premier, Joseph Stalin, the British prime minister, Winston Churchill, and the U.S. president, Franklin Roosevelt. Stalin pressured Churchill and Roosevelt to agree that Germany must pay severe reparations in the amount of $20 billion—equivalent to approximately $333 billion today.[1] Stalin's vengeful intent was to reduce Germany to a medieval agrarian state. Churchill, having learned the lesson of Versailles, argued against the proposal, but Roosevelt gave in to his own revenge desires and sided with Stalin.

By the time of the Potsdam Conference some five months later (from July 17 to August 2, 1945), two of these leaders had been replaced: Roosevelt had died on April 12, 1945, succeeded by President Harry Truman, and Churchill was abruptly removed from office, succeeded by Prime Minister Clement Attlee. Truman quickly realized that Germany would be unable to pay the reparations that Stalin and Roosevelt had tentatively agreed upon at Yalta.[2] The German state lay in ruin, with cities and infrastructure shattered, housing destroyed, widespread food shortages, and rampant inflation and misery. To avoid another German economic collapse like the one after the Treaty of Versailles, the United States and Great Britain would be required to lend Germany the money necessary to pay reparations—a prospect deemed unacceptable. Unlike Roosevelt, Truman believed it would be in the United States' and Western Europe's own self-interest to preserve and strengthen Germany rather than destroy it—despite Germany having spent the previous six years trying to destroy the United States and Western Europe.

Upon arriving at Potsdam, Truman and his secretary of state, James Byrnes, distanced themselves from Roosevelt's acceptance of Stalin's demands. The Allies had already agreed upon partitioning Germany into four zones for purposes of occupation—U.S., British, French, and Soviet, with the Soviet Union taking the eastern agricultural zone. Truman and Byrnes proposed that each of the Allies take whatever reparations they wished from their respective zones, leaving each to deal with the consequences.[3] Stalin acquiesced, with the proviso, to which all parties agreed, that the Soviet Union would receive a supplemental percentage of industrial equipment from the other zones. This resulted in what became known as the Potsdam Protocol.[4] From Potsdam was born the Marshall Plan by which the United States provided massive funding to rebuild all of Western Europe, *including Germany*.[5] From the Marshall Plan was born, among many other things, the European Union, a common currency, and the unprecedented peace the world has witnessed between the major nations of Western Europe, *including Germany*, since 1945.

President Truman explained the Potsdam Protocol and its significance to the American people during a radio address to the nation on August 9, 1945:

> My fellow Americans:
>
> I have just returned from Berlin, the city from which the Germans intended to rule the world. It is a ghost city. The buildings are in ruins, its economy and its people are in ruins.
>
> Our party also visited what is left of Frankfurt and Darmstadt. We flew over the remains of Kassel, Magdeburg, and other devastated cities. German women and children and old men were wandering over the highways, returning to bombed-out homes or leaving bombed out cities, searching for food and shelter.
>
> War has indeed come home to Germany and to the German people. It has come home in all the frightfulness with which the German leaders started and waged it. The German people are beginning to atone for the crimes of the gangsters whom they placed in power and whom they wholeheartedly approved and obediently followed.
>
> We also saw some of the terrific destruction which the

war had brought to the occupied countries of Western Europe and to England.

How glad I am to be home again! And how grateful to Almighty God that this land of ours has been spared!

We must do all we can to spare her from the ravages of any future breach of the peace. That is why, though the United States wants no territory or profit or selfish advantage out of this war, we are going to maintain the military bases necessary for the complete protection of our interests and of world peace. . . .

We are going to do what we can to make Germany over into a decent nation, so that it may eventually work its way from the economic chaos it has brought upon itself, back into a place in the civilized world.

German industry is to be decentralized in order to do away with concentration of economic power in cartels and monopolies. Chief emphasis is to be on agriculture and peaceful industry. German economic power to make war is to be eliminated. The Germans are not to have a higher standard of living than their former victims, the people of the defeated and occupied countries of Europe.

The economic action taken against Germany at the [Potsdam] conference included another most important item—reparations.

We do not intend again to make the mistake of exacting reparations in money and then lending Germany the money with which to pay. Reparations this time are to be paid in physical assets from those resources of Germany which are not required for her peacetime subsistence.

The first purpose of reparations is to take out of Germany everything with which she can prepare for another war. Its second purpose is to help the devastated countries to bring about their own recovery by means of the equipment and material taken from Germany. . . .

> It was agreed at [Potsdam] that the payment of reparations, from whatever zones taken, should always leave enough resources to enable the German people to subsist without sustained support from other nations.[6]

The European revenge cycle was broken at last. Here we have proof of recovery from the deadliest case of mass revenge addiction in world history. Here we have a formula for preventing mass revenge addiction in the future. And here we have evidence for the universality of the principles of nonjustice articulated in the previous chapters—to abstain from the pursuit of justice in the form of revenge *because it is in your own self-interest.*

The practical benefits to the world of this approach are self-evident: eighty years of a Germany at peace with its neighbors, without rising against them in retaliation, contributing to the welfare of humanity. Against the miserable history of revenge addiction and human violence, such an outcome might be considered the stuff of myth. Yet we of this age have witnessed it with our own eyes. If nations at war and their populations of millions of aggrieved and revenge-addicted citizens can achieve this, how much easier each of us in our own homes, schools, workplaces, and communities?

As I write these concluding words in July 2024, the Council on Foreign Relations' Global Conflict Tracker is reporting nearly thirty violent conflicts around the world, including widespread criminal gang violence in Mexico; criminal gang violence in Haiti; political violence in Venezuela; war between Russia and Ukraine; war in Yemen; civil war in Sudan and Myanmar; military conflicts in Israel, the Palestinian Territories, Lebanon, and Syria; violent instability in Afghanistan and Pakistan; threatened war between China and Taiwan and between Iran and Israel; and threats of nuclear war by North Korea against South Korea, Japan, and the United States.[7] In Ukraine, Russia has just bombed a children's hospital. In Gaza, the death toll from Israeli attacks has just exceeded thirty-nine thousand. In Croatia, a lone gunman has just killed six at a nursing home.

In Pennsylvania, a young man with an assault rifle has just attempted to assassinate the former president Donald Trump. In Illinois, a white male police officer has just shot an unarmed Black woman in the face and killed her, inside her own home, after she called 911 to report a prowler, because she angered him. And in California, North Carolina, Oklahoma, Florida, Vermont, Massachusetts, Texas, Utah, Tennessee, Ohio, Mississippi, Georgia, Kentucky, Virginia, and Arizona, multiple murder-suicides have been reported, wiping out entire families.

This is a dire picture of our current world, but there is good news on the horizon. We now have more insight into why brutality happens and how to stop it. The science of revenge demonstrates that most of the violence and intentionally inflicted suffering we experience and inflict is the result of real or imagined grievances activating powerful, compulsive revenge cravings inside our brains to relieve pain. This book demonstrates that these cravings can be controlled, and the psychological pain of our remembered grievances can be reduced or eliminated. We can no longer say that violence is senseless, or the work of evil forces. We can no longer say that we don't know how to stop it. We do know. We must now act on that knowledge.

When Jesus of Nazareth was asked, "How oft shall my brother sin against me, and I forgive him? till seven times?" he responded, "I say not unto thee, Until seven times: but, until seventy times seven" (Matt. 18:21–22). This was not pious instruction for becoming a saint or a naïve suicide pact. It was practical, scientifically sound, lifesaving advice for preventing violence, restoring peace, and overcoming revenge addiction.

ACKNOWLEDGMENTS

Author acknowledgments tend to be celebratory, but that does not seem appropriate in this case. Too many have suffered from the deadly affliction described in this book, too many have been injured or killed by them, and too many remain in harm's way. The time for celebration will come only when this book achieves its purpose, and that will be up to each reader. To the many brilliant, wonderful people who supported the writing and publishing of this book, agreed to be interviewed for it, improved its content, and conducted and participated in the decades of research upon which it is based, please know that I am deeply grateful. May your efforts change the world so that future generations will also feel gratitude and know peace.

APPENDIX

Limited License, Disclaimer, Assumption of Risk, and Release of Liability

By Using The Nonjustice System, You Agree to Be Legally Bound by the Terms and Conditions Below. If You Do Not Agree, You May Not Use The Nonjustice System.

The Nonjustice System in this book is provided and distributed under license by Bette Press LLC. Subject to the terms and conditions of this License, you are granted a limited, nonexclusive license by Bette Press LLC to use The Nonjustice System for your personal use only and for no other purpose. By using any portion of The Nonjustice System, you, including your administrators, personal representatives, executors, heirs, transferees, successors, and assigns (collectively herein, "you"), are irrevocably agreeing to be bound by the terms of this Limited License, Disclaimer, Assumption of Risk, and Release of Liability ("License"). *If you wish to use The Nonjustice System with another person (for example, as a facilitator), you may not use The Nonjustice System with that person unless you have first ensured that said person has reviewed this License and agreed to its terms.*

You agree to use The Nonjustice System in compliance with all applicable laws and regulations, including local laws of the country or region in which you reside. If you are a consumer, you may have rights in your state or country of residence which would prohibit these limitations from applying to you, and where prohibited they will not apply to you. The Nonjustice System is provided for general informational and spiritual purposes only and should not be relied or acted upon as, and does not constitute, legal, psychological, medical, mental health, financial, or other professional advice or direction. You agree that no lawyer-client or patient-doctor/therapist relationship is created by your use of The Nonjustice System. You agree that The Nonjustice System does not constitute the practice of law, medicine, psychology, or any other professional service or licensed activity. You alone remain responsible for your use of The Nonjustice System and any action or inaction you take arising out of or related to your use of The Nonjustice System. You acknowledge and agree that The Nonjustice System is being distributed and made available to you exclusively and solely by Bette Press LLC and no other person or entity.

PURPOSES AND RISKS OF THE NONJUSTICE SYSTEM: The Nonjustice System is a role play during which a person with an actual or imagined grievance or experience of being wronged or mistreated (the victim) is invited through a series of prompts to imagine what it might be like to prosecute the person(s) who perpetrated the grievance, wrong, or mistreatment (the perpetrator(s)). During the process, the victim is asked to recall the circumstances and details of the wrong(s) or mistreatment in question as they would during a traditional trial, and to imagine the perpetrator(s) defense to the charges. The victim is also asked to imagine what it might be like to judge, convict, sentence, and punish the perpetrator(s). This is done to create a space within the imagination in which to experience getting justice against a transgressor safely, without placing the victim, the perpetrator(s), or others at risk of actual harm or jeopardy. These imagined experiences may cause discomfort or distress and trigger powerful emotions. Although these are common discomforts and emotions of remembering traumatic circumstances and imagining getting justice against perpetrators, *you should not use The Nonjustice System unless you are certain that doing so will not in any way harm you emotionally, mentally, or physically, and that you will not in any way harm the perpetrator(s) or any other person, entity, or property in any way. The purpose of The Nonjustice System is to help reduce and control revenge desires, promote healing, and help people move on safely and productively from the wrongs of the past. If you use The Nonjustice System, then intending to be legally bound, you represent and agree that you will not engage in any conduct, whether by act or omission, that could in any way result in harm to yourself, the perpetrator(s), or any other person, entity, or property. If you experience distress or believe you may be at risk of harm to yourself or others, you agree to immediately contact a trained medical or mental health professional, call your local or national mental health crisis hotline, or contact emergency police or medical services (dial 911 or 988 in the United States). You represent and agree that any harm or damage that you may cause at any time and by any means to yourself or any other person, entity, or property is solely the result of your own independent judgments, decisions, actions, emotions, motivations, and choices and is not related to, caused by, contributed to, and could not have arisen in any way from your use of The Nonjustice System. You also represent and agree that you accept and assume these and all other related risks of using The Non-*

justice System. You forever and irrevocably release and discharge from and agree not to file any cause of action, claim, demand, or lawsuit under any legal, equitable, contract, tort, statutory, regulatory, contribution, or other theory for any legal or other liability in any form whatsoever arising out of or related to your use of The Nonjustice System against the creators, providers, publishers, distributors, and administrators of The Nonjustice System, and the Bette Press LLC Parties (as defined below).

NO WARRANTIES: *TO THE MAXIMUM EXTENT PERMITTED BY APPLICABLE LAW, THE NONJUSTICE SYSTEM IS BEING PROVIDED TO YOU "AS IS" AND "AS APPLICABLE," WITH ALL FAULTS AND WITHOUT WARRANTIES OF ANY KIND, AND BETTE PRESS LLC, THE CREATORS AND PUBLISHERS OF THE NONJUSTICE SYSTEM, JAMES KIMMEL JR., PENGUIN RANDOM HOUSE LLC, BETTE PRESS LLC'S OWNERS, MEMBERS, DIRECTORS, OFFICERS, EMPLOYEES, CONTRACTORS, PRINCIPALS, LICENSORS, AFFILIATES, HEIRS, SUCCESSORS, AND ASSIGNS* (collectively, the *"BETTE PRESS LLC PARTIES") HEREBY DISCLAIM ALL WARRANTIES AND CONDITIONS WITH RESPECT TO THE NONJUSTICE SYSTEM, EITHER EXPRESS, IMPLIED, OR STATUTORY, INCLUDING BUT NOT LIMITED TO THE IMPLIED WARRANTIES AND/OR CONDITIONS OF MERCHANTABILITY, SATISFACTORY QUALITY, FITNESS FOR A PARTICULAR PURPOSE, ACCURACY, QUIET ENJOYMENT, AND NONINFRINGEMENT OF THIRD PARTY RIGHTS. The BETTE PRESS LLC PARTIES* do not guarantee the accuracy, completeness, reliability, content, or outcomes of use of The Nonjustice System.

RISK OF USE: *YOU EXPRESSLY ACKNOWLEDGE AND AGREE THAT, TO THE EXTENT PERMITTED BY APPLICABLE LAW, USE OF THE NONJUSTICE SYSTEM IS AT YOUR SOLE RISK AND THAT THE ENTIRE RISK AS TO SATISFACTORY QUALITY, PERFORMANCE, ACCURACY, OUTCOMES, AND EFFORT IS WITH YOU. YOU ACKNOWLEDGE THAT THE BETTE PRESS LLC PARTIES ARE NOT QUALIFIED EXPERTS IN AND ARE UNAWARE OF THE SUBJECT MATTER OR APPROPRIATENESS OR APPLICATION OF THE NONJUSTICE SYSTEM FOR YOUR PARTICULAR SITUATION, CIRCUMSTANCES, OR GRIEVANCES, HAVE NO SPECIAL OR PARTICULAR EXPERTISE, QUALIFICATIONS, OR SKILLS RELATED THERETO, AND THAT YOU ARE ADVISED TO CONSULT QUALIFIED EXPERTS, ADVISERS, OR TRAINED*

PROFESSIONALS IN THE TOPICS, FIELDS, AND AREAS OF THE NON-JUSTICE SYSTEM AND YOUR PARTICULAR SITUATION, CIRCUM-STANCES, OR GRIEVANCES BEFORE USING OR RELYING UPON THE NONJUSTICE SYSTEM FOR ANY PURPOSE WHATSOEVER.

LIMITATION OF LIABILITY: *TO THE EXTENT NOT PROHIBITED BY APPLICABLE LAW, IN NO EVENT SHALL THE BETTE PRESS LLC PARTIES BE LIABLE TO YOU OR ANY OTHER PERSON OR ENTITY FOR PERSONAL OR PROPERTY INJURY, OR ANY INCIDENTAL, SPE-CIAL, INDIRECT, OR CONSEQUENTIAL DAMAGES WHATSOEVER, INCLUDING, WITHOUT LIMITATION, DAMAGES FOR LOSS OF PROF-ITS, OR ANY OTHER COMMERCIAL DAMAGES OR LOSSES, ARISING OUT OF OR RELATED TO YOUR USE OR INABILITY TO USE THE NONJUSTICE SYSTEM OR ANY SERVICES IN CONJUNCTION WITH THE NONJUSTICE SYSTEM, HOWEVER CAUSED, REGARDLESS OF THE THEORY OF LIABILITY (CONTRACT, STATUTE, REGULATION, ORDINANCE, TORT, OR OTHERWISE) AND EVEN IF THE BETTE PRESS LLC PARTIES HAVE BEEN ADVISED OF THE POSSIBILITY OF SUCH DAMAGES. SOME JURISDICTIONS DO NOT ALLOW THE EX-CLUSION OR LIMITATION OF LIABILITY FOR PERSONAL INJURY, OR OF INCIDENTAL OR CONSEQUENTIAL DAMAGES, SO THIS LIMITA-TION MAY NOT APPLY TO YOU. In no event shall the BETTE PRESS LLC PARTIES' total liability to you or any other person or entity for all damages (other than as may be required by applicable law in cases involving personal injury) exceed the amount of one dollar ($1.00). The foregoing limitations will apply even if the above-stated remedy fails of its essential purpose. YOU HEREBY RELEASE AND AGREE TO WAIVE AND NOT TO FILE OR PURSUE ANY CLAIM OR CAUSE OF ACTION OF ANY KIND THAT YOU MAY HAVE AGAINST THE BETTE PRESS LLC PARTIES ARISING OUT OF OR RELATED TO THE NONJUSTICE SYSTEM OR YOUR USE OF THE NONJUSTICE SYS-TEM.*

CONTROLLING LAW AND SEVERABILITY; FORUM; COMPLETE AGREEMENT: This License shall be governed by and construed in accordance with the laws of the Commonwealth of Pennsylvania, excluding its conflict of law principles. This License shall not be governed by the United Nations Convention on Contracts for the International Sale of Goods, the application of which is expressly excluded. If you are a consumer based in the United Kingdom, this License will be governed by the laws of the jurisdiction of your residence. If for any reason a court of competent jurisdiction finds any provision, or portion thereof, to be unenforceable, the remainder of this License shall continue in full force and effect. Any action arising out of or related to The Nonjustice System, your use of The Nonjustice System or this License shall be pursued exclusively in the state or federal courts of the Commonwealth of Pennsylvania and, specifically the U.S. District Court for the Eastern District of Pennsylvania or the Court of Common Pleas of Chester County, Pennsylvania, and you irrevocably submit to the personal jurisdiction of such specified courts. This License constitutes the entire agreement between you and Bette Press LLC, and for the express benefit of the Bette Press LLC Parties, relating to the use of The Nonjustice System and supersedes all prior or contemporaneous understandings regarding such subject matter. No amendment to or modification of this License will be binding unless in writing and signed by Bette Press LLC.

If you do not acknowledge and agree to all of the preceding terms and conditions, you may not use The Nonjustice System for any purpose.

REFERENCES

Allam, Hannah. "'We Were Blindsided': Families of Extremists Form Group to Fight Hate." *All Things Considered.* NPR, Dec. 12, 2019. www.npr.org/2019/12/12/787295283/we-were-blindsided-families-of-extremists-form-group-to-fight-hate.

Al-Masaeed, Sultan. "Islamic State E-caliphate on Twitter: An Observational Study." *Al-Balqa Journal for Research and Studies* 21, no. 1 (2018). digitalcommons.aaru.edu.jo/albalqa/vol21/iss1/5.

Al-Saggaf, Yeslam. "Online Radicalisation Along a Continuum: From When Individuals Express Grievances to When They Transition into Extremism." Paper presented at the SecureComm: Security and Privacy in Communication Networks, Singapore, 2018.

American Heart Association. "Warning Signs of a Heart Attack." 2022. www.heart.org/en/health-topics/heart-attack/warning-signs-of-a-heart-attack.

American Society of Addiction Medicine. "Definition of Addiction." Updated Nov. 24, 2021. www.asam.org/quality-care/definition-of-addiction.

Anderson, C. A., and B. J. Bushman. "Human Aggression." *Annual Review of Psychology* 53 (2002): 27–51. doi.org/10.1146/annurev.psych.53.100901.135231.

Anthony, James C., Lynn A. Warner, and Ronald C. Kessler. "Comparative Epidemiology of Dependence on Tobacco, Alcohol, Controlled Substances, and Inhalants: Basic Findings from the National Comorbidity Survey." *Experimental and Clinical Psychopharmacology* 2, no. 3 (1994): 244–68. doi.org/10.1037/1064-1297.2.3.244.

Anti-Defamation League. "Ku Klux Klan Robes." Accessed May 10, 2024. www.adl.org/resources/hate-symbol/ku-klux-klan-robes.

APA. *Diagnostic and Statistical Manual of Mental Disorders: DSM-5.* 5th ed. Washington, D.C.: American Psychiatric Association, 2013. doi:10.1176/appi.books.9780890425596.

———. *Diagnostic and Statistical Manual of Mental Disorders: DSM-5-TR.* 5th ed. Washington, D.C.: American Psychiatric Association, 2022.

Aquino, K., T. M. Tripp, and R. J. Bies. "How Employees Respond to Personal Offense: The Effects of Blame Attribution, Victim Status, and Offender Status on Revenge and Reconciliation in the Workplace." *Journal of Applied Psychology* 86, no. 1 (Feb. 2001): 52–59. doi.org/10.1037/0021-9010.86.1.52.

Associated Press. "Musk Says Twitter Is Losing Cash Because Advertising Is Down and the Company Is Carrying Heavy Debt." July 15, 2023. apnews.com/article/twitter-elon-musk-debt-advertising-70f526c407d4c68107f9d1ec4b4e3151.

Balcells, Laia. *Rivalry and Revenge: The Politics of Violence During Civil War.* Cambridge, U.K.: Cambridge University Press, 2017.

Barber, Charles. *Citizen Outlaw: One Man's Journey from Gangleader to Peacekeeper.* New York: HarperCollins, 2019.

Barker, Danielle. "How a Former KKK Member and a Muslim Refugee Became Friends." *USA Today,* July 26, 2019. www.usatoday.com/story/news/humankind/2019/07/26/how-former-kkk-member-and-muslim-refugee-became-friends/1807639001/.

Baumeister, Roy F. *Evil: Inside Human Cruelty and Violence.* New York: W. H. Freeman, 1996.

Beech, Mark. "Disney's 'Lion King' Tops $11.6 Billion on Anniversary, Most Successful Franchise Ever." *Forbes,* Oct. 30, 2019. www.forbes.com/sites/markbeech/2019/10/30/lion-king-tops-116-billion-on-anniversary-most-successful-franchise-ever/?sh=7ad7cd5f1c0a.

Bellamy, Chyrell, James Kimmel, Mark N. Costa, Jack Tsai, Larry Nulton, Elissa Nulton, Alexandra Kimmel, et al. "Peer Support on the 'Inside and Outside': Building Lives and Reducing Recidivism for People with Mental Illness Returning from Jail." *Journal of Public Mental Health* 18, no. 3 (2019): 188–98. doi.org/10.1108/JPMH-02-2019-0028.

Benton, M. L., A. Abraham, A. L. LaBella, P. Abbot, A. Rokas, and J. A. Capra. "The Influence of Evolutionary History on Human Health and Disease." *Nature Reviews Genetics* 22, no. 5 (May 2021): 269–83. doi.org/10.1038/s41576-020-00305-9.

The Berlin (Potsdam) Conference, July 17–August 2, 1945, (a) Protocol of the Proceedings, August 1, 1945. National Archives. Avalon Project, Lillian Goldman Law Library, Yale Law School. avalon.law.yale.edu/20th_century/decade17.asp.

Bernhardt, Erin Levin, and Din Blankenship. *Refuge.* Shout! Factory, 2023. Film. www.imdb.com/title/tt16138938/.

Bernhardt, J. M. "Communication at the Core of Effective Public Health." *American Journal of Public Health* 94, no. 12 (Dec. 2004): 2051–53. doi.org/10.2105/ajph.94.12.2051.

Bernstein, Thomas P. "Mao Zedong and the Famine of 1959–1960: A Study in Wilfulness." *China Quarterly,* no. 186 (2006): 421–45. www.jstor.org/stable/20192620.

Best, Nicholas. *Five Days That Shocked the World: Eyewitness Accounts from Europe at the End of World War II.* New York: Thomas Dunne Books, 2012.

Billingsley, J., and E. A. R. Losin. "The Neural Systems of Forgiveness: An Evolutionary Psychological Perspective." *Frontiers in Psychology* 8 (2017): 737. doi.org/10.3389/fpsyg.2017.00737.

Black, D. W. "The Natural History of Antisocial Personality Disorder." *Journal of Psychiatry* 60, no. 7 (July 2015): 309–14. doi.org/10.1177/070674371506000703.

Blum, K., J. W. Ashford, B. Kateb, D. Sipple, E. Braverman, C. A. Dennen, D. Baron, et al. "Dopaminergic Dysfunction: Role for Genetic & Epigenetic Testing in the New Psychiatry." *Journal of the Neurological Sciences* 453 (Oct. 2023): 120809. doi.org/10.1016/j.jns.2023.120809.

Boon, Susan D., Alishia M. Alibhai, and Vicki L. Deveau. "Reflections on the Costs and Benefits of Exacting Revenge in Romantic Relationships." *Canadian Journal of Behavioural Science* 42, no. 2 (2011): 128–37. doi.org/10.1037/a0022367.

Brandon, Alex, and Ben Finley. "'Bodies Drop' as Walmart Manager Kills 6 in Virginia Attack." Associated Press, Nov. 23, 2022. apnews.com/article/walmart-shooting -chesapeake-virginia-b52927596381aa65efed367ce0c81c83.

Briquelet, Kate. "Would-Be Killers, Click Here for Help." *Daily Beast,* Oct. 14, 2015. www.thedailybeast.com/would-be-killers-click-here-for-help.

Brown, M. E., P. A. Dustman, and J. J. Barthelemy. "Twitter Impact on a Community Trauma: An Examination of Who, What, and Why It Radiated." *Journal of Community Psychology* 49, no. 3 (April 2021): 838–53. doi.org/10.1002/jcop.22330.

Brown, R. A., R. Ramchand, and T. C. Helmus. "What Prevention and Treatment of Substance Dependence Can Tell Us About Addressing Violent Extremism." *Rand Health Quarterly* 9, no. 4 (Aug. 2022): 15.

Brüne, M., G. Juckel, and B. Enzi. "'An Eye for an Eye'? Neural Correlates of Retribution and Forgiveness." *PLoS ONE* 8, no. 8 (2013): e73519. doi.org/10.1371/journal .pone.0073519.

Bruni, Frank. *The Age of Grievance.* New York: Simon & Schuster, 2024.

Buckley, Chris. "Former White Supremacist: This Is How to Tackle Hate and Bigotry." Opinion, CNN, Nov. 12, 2020.

———. "Never Lose Faith in Hope and Healing. I Know Because My Wife Helped Me Leave a Life of Violent Extremism." Opinion, Fox News, Dec. 23, 2023. www .foxnews.com/opinion/never-lose-faith-hope-healing-i-know-because-my-wife-helped -me-leave-life-violent-extremism.

———. Testimony. In *Hearing on Helping Veterans Thrive: The Importance of Peer Support in Preventing Domestic Violent Extremism.* 117th U.S. House of Representatives, March 31, 2022.

Bush, George W. "Address to a Joint Session of Congress and the American People." News release, Sept. 20, 2001. georgewbush-whitehouse.archives.gov/news/releases/2001 /09/print/20010920-8.html.

———. "President Delivers 'State of the Union.'" News release, Jan. 28, 2003. georgewbush-whitehouse.archives.gov/news/releases/2003/01/20030128-19.html.

———. "President Discusses the Future of Iraq." News release, Feb. 26, 2003. georgewbush-whitehouse.archives.gov/news/releases/2003/02/20030226-11.html.

Bushman, B. J., R. F. Baumeister, and C. M. Phillips. "Do People Aggress to Improve Their Mood? Catharsis Beliefs, Affect Regulation Opportunity, and Aggressive Responding." *Journal of Personality and Social Psychology* 81, no. 1 (July 2001): 17–32.

Calhoun, Frederick S., and Stephen Weston. *Contemporary Threat Management: A Practical Guide for Identifying, Assessing, and Managing Individuals of Violent Intent.* Specialized Training Services, 2003.

Campoy, Ana, Peter Sanders, and Russell Gold. "Hash Browns, Then 4 Minutes of Chaos. Role of Texas Shooter's Muslim Faith Is Examined; Policewoman Hailed as Hero." *Wall Street Journal,* Nov. 9, 2009. www.wsj.com/articles /SB125750297355533413.

Carlsmith, K. M., T. D. Wilson, and D. T. Gilbert. "The Paradoxical Consequences of Revenge." *Journal of Personality and Social Psychology* 95, no. 6 (Dec. 2008): 1316–24. doi.org/10.1037/a0012165.

Center for Preventive Action. "Global Conflict Tracker." Council on Foreign Relations, 2024. Accessed July 22, 2024. www.cfr.org/global-conflict-tracker/.

Chang, Jung, and Jon Halliday. *Mao: The Unknown Story.* New York: Anchor, 2006. Kindle.

Chernyak, N., K. L. Leimgruber, Y. C. Dunham, J. Hu, and P. R. Blake. "Paying Back People Who Harmed Us but Not People Who Helped Us: Direct Negative Reciprocity Precedes Direct Positive Reciprocity in Early Development." *Psychological Science* 30, no. 9 (Sept. 2019): 1273–86. doi.org/10.1177/0956797619854975.

Chester, D. S., and C. N. DeWall. "Combating the Sting of Rejection with the Pleasure of Revenge: A New Look at How Emotion Shapes Aggression." *Journal of Personality and Social Psychology* 112, no. 3 (March 2017): 413–30. doi.org/10.1037/pspi0000080.

Chester, D. S., and C. N. DeWall. "The Pleasure of Revenge: Retaliatory Aggression Arises from a Neural Imbalance Toward Reward." *Social Cognitive and Affective Neuroscience* 11, no. 7 (July 2016): 1173–82. doi.org/10.1093/scan/nsv082.

Chester, D. S., C. N. DeWall, K. J. Derefinko, S. Estus, D. R. Lynam, J. R. Peters, and Y. Jiang. "Looking for Reward in All the Wrong Places: Dopamine Receptor Gene Polymorphisms Indirectly Affect Aggression Through Sensation-Seeking." *Social Neuroscience* 11, no. 5 (Oct. 2016): 487–94. doi.org/10.1080/17470919.2015.1119191.

Chester, D. S., C. N. DeWall, and B. Enjaian. "Sadism and Aggressive Behavior: Inflicting Pain to Feel Pleasure." *Personality and Social Psychology Bulletin* 45, no. 8 (Aug. 2019): 1252–68. doi.org/10.1177/0146167218816327.

Chester, D. S., D. R. Lynam, R. Milich, and C. N. DeWall. "Neural Mechanisms of the Rejection-Aggression Link." *Social Cognitive and Affective Neuroscience* 13, no. 5 (May 2018): 501–12. doi.org/10.1093/scan/nsy025.

Childress, A. R., R. N. Ehrman, Z. Wang, Y. Li, N. Sciortino, J. Hakun, W. Jens, et al. "Prelude to Passion: Limbic Activation by 'Unseen' Drug and Sexual Cues." *PLoS ONE* 3, no. 1 (Jan. 2008): e1506. doi.org/10.1371/journal.pone.0001506.

Cho, Seung-Hui. Manifesto. SchoolShooters.Info: Resources on School Shootings, Perpetrators, and Prevention. schoolshooters.info/sites/default/files/cho_manifesto_1.1 .pdf.

Cílek, Roman. *Oprátka za osm mrtvých* [Noose for eight dead]. Machine translated by Google. MarieTum, 2014.

City of Chesapeake (@AboutChesapeake). "As the investigation has progressed, detectives conducted a forensic analysis of the suspect's phone, which was located at the scene. This note was located in the device." Twitter, Nov. 25, 2022, 9:00 a.m., x.com /AboutChesapeake/status/1596141677508710403.

Clarkson, Brett. "Autopsy Report Details Scope of Injuries from Beating That Killed Rancho Student." *Las Vegas Review-Journal,* March 6, 2024. www.reviewjournal.com /crime/homicides/autopsy-report-details-scope-of-injuries-from-beating-that-killed -rancho-student-3012737/.

Copeland-Linder, N., S. B. Johnson, D. L. Haynie, S. E. Chung, and T. L. Cheng. "Retaliatory Attitudes and Violent Behaviors Among Assault-Injured Youth." *Journal of Adolescent Health* 50, no. 3 (March 2012): 215–20. doi.org/10.1016/j.jado-health.2011.04.005.

Cox, Kate, William Marcellino, Jacopo Bellasio, Antonia Ward, Katerina Galai, Sofia Meranto, and Giacomo Persi Paoli. *Social Media in Africa: A Double-Edged Sword for Security and Development.* RAND Corporation, Nov. 5, 2018.

Cramer, S. C., M. Sur, B. H. Dobkin, C. O'Brien, T. D. Sanger, J. Q. Trojanowski, J. M. Rumsey, et al. "Harnessing Neuroplasticity for Clinical Applications." *Brain* 134, no. 6 (June 2011): 1591–609. doi.org/10.1093/brain/awr039.

Crockett, M. J., A. Apergis-Schoute, B. Herrmann, M. D. Lieberman, U. Müller, T. W. Robbins, and L. Clark. "Serotonin Modulates Striatal Responses to Fairness and Retaliation in Humans." *Journal of Neuroscience* 33, no. 8 (Feb. 2013): 3505–13. doi. org/10.1523/jneurosci.2761-12.2013.

Crombag, Hans, Eric Rassin, and Robert Horselenberg. "On Vengeance." *Psychology, Crime, and Law* 9, no. 4 (2003): 333–44. doi.org/10.1080/1068316031000068647.

Daly, M., and M. Wilson. "Evolutionary Social Psychology and Family Homicide." *Science* 242, no. 4878 (Oct. 1988): 519–24. doi.org/10.1126/science.3175672.

Davies, Robert Williams, and Stephen G. Wheatcroft. "The Years of Hunger: Soviet Agriculture, 1931–1933." In *The Industrialisation of Soviet Russia.* Vol. 5. London: Palgrave Macmillan, 2009.

DeCamp, Whitney, and Brian Newby. "From Bullied to Deviant: The Victim–Offender Overlap Among Bullying Victims." *Youth Violence and Juvenile Justice* 13, no. 1 (2015): 3–17. doi.org/10.1177/1541204014521250.

Denham, Hannah. "'Lion King' Has Been Clouded by Intellectual Property Controversy for 25 Years. Here's the Story Behind It." *Seattle Times,* July 26, 2019. www .seattletimes.com/business/lion-king-has-been-clouded-by-intellectual-property -controversy-for-25-years-heres-the-story-behind-it/.

de Quervain, D. J., U. Fischbacher, V. Treyer, M. Schellhammer, U. Schnyder, A. Buck, and E. Fehr. "The Neural Basis of Altruistic Punishment." *Science* 305, no. 5688 (Aug. 2004): 1254–58. doi.org/10.1126/science.1100735.

de Waal, Frans B. M. "The Chimpanzee's Sense of Social Regularity and Its Relation to the Human Sense of Justice." *American Behavioral Scientist* 34, no. 3 (1991): 335–49. doi.org/10.1177/0002764291034003005.

Dikötter, Frank. *The Cultural Revolution: A People's History, 1962–1976.* New York: Bloomsbury, 2016.

Djilas, Milovan. *Conversations with Stalin.* New York: Harcourt, Brace & World, 1962.

D'Souza, Amanda, Ronald Weitzer, and Rod K. Brunson. "Federal Investigations of Police Misconduct: A Multi-city Comparison." *Crime, Law, and Social Change* 71 (2019): 461–82. doi.org/10.1007/s10611-018-9797-4.

Duff, Nancy J. "Plagues and Concern for the Neighbor." *Theology Today* 77, no. 4 (2021): 353–58. doi.org/10.1177/0040573620965665.

Eadeh, Fade R., Stephanie A. Peak, and Alan J. Lambert. "The Bittersweet Taste of Revenge: On the Negative and Positive Consequences of Retaliation." *Journal of Experimental Social Psychology* 68 (2017): 27–39. doi.org/10.1016/j.jesp.2016.04.007.

Eder, A. B., V. Mitschke, and M. Gollwitzer. "What Stops Revenge Taking? Effects of Observed Emotional Reactions on Revenge Seeking." *Aggressive Behavior* 46, no. 4 (July 2020): 305–16. doi.org/10.1002/ab.21890.

Ericksen, Karen Paige, and Heather Horton. "'Blood Feuds': Cross-Cultural Variations in Kin Group Vengeance." *Behavioral Science Research* 26, no. 1–4 (1992): 57–85. doi.org /10.1177/106939719202600103.

Evans, Alexadra T., and Heather J. Williams. *How Extremism Operates Online: A Primer.* RAND Corporation, 2022. www.rand.org/pubs/perspectives/PEA1458-2.html.

Febo, M., K. Blum, R. D. Badgaiyan, D. Baron, P. K. Thanos, L. M. Colon-Perez, Z. Demortrovics, and M. S. Gold. "Dopamine Homeostasis: Brain Functional Connectivity in Reward Deficiency Syndrome." *Frontiers in Bioscience-Landmark* 22, no. 4 (Jan. 2017): 669–91. doi.org/10.2741/4509.

Finley, Ben. "Witness: Walmart Shooter Seemed to Target Certain People." Associated Press, Nov. 24, 2022. apnews.com/article/business-shootings-virginia-holidays -51f60562dd259f73ce19c1b4d2f20ded.

Finley, Ben, and Matthew Barakat. "Walmart Shooter Left 'Death Note,' Bought Gun Day of Killing." Associated Press, Nov. 25, 2022. apnews.com/article/business -shootings-virginia-b36d3d89e8677cb2ae3d9a1702c3897d.

Flint, Joe, and Patience Haggin. "Apple and Disney Among Companies Stopping Ads on X." *Wall Street Journal,* Nov. 18, 2023. www.wsj.com/business/media/disney-lions -gate-pause-ads-on-x-after-musk-agrees-with-antisemitic-tweet-641c3ea4.

Flood, Charles Bracelen. "Lance Corporal Adolf Hitler on the Western Front, 1914– 1918." *Kentucky Review* 5, no. 3 (1985). uknowledge.uky.edu/kentucky-review/vol5 /iss3/2.

Fluck, Julia. "Why Do Students Bully? An Analysis of Motives Behind Violence in Schools." *Youth and Society* 49, no. 5 (2017): 567–87.

Foulkes, Lucy. "Sadism: Review of an Elusive Construct." *Personality and Individual Differences* 151 (2019): 109500. doi.org/10.1016/j.paid.2019.07.010.

Fourie, M. M., R. Hortensius, and J. Decety. "Parsing the Components of Forgiveness: Psychological and Neural Mechanisms." *Neuroscience and Biobehavioral Reviews* 112 (May 2020): 437–51. doi.org/10.1016/j.neubiorev.2020.02.020.

Fox, James Alan. "Mass Killing Database: Revealing Trends, Details, and Anguish of Every US Event Since 2006." *USA Today,* Aug. 18, 2022. www.usatoday.com/in-depth /graphics/2022/08/18/mass-killings-database-us-events-since-2006/9705311002/.

Freud, Sigmund. *Reflections on War and Death.* Translated by A. Brill and A. Kuttner. New York: Moffat, Yard, 1918.

Funk, F., V. McGeer, and M. Gollwitzer. "Get the Message: Punishment Is Satisfying if the Transgressor Responds to Its Communicative Intent." *Personality and Social Psychology Bulletin* 40, no. 8 (Aug. 2014): 986–97. doi.org/10.1177/0146167214533130.

Gandhi, Mahatma. *Young India, 1919–1922.* 2nd ed. New York: B. W. Huebsch, 1924.

Garbarino, James. *Listening to Killers: Lessons Learned from My Twenty Years as a Psychological Expert Witness in Murder Cases.* Oakland: University of California Press, 2015. Kindle.

Gerstenfeld, Phyllis B. *Hate Crimes: Causes, Controls, and Controversies.* 4th ed. Thousand Oaks, Calif.: Sage Publications, 2017.

Ghatak, Sambuddha, and Brandon C. Prins. "The Homegrown Threat: State Strength, Grievance, and Domestic Terrorism." *International Interactions* 43, no. 2 (2017): 217–47. doi.org/10.1080/03050629.2016.1128431.

Gilligan, James. *Violence: Our Deadly Epidemic and Its Causes.* New York: Putnam, 1996.

Girgis, R. R., R. T. Rogers, H. Hesson, J. A. Lieberman, P. S. Appelbaum, and G. Brucato. "Mass Murders Involving Firearms and Other Methods in School, College, and University Settings: Findings from the Columbia Mass Murder Database." *Journal of Forensic Sciences* 68, no. 1 (Jan. 2023): 207–11. doi.org/10.1111/1556-4029.15161.

Glatter, K. A., and P. Finkelman. "History of the Plague: An Ancient Pandemic for the Age of COVID-19." *American Journal of Medicine* 134, no. 2 (Feb. 2021): 176–81. doi.org/10.1016/j.amjmed.2020.08.019.

Global Commission on Drug Policy. *War on Drugs.* Report of the Global Commission on Drug Policy, June 2011. www.globalcommissionondrugs.org/reports/the-war-on-drugs.

Golden, S. A., C. Heins, M. Venniro, D. Caprioli, M. Zhang, D. H. Epstein, and Y. Shaham. "Compulsive Addiction-Like Aggressive Behavior in Mice." *Biological Psychiatry* 82, no. 4 (Aug. 2017): 239–48. doi.org/10.1016/j.biopsych.2017.03.004.

Golden, S. A., M. Jin, C. Heins, M. Venniro, M. Michaelides, and Y. Shaham. "Nucleus Accumbens Drd1-Expressing Neurons Control Aggression Self-Administration and Aggression Seeking in Mice." *Journal of Neuroscience* 39, no. 13 (March 2019): 2482–96. doi.org/10.1523/jneurosci.2409-18.2019.

Gollwitzer, Mario, and Markus Denzler. "What Makes Revenge Sweet: Seeing the Offender Suffer or Delivering a Message?" *Journal of Experimental Social Psychology* 45 (2009): 840–44. doi.org/10.1016/j.jesp.2009.03.001.

Gollwitzer, Mario, Milena Meder, and Manfred Schmitt. "What Gives Victims Satisfaction When They Seek Revenge?" *European Journal of Social Psychology* 41 (2011): 364–74. doi.org/10.1002/ejsp.782.

Gollwitzer, Mario, L. J. Skitka, D. Wisneski, A. Sjöström, P. Liberman, S. J. Nazir, and B. J. Bushman. "Vicarious Revenge and the Death of Osama bin Laden." *Personality and Social Psychology Bulletin* 40, no. 5 (May 2014): 604–16. doi.org/10.1177/0146167214521466.

Grant, J. E., M. N. Potenza, A. Weinstein, and D. A. Gorelick. "Introduction to Behavioral Addictions." *American Journal of Drug and Alcohol Abuse* 36, no. 5 (Sept. 2010): 233–41. doi.org/10.3109/00952990.2010.491884.

Graziosi, Andrea. "Political Famines in the USSR and China: A Comparative Analysis." *Journal of Cold War Studies* 19, no. 3 (2017): 42–103. muse.jhu.edu/article/668158.

Gregory, Paul R., Hsiao-ting Lin, and Lisa Nguyen. "Chiang Chooses His Enemies." *Hoover Digest,* April 20, 2010. www.hoover.org/research/chiang-chooses-his-enemies.

Grites, Karen. *Step Back or Get Back?* Charleston, S.C.: Palmetto Publishing, 2024.

Guerrero, Jean. "Guerrero: Why Elon Musk, the Bully, Is Seen by Many, Including Liberals, as a Hero." Opinion, *Los Angeles Times,* Dec. 4, 2023. www.latimes.com/opinion/story/2023-12-04/elon-musk-racism-x-bully-savior-culture.

Guess, A. M., N. Malhotra, J. Pan, P. Barberá, H. Allcott, T. Brown, A. Crespo-Tenorio, et al. "How Do Social Media Feed Algorithms Affect Attitudes and Behavior in an Election Campaign?" *Science* 381, no. 6656 (July 2023): 398–404. doi.org/10.1126/science.abp9364.

Hadlock, Charles, and Erin McClam. "Hasan Found Guilty of Premeditated Murder in 2009 Fort Hood Rampage." NBC News, Aug. 24, 2013. www.nbcnews.com/news/us-news/hasan-found-guilty-premeditated-murder-2009-fort-hood-rampage-flna8C10989186.

Hagey, Keach, and Jeff Horwitz. "Facebook Tried to Make Its Platform a Healthier Place. It Got Angrier Instead." *Wall Street Journal,* Sept. 15, 2021. www.wsj.com/articles/facebook-algorithm-change-zuckerberg-11631654215?mod=article_inline.

Hahn, R., D. Fuqua-Whitley, H. Wethington, J. Lowy, A. Crosby, M. Fullilove, R. Johnson, et al. "Effectiveness of Universal School-Based Programs to Prevent Violent and Aggressive Behavior: A Systematic Review." Supplement, *American Journal of Preventive Medicine* 33, no. 2 (Aug. 2007): S114–29. doi.org/10.1016/j.amepre.2007.04.012.

Halperin, Mark, and John Heilemann. *Double Down: Game Change 2012.* New York: Penguin, 2013.

Hamlin, J. K., K. Wynn, P. Bloom, and N. Mahajan. "How Infants and Toddlers React to Antisocial Others." *Proceedings of the National Academy of Sciences of the United States of America* 108, no. 50 (Dec. 2011): 19931–36. doi.org/10.1073/pnas.1110306108.

Heilig, M., J. MacKillop, D. Martinez, J. Rehm, L. Leggio, and L. J. M. J. Vanderschuren. "Addiction as a Brain Disease Revised: Why It Still Matters, and the Need for Consilience." *Neuropsychopharmacology* 46, no. 10 (Sept. 2021): 1715–23. doi.org/10.1038/s41386-020-00950-y.

Hendrix, Steve. "In the Army and the Klan, He Hated Muslims. Now One Was Coming to Chris Buckley's Home." *Washington Post,* June 5, 2018. www.washingtonpost.com/news/local/wp/2018/06/05/feature/in-the-army-and-the-klan-he-hated-muslims-now-one-was-coming-to-his-home/.

Hickey, Daniel, Matheus Schmitz, Daniel Fessler, Paul E. Smaldino, Goran Muric, and Keith Burghardt. "Auditing Elon Musk's Impact on Hate Speech and Bots." *Proceedings of the International AAAI Conference on Web and Social Media* 17, no. 1 (2023): 1133–37. doi.org/10.1609/icwsm.v17i1.22222.

Hinnershitz, Stephanie. "The Marshall Plan and Postwar Economic Recovery." National WWII Museum, March 30, 2022. www.nationalww2museum.org/war/articles/marshall-plan-and-postwar-economic-recovery.

Hitler, Adolf. *Adolf Hitler Collection of Speeches, 1922–1945.* Internet Archive, 1945. archive.org/details/AdolfHitlerCollectionOfSpeeches19221945.

———. *Mein Kampf.* Translated by Ralph Manheim. Boston: Houghton Mifflin, 1943.

———. "Speech of 18 September 1922." Translated by Norman H. Baynes. In *Hitler's Speeches,* 107–8. London: Oxford University Press, 1942.

Hofmann, S. G., A. Asnaani, I. J. J. Vonk, A. T. Sawyer, and A. Fang. "The Efficacy of Cognitive Behavioral Therapy: A Review of Meta-analyses." *Cognitive Therapy and Research* 36 (July 31, 2012): 427–440. doi 10.1007/s10608-012-9476-1.

Holder, Eric. Statement. U.S. House of Representatives. May 3, 2011. www.justice.gov/opa/speech/statement-attorney-general-eric-holder-house-judiciary-committee.

Horney, K. "The Value of Vindictiveness." *American Journal of Psychoanalysis* 8 (1948): 3–12. doi.org/10.1007/BF01871591.

Horwitz, Jeff. "The Facebook Whistleblower, Frances Haugen, Says She Wants to Fix the Company, Not Harm It." *Wall Street Journal,* Oct. 3, 2021. www.wsj.com/articles/facebook-whistleblower-frances-haugen-says-she-wants-to-fix-the-company-not-harm-it-11633304122.

Horwitz, Jeff, and Justin Scheck. "Facebook Increasingly Suppresses Political Movements It Deems Dangerous." *Wall Street Journal,* Oct. 22, 2021. www.wsj.com/articles/facebook-suppresses-political-movements-patriot-party-11634937358?mod=article_inline.

Hughes, Paul M., and Brandon Warmke. "Forgiveness." In *The Stanford Encyclopedia of Philosophy,* edited by Edward N. Zalta. Spring 2022 Edition. plato.stanford.edu/archives/spr2022/entries/forgiveness/.

Hunt, Richard M. "Myths, Guilt, and Shame in Pre-Nazi Germany." *Virginia Quarterly Review* 34, no. 3 (1958): 355–71. www.jstor.org/stable/26442614.

Ibssa, Lalee, and Libby Cathey. "Trump Will Stay in 2024 Presidential Race Even if Indicted, Tells CPAC Crowd: 'I Am Your Retribution.'" ABC News, March 4, 2023. abcnews.go.com/Politics/trump-stay-2024-presidential-race-indicted-tells-cpac/story?id=97628469.

Isaacson, Walter. *Elon Musk.* New York: Simon & Schuster, 2023.

Jackson, J. C., V. K. Choi, and M. J. Gelfand. "Revenge: A Multilevel Review and Synthesis." *Annual Review of Psychology* 70 (Jan. 2019): 319–45. doi.org/10.1146/annurev-psych-010418-103305.

Jacobs, B. A., and R. Wright. *Street Justice: Retaliation in the Criminal Underworld.* New York: Cambridge University Press, 2006.

Jalabadze, Natia. "The Resurgence of Blood Feud in the Georgian Lowlands." *Caucasus Analytical Digest* 42 (2012): 7–9.

Javed, Jeffrey A. *Righteous Revolutionaries: Morality, Mobilization, and Violence in the Making of the Chinese State.* Ann Arbor: University of Michigan Press, 2022.

Jensen, K., J. Call, and M. Tomasello. "Chimpanzees Are Vengeful but Not Spiteful." *Proceedings of the National Academy of Sciences of the United States of America* 104, no. 32 (Aug. 2007): 13046–50. doi.org/10.1073/pnas.0705555104.

Johannes, Laura, and Mark Maremont. "U.S. Army Is in Bind over Worries About Safety of Its Anthrax Vaccine." *Wall Street Journal,* Oct. 12, 2001. www.wsj.com/articles/SB1002833153667626000.

Johnson-Migalski, Leigh. "A Paradoxical Strategy for Suicidal Clients: A More Useful Form of Revenge." *Journal of Individual Psychology* 67, no. 1 (2001): 31–40.

Karnib, N., and M. J. van Staaden. "The Deep Roots of Addiction: A Comparative Perspective." *Brain, Behavior, and Evolution* 95, no. 5 (2020): 222–29. doi.org/10.1159/000514180.

Kelty, S. F., G. Hall, and A. O'Brien-Malone. "You Have to Hit Some People! Endorsing Violent Sentiments and the Experience of Grievance Escalation in Australia." *Psychiatry, Psychology, and Law* 19, no. 3 (2012): 299–313.

Kershaw, Ian. *Hitler: A Biography.* New York: W. W. Norton, 2008.

Keynes, John Maynard. *The Economic Consequences of the Peace.* London: Macmillan, 1919.

Kimmel, James, Jr. *Suing for Peace: A Guide for Resolving Life's Conflicts.* Charlottesville, Va.: Hampton Roads, 2005.

———. *The Trial of Fallen Angels.* New York: Penguin, 2012.

———. "Website for Would-Be Killers." *Newshour,* BBC, Oct. 14, 2015. www.bbc.co .uk/programmes/p0357mvt.

———. "What the Science of Addiction Tells Us About Trump." Opinion, *Politico,* Dec. 12, 2020. www.politico.com/news/magazine/2020/12/12/trump-grievance -addiction-444570.

Kimmel, James, Jr., and Michael Rowe. "A Behavioral Addiction Model of Revenge, Violence, and Gun Abuse." Supplement, *Journal of Law, Medicine, and Ethics* 48, no. 4 (Dec. 2020): 172–78. doi.org/10.1177/1073110520979419.

Klausen, M. K., M. Thomsen, G. Wortwein, and A. Fink-Jensen. "The Role of Glucagon-Like Peptide 1 (GLP-1) in Addictive Disorders." *British Journal of Pharmacology* 179, no. 4 (Feb. 2022): 625–41. doi.org/10.1111/bph.15677.

Klimecki, O. M., D. Sander, and P. Vuilleumier. "Distinct Brain Areas Involved in Anger Versus Punishment During Social Interactions." *Scientific Reports* 8, no. 1 (July 2018): 10556. doi.org/10.1038/s41598-018-28863-3.

Knoll, J. L., IV. "Mass Murder: Causes, Classification, and Prevention." *Psychiatric Clinics of North America* 35, no. 4 (Dec. 2012): 757–80. doi.org/10.1016/j.psc.2012.08.001.

———. "The 'Pseudocommando' Mass Murderer: Part I, The Psychology of Revenge and Obliteration." *Journal of the American Academy of Psychiatry and the Law* 38, no. 1 (2010): 87–94.

———. "The 'Pseudocommando' Mass Murderer: Part II, The Language of Revenge." *Journal of the American Academy of Psychiatry and the Law* 38, no. 2 (2010): 263–72.

Koob, G. F., and N. D. Volkow. "Neurobiology of Addiction: A Neurocircuitry Analysis." *Lancet Psychiatry* 3, no. 8 (Aug. 2016): 760–73. doi.org/10.1016/s2215 -0366(16)00104-8.

Kotyuk, E., A. Magi, A. Eisinger, O. Király, A. Vereczkei, C. Barta, M. D. Griffiths, et al. "Co-occurrences of Substance Use and Other Potentially Addictive Behaviors: Epidemiological Results from the Psychological and Genetic Factors of the Addictive Behaviors (PGA) Study." *Journal of Behavioral Addictions* 9, no. 2 (June 2020): 272–88. doi.org/10.1556/2006.2020.00033.

Kramer, Heinrich. *The Hammer of Witches: A Complete Translation of the "Malleus Maleficarum."* Translated by Christopher S. Mackay. Cambridge, U.K.: Cambridge University Press, 2009.

Kristof, Nicholas D. "A Tale of Red Guards and Cannibals." *New York Times,* Jan. 6, 1993. www.nytimes.com/1993/01/06/world/a-tale-of-red-guards-and-cannibals.html.

Kshtriya, Sowmya, Ani Kalayjian, Sarah R. Lowe, Daria Diakonova-Curtis, and Loren Toussaint. "Exploring the Association Between Forgiveness, Meaning-Making, and Post-traumatic Stress Symptoms: The Case of Hurricane Maria in Puerto Rico." *International Journal of Education Research* 115 (2022). doi.org/10.1016/j.ijer.2022.102020.

Kuklick, Bruce. "The Division of Germany and American Policy on Reparations." *Western Political Quarterly* 23, no. 2 (1970): 276–93. www.jstor.org/stable/447072.

Lambert, Alan J., Stephanie A. Peak, Fade R. Eadeh, and John Paul Schott. "How Do You Feel Now? On the Perceptual Distortion of Extremely Recent Changes in Anger." *Journal of Experimental Social Psychology* 52 (2014): 82–95. doi.org/10.1016/j.jesp.2014.01.004.

Lanchin, Mike. "Trotsky's Grandson Recalls Ice Pick Killing." BBC News, Aug. 28, 2012. www.bbc.com/news/magazine-19356256.

Langhinrichsen-Rohling, Jennifer, Adrianne McCullars, and Tiffany A. Misra. "Motivations for Men and Women's Intimate Partner Violence Perpetration: A Comprehensive Review." *Partner Abuse* 3 (Nov. 2012): 429–68. doi.org/10.1891/1946-6560.3.4.429.

Langley, Marty, and Josh Sugarmann. *Lost Youth: A County-by-County Analysis of 2013 California Homicide Victims Ages 10 to 24.* Violence Policy Center, Nov. 2015. www.vpc.org/studies/cayouth2015.pdf.

Lankford, Adam, and James Silver. "Why Have Public Mass Shootings Become More Deadly? Assessing How Perpetrators' Motives and Methods Have Changed over Time." *Criminology and Public Policy* 19 (2020): 37–60. doi.org/10.1111/1745-9133.12472.

Larner, Christina. *Enemies of God: The Witch-Hunt in Scotland.* London: Chatto & Windus, 1981.

Lee, Bandy X. *The Dangerous Case of Donald Trump: 37 Psychiatrists and Mental Health Experts Assess a President.* New York: Thomas Dunne Books, 2019.

———. *Violence: An Interdisciplinary Approach to Causes, Consequences, and Cures.* Hoboken, N.J.: John Wiley & Sons, 2019.

Leggio, L., C. S. Hendershot, M. Farokhnia, A. Fink-Jensen, M. K. Klausen, J. P. Schacht, and W. K. Simmons. "GLP-1 Receptor Agonists Are Promising but Unproven Treatments for Alcohol and Substance Use Disorders." *Nature Medicine* 29, no. 12 (Dec. 2023): 2993–95. doi.org/10.1038/s41591-023-02634-8.

Lembke, Anna. *Dopamine Nation: Finding Balance in the Age of Indulgence.* New York: Dutton, 2021.

Leshner, A. I. "Addiction Is a Brain Disease, and It Matters." *Science* 278, no. 5335 (Oct. 1997): 45–47. doi.org/10.1126/science.278.5335.45.

Lewis, Marc. *The Biology of Desire: Why Addiction Is Not a Disease.* New York: PublicAffairs, 2016.

Loney, Alexander C. *The Ethics of Revenge and the Meanings of the "Odyssey."* New York: Oxford University Press, 2019.

Lundahl, Brad W., C. Kunz., C. Brownell, D. Tollefson, and B. L. Burke. "A Meta-Analysis of Motivational Interviewing: Twenty-Five Years of Empirical Studies." *Research on Social Practice* 20(2) (2010): 137-160. doi: 10.1177/1049731509347850.

Magdaleno, Johnny. "Welcome to the Youth Murder Capital of California." *Vice,* July 27, 2016. www.vice.com/en/article/qv55pp/salinas-the-youth-murder-capital-of -california.

Mahoney, J. J., M. W. Haut, J. Carpenter, M. Ranjan, D. G. Y. Thompson-Lake, J. L. Marton, W. Zheng, et al. "Low-Intensity Focused Ultrasound Targeting the Nucleus Accumbens as a Potential Treatment for Substance Use Disorder: Safety and Feasibility Clinical Trial." *Frontiers in Psychiatry* 14 (2023): 1211566. doi.org/10.3389/fpsyt.2023 .1211566.

Mao Tse-tung. "On the Correct Handling of Contradictions Among the People." In *Selected Works of Mao Tse-tung,* Vol. V, 384–421. Peking: Foreign Languages Press, 1977.

———. "Report on an Investigation of the Peasant Movement in Hunan." In *Selected Works of Mao Tse-tung,* Vol. 1, 23–59. Peking: Foreign Languages Press, 1967.

Maresville, Emilie de Sainte, Matthew Cullinan, Cho Park, and Ivan Pereira. "How an Undercover Grand Knighthawk Foiled a Murder Plot Concocted by KKK Law Enforcement Members." ABC News, April 27, 2023. abcnews.go.com/US/undercover -grand-knighthawk-foiled-murder-plot-concocted-kkk/story?id=97909060.

"Markets: Meta Platforms Inc." *Wall Street Journal.* www.wsj.com/market-data/quotes /META/financials/annual/income-statement.

Matejkowski, J. C., S. W. Cullen, and P. L. Solomon. "Characteristics of Persons with Severe Mental Illness Who Have Been Incarcerated for Murder." *Journal of the American Academy of Psychiatry and the Law* 36, no. 1 (2008): 74–86.

McAuliffe, C., E. Arensman, H. S. Keeley, P. Corcoran, and A. P. Fitzgerald. "Motives and Suicide Intent Underlying Hospital Treated Deliberate Self-Harm and Their Association with Repetition." *Suicide and Life-Threatening Behavior* 37, no. 4 (Aug. 2007): 397–408. doi.org/10.1521/suli.2007.37.4.397.

McCullough, Michael E. *Beyond Revenge: The Evolution of the Forgiveness Instinct.* San Francisco: Jossey-Bass, 2008.

McCullough, Michael E., C. Garth Bellah, Shelley D. Kilpatrick, and Judith L. Johnson. "Vengefulness: Relationships with Forgiveness, Rumination, Well-Being, and the Big Five." *Personality and Social Psychology Bulletin* 27, no. 5 (2001): 601–10. doi.org/10 .1177/0146167201275008.

McCullough, Michael E., R. Kurzban, and B. A. Tabak. "Cognitive Systems for Revenge and Forgiveness." *Behavioral and Brain Sciences* 36, no. 1 (Feb. 2013): 1–15. doi .org/10.1017/s0140525x11002160.

McIntyre, Douglas A. "This Is the Most Profitable Kids Movie of All Time." *24/7 Wall St.,* April 7, 2022. 247wallst.com/media/2022/04/07/bambi-is-the-most-profitable-kids -movie-of-all-time/.

McLellan, A. T., D. C. Lewis, C. P. O'Brien, and H. D. Kleber. "Drug Dependence, a Chronic Medical Illness: Implications for Treatment, Insurance, and Outcomes Evaluation." *JAMA* 284, no. 13 (Oct. 2000): 1689–95. doi.org/10.1001/jama.284.13.1689.

McNeal, Robert H. *Stalin: Man and Ruler.* New York: Macmillan, 1988.

Meindl, J. N., and J. W. Ivy. "Mass Shootings: The Role of the Media in Promoting Generalized Imitation." *American Journal of Public Health* 107, no. 3 (March 2017): 368–70. doi.org/10.2105/ajph.2016.303611.

Montefiore, Simon Sebag. *Stalin: The Court of the Red Tsar.* New York: Knopf, 2004.

———. *Young Stalin.* New York: Vintage, 2009. Kindle.

Morrow, Allison. "With Antisemitic Tweet, Elon Musk Reveals His 'Actual Truth.'" CNN, Nov. 17, 2023. www.cnn.com/2023/11/17/business/elon-musk-reveals-his-actual -truth/index.html.

Murdoch, Dan, dir. *KKK: The Fight for White Supremacy.* BBC, 2015. www.bbc.co.uk /programmes/b06fq188.

Nagorski, Andrew. *The Greatest Battle: The Battle for Moscow, 1941–42.* New York: Simon & Schuster, 2007.

Nash Information Services. "All Time Worldwide Box Office for Walt Disney Movies." The Numbers, April 21, 2024. www.the-numbers.com/box-office-records/worldwide/all -movies/theatrical-distributors/walt-disney.

———. "Box Office History for Bambi Movies." The Numbers, April 21, 2024. m.the -numbers.com/movies/franchise/Bambi.

Nassauer, Sarah. "Walmart Investigated in Early 2020 Complaints About Chesapeake Shooter from Co-workers." *Wall Street Journal,* Dec. 9, 2022. www.wsj.com/articles /walmart-investigated-in-early-2020-complaints-about-chesapeake-shooter-from-co -workers-11670611325.

National Center for Health Statistics. "Assault or Homicide." Centers for Disease Control and Prevention, Dec. 29, 2023. www.cdc.gov/nchs/fastats/homicide.htm.

National Center for Injury Prevention and Control. "National Violent Death Reporting System." Centers for Disease Control and Prevention. www.cdc.gov/injury/wisqars /nvdrs.html.

National Threat Assessment Center. "Protecting America's Schools: A U.S. Secret Service Analysis of Targeted School Violence." U.S. Secret Service, Department of Homeland Security, 2019. www.secretservice.gov/sites/default/files/2020-04/Protecting _Americas_Schools.pdf.

National WWII Museum. "Research Starters: Worldwide Deaths in World War 2." National WWII Museum. www.nationalww2museum.org/students-teachers/student -resources/research-starters/research-starters-worldwide-deaths-world-war.

Nicholson, Joanne, Sean Keeling, and Marigold Black. *Countering Violent Extremism Online: Understanding Adversity and Adaptation in an Increasingly Complex Digital Environment.* RAND Corporation, June 28, 2023. www.rand.org/pubs/research_reports /RRA2773-1.html.

Noar, S. M., M. Chabot, and R. S. Zimmerman. "Applying Health Behavior Theory to Multiple Behavior Change: Considerations and Approaches." *Preventive Medicine* 46, no. 3 (March 2008): 275–80. doi.org/10.1016/j.ypmed.2007.08.001.

Obama, Barack. "President Obama on Death of Osama bin Laden." News release, May 1, 2011. obamawhitehouse.archives.gov/photos-and-video/video/2011/05/01/president -obama-death-osama-bin-laden#transcript.

Office of the Surgeon General. *Social Media and Youth Mental Health: The U.S. Surgeon General's Advisory.* U.S. Department of Health and Human Services, 2023.

O'Sullivan, Donie, Tara Subramaniam, and Clare Duffy. "Not Stopping 'Stop the Steal': Facebook Papers Paint Damning Picture of Company's Role in Insurrection." CNN,

Oct. 24, 2021. www.cnn.com/2021/10/22/business/january-6-insurrection-facebook-papers/index.html.

Ott, Brian L., and Carrisa S. Hoelscher. "The Digital Authoritarian: On the Evolution and Spread of Toxic Leadership." *World* 4 (2023): 726–44. doi.org/10.3390/world4040046.

Papachristos, Andrew V., David M. Hureau, and Anthony A. Braga. "The Corner and the Crew: The Influence of Geography and Social Networks on Gang Violence." *American Sociological Review* 78, no. 3 (2013): 417–47. doi.org/10.1177/0003122413486800.

Pathé, Michele, Debbie J. Haworth, Terri-ann Goodwin, Amanda G. Holman, Stephen J. Amos, Paul Winterbourne, and Leanne Day. "Establishing a Joint Agency Response to the Threat of Lone Actor Grievance-Fueled Violence." *Journal of Forensic Psychiatry and Psychology* 29, no. 1 (2017): 37–52. doi.org/10.1080/14789949.2017.1335762.

Pennsylvania Psychological Association. *Resolution on Violence Motivation Research and Prevention.* Sept. 6, 2017.

Peterson, Jillian, and James Densley. "Key Findings." Violence Prevention Project, April 21, 2024. www.theviolenceproject.org/key-findings/.

Petry, N. M., K. Zajac, and M. K. Ginley. "Behavioral Addictions as Mental Disorders: To Be or Not to Be?" *Annual Review of Clinical Psychology* 14 (May 2018): 399–423. doi.org/10.1146/annurev-clinpsy-032816-045120.

Phillips, Aleks. "Full List of Capitol Rioters Jailed So Far and the Sentences They Are Serving." *Newsweek,* Sept. 12, 2023. www.newsweek.com/full-list-capitol-rioters-jailed-sentences-january-6-1826075.

Pickard, Hanna. "Is Addiction a Brain Disease? A Plea for Agnosticism and Heterogeneity." *Psychopharmacology* 239, no. 4 (April 2022): 993–1007. doi.org/10.1007/s00213-021-06013-4.

Pines, Yuri. "Legalism in Chinese Philosophy." In *The Stanford Encyclopedia of Philosophy,* edited by Edward N. Zalta and Uri Nodelman. Summer 2023 Edition. plato.stanford.edu/archives/sum2023/entries/chinese-legalism/.

Pinker, Steven. *The Better Angels of Our Nature: Why Violence Has Declined.* New York: Penguin, 2011. Kindle.

Prins, H., G. Tennent, and K. Trick. "Motives for Arson (Fire Raising)." *Medicine, Science, and the Law* 25, no. 4 (Oct. 1985): 275–78. doi.org/10.1177/002580248502500409.

Ramírez, J. Martin, Marie-Claude Bonniot-Cabanac, and Michel Cabanac. "Can Aggression Provide Pleasure?" *European Psychologist* 10, no. 2 (2005): 136–45. doi.org/10.1027/1016-9040.10.2.136.

Reich, Robert. "Bullying Adversaries. Demeaning Critics. Craving Attention. Who Does Musk Remind You Of?" Opinion, *Newsweek,* Dec. 29, 2022. www.newsweek.com/bullying-adversaries-demeaning-critics-craving-attention-who-does-musk-remind-you-opinion-1770186.

Remme, Tilman. "The Battle for Berlin in World War Two." BBC, March 10, 2011. www.bbc.co.uk/history/worldwars/wwtwo/berlin_01.shtml.

Reynolds, Julia. *Blood in the Fields: Ten Years Inside California's Nuestra Familia Gang.* Chicago: Chicago Review Press, 2014.

Ricciardi, E., G. Rota, L. Sani, C. Gentili, A. Gaglianese, M. Guazzelli, and P. Pietrini. "How the Brain Heals Emotional Wounds: The Functional Neuroanatomy of Forgiveness." *Frontiers in Human Neuroscience* 7 (2013): 839. doi.org/10.3389/fnhum.2013.00839.

Rosen, I. C. "Revenge—the Hate That Dare Not Speak Its Name: A Psychoanalytic Perspective." *Journal of the American Psychoanalytic Association* 55, no. 2 (Spring 2007): 595–620. doi.org/10.1177/00030651070550021501.

Rowe, M., J. Kimmel Jr., A. J. Pavlo, K. D. Antunes, C. D. Bellamy, M. J. O'Connell, L. Ocasio, et al. "A Pilot Study of Motive Control to Reduce Vengeance Cravings." *Journal of the American Academy of Psychiatry and the Law* 46, no. 4 (Dec. 2018): 486–97. doi:10.29158/JAAPL.003792-18.

Rubin, Olivia, Alexander Malin, and Will Steakin. "By the Numbers: How the Jan. 6 Investigation Is Shaping Up 1 Year Later." ABC News, Jan. 4, 2022. abcnews.go.com/US/numbers-jan-investigation-shaping-year/story?id=82057743.

Runions, K. C. "Toward a Conceptual Model of Motive and Self-Control in Cyber-aggression: Rage, Revenge, Reward, and Recreation." *Journal of Youth and Adolescence* 42, no. 5 (May 2013): 751–71. doi.org/10.1007/s10964-013-9936-2.

Sala, Nohemi, Ana Pantoja-Pérez, Juan Luis Arsuaga, Adrián Pablos, and Ignacio Martínez. "The Sima de los Huesos Crania: Analysis of the Cranial Breakage Patterns." *Journal of Archaeological Science* 72 (2016): 25–43. doi.org/10.1016/j.jas.2016.06.001.

Sanfey, A. G., J. K. Rilling, J. A. Aronson, L. E. Nystrom, and J. D. Cohen. "The Neural Basis of Economic Decision-Making in the Ultimatum Game." *Science* 300, no. 5626 (June 2003): 1755–58. doi.org/10.1126/science.1082976.

Sataline, S. "Gunman Kills 2 in Crowded Restaurant." *Hartford Courant,* May 26, 1993. www.courant.com/1993/05/26/gunman-kills-2-in-crowded-restaurant.

Schmid, Alex P. *The Routledge Handbook of Terrorism Research.* New York: Routledge, 2011.

Schumaker, Erin. "Is It Possible to Cure the Desire for Revenge?" *GEN,* Medium, Sept. 19, 2019. gen.medium.com/is-it-possible-to-cure-the-desire-for-revenge-d1697b58de2f.

Schumann, Karina, and Michael Ross. "The Benefits, Costs, and Paradox of Revenge." *Social and Personality Psychology Compass* 4, no. 12 (2010): 1193–205. doi.org/10.1111/j.1751-9004.2010.00322.x.

Schuttenberg, E. M., J. T. Sneider, D. H. Rosmarin, J. E. Cohen-Gilbert, E. N. Oot, A. M. Seraikas, E. R. Stein, et al. "Forgiveness Mediates the Relationship Between Middle Frontal Gyrus Volume and Clinical Symptoms in Adolescents." *Frontiers in Human Neuroscience* 16 (2022): 782893. doi.org/10.3389/fnhum.2022.782893.

Schwartz, H. I. "The Mind of the Mass School Shooter." *Journal of the American Academy of Psychiatry and the Law* 51, no. 3 (Sept. 2023): 314–19. doi.org/10.29158/jaapl.230041-23.

Shipler, D. K. "Anatomies of a Murderer." *New York Times,* Nov. 18, 1990, sec. 7, p. 3. www.nytimes.com/1990/11/18/books/anatomies-of-a-murderer.html.

Shrier, William L. *The Rise and Fall of the Third Reich.* New York: Simon & Schuster, 1960.

Silver, James, Andre Simons, and Sarah Craun. "A Study of the Pre-attack Behaviors of Active Shooters in the United States Between 2000 and 2013." Federal Bureau of Investigation, U.S. Department of Justice, June 2018. www.fbi.gov/file-repository/pre -attack-behaviors-of-active-shooters-in-us-2000-2013.pdf/view.

Silverman, Craig, Craig Timberg, Jeff Kao, and Jeremy B. Merrill. "Facebook Hosted Surge of Misinformation and Insurrection Threats in Months Leading Up to Jan. 6 Attack, Records Show." ProPublica, Jan. 4, 2022. www.propublica.org/article/facebook -hosted-surge-of-misinformation-and-insurrection-threats-in-months-leading-up-to -jan-6-attack-records-show.

Šimić, G., M. Tkalčić, V. Vukić, D. Mulc, E. Španić, M. Šagud, F. E. Olucha-Bordonau, et al. "Understanding Emotions: Origins and Roles of the Amygdala." *Biomolecules* 11, no. 6 (May 2021). doi.org/10.3390/biom11060823.

Simms, Brendan. "Against a 'World of Enemies': The Impact of the First World War on the Development of Hitler's Ideology." *International Affairs* 90, no. 2 (2014): 317–36. doi.org/10.1111/1468-2346.12111.

Singer, T., B. Seymour, J. P. O'Doherty, K. E. Stephan, R. J. Dolan, and C. D. Frith. "Empathic Neural Responses Are Modulated by the Perceived Fairness of Others." *Nature* 439, no. 7075 (Jan. 2006): 466–69. doi.org/10.1038/nature04271.

Sjöström, Arne, Zoe Magraw-Mickelson, and Mario Gollwitzer. "What Makes Displaced Revenge Taste Sweet: Retributing Displaced Responsibility or Sending a Message to the Original Perpetrator?" *European Journal of Social Psychology* 48, no. 4 (2018): 490–506. doi.org/10.1002/ejsp.2345.

Skeem, J. L., C. Schubert, C. Odgers, E. P. Mulvey, W. Gardner, and C. Lidz. "Psychiatric Symptoms and Community Violence Among High-Risk Patients: A Test of the Relationship at the Weekly Level." *Journal of Consulting and Clinical Psychology* 74, no. 5 (2006): 967–79. doi.org/10.1037/0022-006x.74.5.967.

Smith, D. E. "The Evolution of Addiction Medicine as a Medical Specialty." *Virtual Mentor* 13, no. 12 (2011): 900–905. doi.org/10.1001/virtualmentor.2011.13.12.mhst1 -1112.

Sood, Aradhana Bela. "Getting into the Mind of the Killer: A Psychological Autopsy of Seung-Hui Cho." In *The Virginia Tech Massacre: Strategies and Challenges for Improving Mental Health Policy on Campus and Beyond,* edited by Aradhana Bela Sood and Robert Cohen. Oxford: Oxford University Press, 2014.

Spence, Jonathan. *Mao Zedong: A Life.* New York: Penguin, 2006. Kindle.

Stead, M., K. Angus, T. Langley, S. V. Katikireddi, K. Hinds, S. Hilton, S. Lewis, et al. "Mass Media to Communicate Public Health Messages in Six Health Topic Areas: A Systematic Review and Other Reviews of the Evidence." *Public Health Research* 7, no. 8 (2019). doi.org/10.3310/phr07080.

Steadman, H. J., E. P. Mulvey, J. Monahan, P. C. Robbins, P. S. Appelbaum, T. Grisso, L. H. Roth, and E. Silver. "Violence by People Discharged from Acute Psychiatric Inpatient Facilities and by Others in the Same Neighborhoods." *Archives of General Psychiatry* 55, no. 5 (May 1998): 393–401. doi.org/10.1001/archpsyc.55.5.393.

Stern, Jessica E., Megan K. McBride, Jessa L. Mellea, and Elena Savoia. "Practices and Needs in Reintegration Programs for Violent Extremist Offenders in the United States:

The Extremist Perspective." *Studies in Conflict and Terrorism* (2023). doi.org/10.1080 /1057610X.2023.2204668.

Stewart, Samantha, Thomas Buckley, and Bloomberg. "Elon Musk Is So Irate at Disney for Pulling Ads from X That He Says CEO Bob Iger 'Should Be Fired Immediately.'" *Fortune,* Dec. 7, 2023. fortune.com/2023/12/07/elon-musk-x-bob-iger-fight-disney -pulls-ads/.

Strobel, A., J. Zimmermann, A. Schmitz, M. Reuter, S. Lis, S. Windmann, and P. Kirsch. "Beyond Revenge: Neural and Genetic Bases of Altruistic Punishment." *Neuro-image* 54, no. 1 (Jan. 2011): 671–80. doi.org/10.1016/j.neuroimage.2010.07.051.

Sussman, S., and A. N. Sussman. "Considering the Definition of Addiction." *International Journal of Environmental Research and Public Health* 8, no. 10 (Oct. 2011): 4025– 38. doi.org/10.3390/ijerph8104025.

Sutherland, Paige, and Meghna Chakrabarti. "The U.S. Military Promised to Counter Extremism. Has the Pentagon Made Progress?" *On Point,* NPR, May 19, 2023. www .wbur.org/onpoint/2023/05/19/pentagon-extremism-military-security.

Tabibnia, G., A. B. Satpute, and M. D. Lieberman. "The Sunny Side of Fairness: Prefer-ence for Fairness Activates Reward Circuitry (and Disregarding Unfairness Activates Self-Control Circuitry)." *Psychological Science* 19, no. 4 (April 2008): 339–47. doi.org/10 .1111/j.1467-9280.2008.02091.x.

Takahashi, H., M. Kato, M. Matsuura, D. Mobbs, T. Suhara, and Y. Okubo. "When Your Gain Is My Pain and Your Pain Is My Gain: Neural Correlates of Envy and Schaden-freude." *Science* 323, no. 5916 (Feb. 2009): 937–39. doi.org/10.1126/science.1165604.

Taniguchi, N., N. Hironaga, T. Mitsudo, S. Tamura, K. Yamaura, and S. Tobimatsu. "Late Responses in the Anterior Insula Reflect the Cognitive Component of Pain: Evi-dence of Nonpain Processing." *Pain Reports* 7, no. 2 (March–April 2022): e984. doi.org /10.1097/pr9.0000000000000984.

ten Boom, Annemarie, and Karlijn F. Kuijpers. "Victims' Needs as Basic Human Needs." *International Review of Victimology* 18, no. 2 (2012). doi.org/10.1177 /0269758011432060.

Threadgill, A. H., and P. A. Gable. "Revenge Is Sweet: Investigation of the Effects of Approach-Motivated Anger on the RewP in the Motivated Anger Delay (MAD) Para-digm." *Human Brain Mapping* 41, no. 17 (Dec. 2020): 5032–56. doi.org/10.1002/hbm .25177.

Toussaint, L., A. J. Gall, A. Cheadle, and D. R. Williams. "Let It Rest: Sleep and Health as Positive Correlates of Forgiveness of Others and Self-Forgiveness." *Psychology and Health* 35, no. 3 (March 2020): 302–17. doi.org/10.1080/08870446.2019.1644335.

Toussaint, L., J. A. Lee, M. H. Hyun, G. S. Shields, and G. M. Slavich. "Forgiveness, Rumination, and Depression in the United States and Korea: A Cross-Cultural Media-tion Study." *Journal of Clinical Psychology* 79, no. 1 (Jan. 2023): 143–57. doi.org/10.1002 /jclp.23376.

Toussaint, L., G. S. Shields, G. Dorn, and G. M. Slavich. "Effects of Lifetime Stress Exposure on Mental and Physical Health in Young Adulthood: How Stress Degrades and Forgiveness Protects Health." *Journal of Health Psychology* 21, no. 6 (June 2016): 1004–14. doi.org/10.1177/1359105314544132.

Toussaint, L., G. S. Shields, E. Green, K. Kennedy, S. Travers, and G. M. Slavich. "Hostility, Forgiveness, and Cognitive Impairment over 10 Years in a National Sample of American Adults." *Health Psychology* 37, no. 12 (Dec. 2018): 1102–6. doi.org/10.1037/hea0000686.

Toussaint, L., S. B. Skalski-Bednarz, J. P. Lanoix, K. Konaszewski, and J. Surzykiewicz. "The Relationship Between Forgiveness and Health Outcomes Among People Living with HIV: A Cross-Sectional Study in France." *AIDS and Behavior* 27, no. 10 (Oct. 2023): 3332–41. doi.org/10.1007/s10461-023-04052-w.

Toussaint, L., and E. L. Worthington Jr. "Forgiveness and Mental Health." In *Encyclopedia of Mental Health*, edited by H. S. Friedman and C. H. Markey, 53–58. Amsterdam: Academic Press, 2023.

Tremblay, R. E. "Early Development of Physical Aggression and Early Risk Factors for Chronic Physical Aggression in Humans." In *Neuroscience of Aggression*, edited by Klaus A. Miczek and Andreas Meyer-Lindenberg, 315–27. Heidelberg: Springer, 2014. doi.org/10.1007/7854_2013_262.

Truman, Harry S. "August 9, 1945: Radio Report to the American People on the Potsdam Conference." University of Virginia, Miller Center. millercenter.org/the-presidency/presidential-speeches/august-9-1945-radio-report-american-people-potsdam-conference.

Ttofi, Maria M., David P. Farrington, and Friedrich Lösel. "School Bullying as a Predictor of Violence Later in Life: A Systematic Review and Meta-analysis of Prospective Longitudinal Studies." *Aggression and Violent Behavior* 17, no. 5 (2012): 405–18. doi.org/10.1016/j.avb.2012.05.002.

Tucker, Robert C. *Stalin in Power: The Revolution from Above, 1928–1941.* New York: W. W. Norton, 1992.

Uildriks, Niels, and Piet van Reenen. "Human Rights Violations by the Police." *Human Rights Review* 2, no. 2 (2001): 64–92.

United Nations Office on Drugs and Crime. *Global Study on Homicide 2023.* United Nations, 2023. www.unodc.org/documents/data-and-analysis/gsh/2023/Global_study_on_homicide_2023_web.pdf.

———. *World Drug Report 2023.* United Nations, 2023. www.unodc.org/res/WDR-2023/WDR23_Exsum_fin_SP.pdf.

USA Today. "Chilling Images from the Capitol Riot: Jan. 6 Insurrection in Photos." Jan. 3, 2022. www.usatoday.com/picture-gallery/news/politics/2022/01/03/jan-6-insurrection-photos-capitol-riot/9052798002/.

U.S. Department of Justice, Office of Justice Programs. "U.S. Correctional Population Continued to Decline in 2021." News release, Feb. 23, 2023. bjs.ojp.gov/sites/g/files/xyckuh236/files/media/document/cpus21st%20and%20ppus21_prB.pdf.

Useinova, K. R., and A. T. Bazarbaeva. "On the Question of the Relationship Between the Institutions of 'Blood Feud' and 'Talion.'" *Journal of Actual Problems of Jurisprudence* 89, no. 1 (2019): 14–20.

van der Kolk, Bessel. *The Body Keeps the Score: Brain, Mind, and Body in the Healing of Trauma.* New York: Penguin, 2015.

———. "How Trauma Lodges in the Body, Revisited." By Krista Tippett. *On Being*, July 11, 2013. onbeing.org/programs/bessel-van-der-kolk-how-trauma-lodges-in-the-body-revisited/.

Varjas, K., J. Talley, J. Meyers, L. Parris, and H. Cutts. "High School Students' Perceptions of Motivations for Cyberbullying: An Exploratory Study." *Western Journal of Emergency Medicine* 11, no. 3 (Aug. 2010): 269–73.

Venosa, Ali. "Mass Shootings on the Rise: James Kimmel Jr. Says Internet-Based, Preventive Approach Can Help." *Medical Daily*, Oct. 14, 2015. www.medicaldaily.com/mass-shootings-rise-james-kimmel-jr-says-internet-based-preventive-approach-can-help-357226.

Virginia Tech Review Panel. *Mass Shootings at Virginia Tech, April 16, 2007: Report of the Virginia Tech Review Panel Presented to Timothy M. Kaine, Governor, Commonwealth of Virginia*. Aug. 2007. scholar.lib.vt.edu/prevail/docs/VTReviewPanelReport.pdf.

Volkow, Nora D. "What Does It Mean When We Call Addiction a Brain Disorder?" *Scientific American*, March 23, 2018. www.scientificamerican.com/blog/observations/what-does-it-mean-when-we-call-addiction-a-brain-disorder/.

Volkow, Nora D., G. F. Koob, and A. T. McLellan. "Neurobiologic Advances from the Brain Disease Model of Addiction." *New England Journal of Medicine* 374, no. 4 (Jan. 2016): 363–71. doi.org/10.1056/NEJMra1511480.

Volkow, Nora D., G. J. Wang, F. Telang, J. S. Fowler, J. Logan, A. R. Childress, M. Jayne, et al. "Cocaine Cues and Dopamine in Dorsal Striatum: Mechanism of Craving in Cocaine Addiction." *Journal of Neuroscience* 26, no. 24 (June 2006): 6583–88. doi.org/10.1523/jneurosci.1544-06.2006.

Volsky, Igor, and Victoria Fleisher. "This Effort to Prevent Mass Shootings Is So Obvious. So Why Aren't We Pursuing It?" Think Progress, Oct. 29, 2015. archive.thinkprogress.org/this-effort-to-prevent-mass-shootings-is-so-obvious-so-why-arent-we-pursuing-it-faf01c89f2a1/.

Wakefield, Jerome C. "Addiction and the Concept of Disorder, Part 1: Why Addiction Is a Medical Disorder." *Neuroethics* 10 (2017): 39–53. doi.org/10.1007/s12152-016-9300-9.

Wakefield, M. A., B. Loken, and R. C. Hornik. "Use of Mass Media Campaigns to Change Health Behaviour." *Lancet* 376, no. 9748 (Oct. 2010): 1261–71. doi.org/10.1016/s0140-6736(10)60809-4.

Walsh, Nick Paton. "The Valley of Death." *Guardian*, July 30, 2002. www.theguardian.com/g2/story/0,,765316,00.html.

Watson Institute for International and Public Affairs. "Costs of War: Human and Budgetary Costs to Date of the U.S. War in Afghanistan, 2001–2022." Brown University, May 15, 2024. watson.brown.edu/costsofwar/figures/2021/human-and-budgetary-costs-date-us-war-afghanistan-2001-202.

Webb, Marcia, Trina A. Colburn, Dawn Heisler, Steve Call, and Sarah A. Chickering. "Clinical Correlates of Dispositional Forgiveness." *Journal of Applied Social Psychology* 38, no. 10 (2008): 2495–517. doi.org/10.1111/j.1559-1816.2008.00401.x.

Wells, Georgia, Deepa Seetharaman, and Jeff Horwitz. "Is Facebook Bad for You? It Is for About 360 Million Users, Company Surveys Suggest." *Wall Street Journal*, Nov. 5,

2021. www.wsj.com/articles/facebook-bad-for-you-360-million-users-say-yes-company -documents-facebook-files-11636124681?mod=article_inline.

Wemheuer, Felix. "Dealing with Responsibility for the Great Leap Famine in the People's Republic of China." *China Quarterly*, no. 201 (March 2010): 176–94. www.jstor .org/stable/20749353.

White, Matthew. *Atrocities: The 100 Deadliest Episodes in Human History*. New York: W. W. Norton, 2013. Kindle.

Will, G. J., E. A. Crone, P. A. van Lier, and B. Güroğlu. "Neural Correlates of Retaliatory and Prosocial Reactions to Social Exclusion: Associations with Chronic Peer Rejection." *Developmental Cognitive Neuroscience* 19 (June 2016): 288–97. doi.org/10.1016 /j.dcn.2016.05.004.

Williams, Heather J., and Alexandra T. Evans. *Extremist Use of Online Spaces*. RAND Corporation, April 27, 2022. www.rand.org/pubs/testimonies/CTA1458-1.html.

Wilson, A. B., J. Draine, T. Hadley, S. Metraux, and A. Evans. "Examining the Impact of Mental Illness and Substance Use on Recidivism in a County Jail." *International Journal of Law and Psychiatry* 34, no. 4 (July–Aug. 2011): 264–68. doi.org/10.1016/j.ijlp .2011.07.004.

Windrem, Robert. "Va. Tech Killer's Strange 'Manifesto.'" NBC News, April 18, 2007. www.nbcnews.com/id/wbna18187368.

Woodcock, Claire. "Archivists Are Putting Terrorist Manifestos Online. Should They Stay There?" *Vice*, Feb. 14, 2022. www.vice.com/en/article/bvn5g3/archivists-are-putting -terrorist-manifestos-online-should-they-stay-there.

World Health Organization. *Global Status Report on Alcohol and Health 2018*. iris.who .int/bitstream/handle/10665/274603/9789241565639-eng.pdf?sequence=1.

———. "Injuries and Violence." June 19, 2024. www.who.int/news-room/fact-sheets /detail/injuries-and-violence.

———. *WHO Report on the Global Tobacco Epidemic, 2023*. iris.who.int/bitstream /handle/10665/372043/9789240077164-eng.pdf?sequence=1.

Worthington, Everett L., Jr. *The Science of Forgiveness*. John Templeton Foundation, April 2020. www.templeton.org/wp-content/uploads/2020/06/Forgiveness_final.pdf.

Worthington, Everett L., Jr., C. V. Witvliet, P. Pietrini, and A. J. Miller. "Forgiveness, Health, and Well-Being: A Review of Evidence for Emotional Versus Decisional Forgiveness, Dispositional Forgivingness, and Reduced Unforgiveness." *Journal of Behavioral Medicine* 30, no. 4 (Aug. 2007): 291–302. doi.org/10.1007/s10865-007-9105-8.

X. "An Update to the Twitter Transparency Center." July 14, 2021. blog.x.com/en_us /topics/company/2021/an-update-to-the-twitter-transparency-center.

Xun, Zhou. "Violence in Revolutionary China: 1949–1963." In *The Cambridge World History of Violence*, edited by Louise Edwards, Nigel Penn, and Jay Winter. Cambridge, U.K.: Cambridge University Press, 2020.

Yamat, Rio. "Judge Orders Las Vegas High Schoolers Held on No Bail in Classmate's Deadly Beating." Associated Press, Nov. 17, 2023. apnews.com/article/las-vegas-school -beating-suspects-jonathan-lewis-93769353dec2f44aca7b947b3d3c11b3.

———. "A Las Vegas High School Grapples with How a Feud over Stolen Items Escalated into a Fatal Beating." Associated Press, Nov. 22, 2023. apnews.com/article/las-vegas-high-school-brawl-teen-killed-3373508c4772c0f5c0e222449bee64ec.

Yau, Y. H., and M. N. Potenza. "Gambling Disorder and Other Behavioral Addictions: Recognition and Treatment." *Harvard Review of Psychiatry* 23, no. 2 (March–April 2015): 134–46. doi.org/10.1097/hrp.0000000000000051.

Zafar, R., M. Siegel, R. Harding, T. Barba, C. Agnorelli, S. Suseelan, L. Roseman, et al. "Psychedelic Therapy in the Treatment of Addiction: The Past, Present, and Future." *Frontiers in Psychiatry* 14 (2023): 1183740. doi.org/10.3389/fpsyt.2023.1183740.

Zenko, Micah. "Obama's Final Drone Strike Data." Council on Foreign Relations, Jan. 20, 2017. www.cfr.org/blog/obamas-final-drone-strike-data.

NOTES

INTRODUCTION: A REVENGE REVOLUTION

1. Kimmel and Rowe, "Behavioral Addiction Model of Revenge, Violence, and Gun Abuse"; Anderson and Bushman, "Human Aggression"; Pinker, *Better Angels of Our Nature*, 529–47; Jackson, Choi, and Gelfand, "Revenge"; Daly and Wilson, "Evolutionary Social Psychology and Family Homicide"; Langhinrichsen-Rohling, McCullars, and Misra, "Motivations for Men and Women's Intimate Partner Violence Perpetration"; Copeland-Linder et al., "Retaliatory Attitudes and Violent Behaviors Among Assault-Injured Youth"; Fluck, "Why Do Students Bully?"; Papachristos, Hureau, and Braga, "The Corner and the Crew"; Jacobs and Wright, *Street Justice*, 1–8; Pathé et al., "Establishing a Joint Agency Response to the Threat of Lone Actor Grievance-Fueled Violence"; D'Souza, Weitzer, and Brunson, "Federal Investigations of Police Misconduct"; Uildriks and Van Reenen, "Human Rights Violations by the Police"; Prins, Tennent, and Trick, "Motives for Arson (Fire Raising)"; Aquino, Tripp, and Bies, "How Employees Respond to Personal Offense"; Ghatak and Prins, "Homegrown Threat"; Schmid, *Routledge Handbook of Terrorism Research*, 6; Balcells, *Rivalry and Revenge*, 5–8, 39–45, 182–83, 90–93.

2. Eder, Mitschke, and Gollwitzer, "What Stops Revenge Taking?"; Funk, McGeer, and Gollwitzer, "Get the Message"; Eadeh, Peak, and Lambert, "Bittersweet Taste of Revenge."

3. Carlsmith, Wilson, and Gilbert, "Paradoxical Consequences of Revenge"; Eadeh, Peak, and Lambert, "Bittersweet Taste of Revenge"; Lambert et al., "How Do You Feel Now?"; Funk, McGeer, and Gollwitzer, "Get the Message"; Boon, Alibhai, and Deveau, "Reflections on the Costs and Benefits of Exacting Revenge in Romantic Relationships."

4. Jackson, Choi, and Gelfand, "Revenge."

5. Ericksen and Horton, "'Blood Feuds'"; McCullough, Kurzban, and Tabak, "Cognitive Systems for Revenge and Forgiveness."

6. de Waal, "Chimpanzee's Sense of Social Regularity and Its Relation to the Human Sense of Justice"; Jensen, Call, and Tomasello, "Chimpanzees Are Vengeful but Not Spiteful"; Daly and Wilson, "Evolutionary Social Psychology and Family Homicide"; Chernyak et al., "Paying Back People Who Harmed Us but Not People Who Helped Us"; Hamlin et al., "How Infants and Toddlers React to Antisocial Others."

7. Jackson, Choi, and Gelfand, "Revenge"; McCullough, Kurzban, and Tabak, "Cognitive Systems for Revenge and Forgiveness."

8. McCullough, *Beyond Revenge,* xviii–xxiv.

9. Black, "Natural History of Antisocial Personality Disorder."

10. Garbarino, *Listening to Killers*, 25.

11. Gollwitzer et al., "Vicarious Revenge and the Death of Osama bin Laden."

12. McCullough et al., "Vengefulness."

13. See references in note 1 above; National Center for Injury Prevention and Control, "National Violent Death Reporting System" (most common circumstance of all violent deaths not precipitated by another crime is "injury occurred during an argument"); Matejkowski, Cullen, and Solomon, "Characteristics of Persons with Severe Mental Illness Who Have Been Incarcerated for Murder"; Skeem et al., "Psychiatric Symptoms and Community Violence Among High-Risk Patients."

14. Kimmel and Rowe, "Behavioral Addiction Model of Revenge, Violence, and Gun Abuse."

15. Blum et al., "Dopaminergic Dysfunction"; Šimić et al., "Understanding Emotions"; Lembke, *Dopamine Nation*, 47–62; Febo et al., "Dopamine Homeostasis."

16. Singer et al., "Empathic Neural Responses Are Modulated by the Perceived Fairness of Others"; Sanfey et al., "Neural Basis of Economic Decision-Making in the Ultimatum Game"; Blum et al., "Dopaminergic Dysfunction"; Billingsley and Losin, "Neural Systems of Forgiveness"; Taniguchi et al., "Late Responses in the Anterior Insula Reflect the Cognitive Component of Pain."

17. de Quervain et al., "Neural Basis of Altruistic Punishment"; Singer et al., "Empathic Neural Responses Are Modulated by the Perceived Fairness of Others"; Strobel et al., "Beyond Revenge"; Brüne, Juckel, and Enzi, "'An Eye for an Eye'?"; Crockett et al., "Serotonin Modulates Striatal Responses to Fairness and Retaliation in Humans"; Chester and DeWall, "Pleasure of Revenge"; Chester et al., "Looking for Reward in All the Wrong Places"; Chester et al., "Neural Mechanisms of the Rejection-Aggression Link."

18. Šimić et al., "Understanding Emotions"; Lembke, *Dopamine Nation*, 47–62.

19. Koob and Volkow, "Neurobiology of Addiction."

20. Volkow, Koob, and McLellan, "Neurobiologic Advances from the Brain Disease Model of Addiction"; Koob and Volkow, "Neurobiology of Addiction."

21. Koob and Volkow, "Neurobiology of Addiction"; Cramer et al., "Harnessing Neuroplasticity for Clinical Applications."

22. Kimmel and Rowe, "Behavioral Addiction Model of Revenge, Violence, and Gun Abuse"; Chester and DeWall, "Pleasure of Revenge"; Chester and DeWall, "Combating the Sting of Rejection with the Pleasure of Revenge."

23. Writing in 1948, the psychoanalyst Karen Horney might have been the first mental health professional to have hinted at the compulsive nature of revenge, observing that "often there is no more holding back a person driven toward revenge than an alcoholic determined to go on a binge." Horney, "Value of Vindictiveness."

24. Loney, *Ethics of Revenge and the Meanings of the "Odyssey,"* 193–226.

25. Schumann and Ross, "Benefits, Costs, and Paradox of Revenge"; Crombag, Rassin, and Horselenberg, "On Vengeance."

26. Kimmel, *Suing for Peace*.

27. Kimmel, *Trial of Fallen Angels*.

CHAPTER 1: THE DEADLIEST ADDICTION

1. Excerpts of Hepnarová's letter and testimony come from Cílek, *Oprátka za osm mrtvých*.

2. Freud, *Reflections on War and Death*, 64.

3. Pinker, *Better Angels of Our Nature*.

4. American Society of Addiction Medicine, "Definition of Addiction."

5. Grant et al., "Introduction to Behavioral Addictions."

6. Sjöström, Magraw-Mickelson, and Gollwitzer, "What Makes Displaced Revenge Taste Sweet."

7. Volkow, Koob, and McLellan, "Neurobiologic Advances from the Brain Disease Model of Addiction"; Koob and Volkow, "Neurobiology of Addiction."

8. Chester and DeWall, "Pleasure of Revenge"; Strobel et al., "Beyond Revenge"; Golden et al., "Nucleus Accumbens Drd1-Expressing Neurons Control Aggression Self-Administration and Aggression Seeking in Mice."

9. A. I. Leshner, "Addiction Is a Brain Disease, and It Matters." *Science* 278, no. 5335 (October 1997), https://doi.org/10.1126/science.278.5335.45.

10. McLellan et al., "Drug Dependence, a Chronic Medical Illness."

11. Pickard, "Is Addiction a Brain Disease?"; Smith, "Evolution of Addiction Medicine as a Medical Specialty."

12. Volkow, "What Does It Mean When We Call Addiction a Brain Disorder?"

13. Lewis, *Biology of Desire.*

14. Heilig et al., "Addiction as a Brain Disease Revised"; Wakefield, "Addiction and the Concept of Disorder, Part 1"; Volkow, Koob, and McLellan, "Neurobiologic Advances from the Brain Disease Model of Addiction"; Volkow, "What Does It Mean When We Call Addiction a Brain Disorder?"

15. APA, *Diagnostic and Statistical Manual of Mental Disorders: DSM-5,* 20. When I use the phrase "brain disease model of revenge addiction" in this book, I mean it in a broad, colloquial sense, inclusive of mental disorder and mirroring the American Psychiatric Association's diagnostic criteria for substance use disorders. Ibid., 483. In the next chapter, I discuss how those diagnostic criteria could theoretically be modified to apply to revenge seeking.

16. This in no way minimizes the death toll caused by other addictions. Tobacco use is currently estimated to kill 8 million people worldwide each year. World Health Organization, *Report on the Global Tobacco Epidemic.* Alcohol use kills 3 million annually. World Health Organization, *Global Status Report on Alcohol and Health.* Narcotics use kills 500,000 annually. United Nations Office on Drugs and Crime, *World Drug Report 2023.* Homicide claims about 458,000 lives annually, but this does not account for major wars and other atrocities that can cause violent deaths to soar into the millions. United Nations Office on Drugs and Crime, *Global Study on Homicide 2023.*

17. White, *Atrocities.*

18. Pinker, *Better Angels of Our Nature,* 508; Gerstenfeld, *Hate Crimes,* 5–6.

19. Baumeister, *Evil;* Gilligan, *Violence;* Pinker, *Better Angels of Our Nature,* 488–96.

20. Baumeister, *Evil,* 49 (quoting Gacy).

21. Global Commission on Drug Policy, *War on Drugs.*

22. Pinker, *Better Angels of Our Nature,* 349; Bruni, *Age of Grievance.*

23. Lee, *Violence,* 25–43.

CHAPTER 2: QUEST TO FIND A KILLER

1. Ttofi, Farrington, and Lösel, "School Bullying as a Predictor of Violence Later in Life"; DeCamp and Newby, "From Bullied to Deviant"; Copeland-Linder et al., "Retaliatory Attitudes and Violent Behaviors Among Assault-Injured Youth"; Fluck, "Why Do Students Bully?"

2. APA, *Diagnostic and Statistical Manual of Mental Disorders: DSM-5-TR.*

3. de Quervain et al., "Neural Basis of Altruistic Punishment."

4. Ibid.

5. Singer et al., "Empathic Neural Responses Are Modulated by the Perceived Fairness of Others."
6. Ibid.
7. Volkow et al., "Cocaine Cues and Dopamine in Dorsal Striatum."
8. Childress et al., "Prelude to Passion."
9. Wilson et al., "Examining the Impact of Mental Illness and Substance Use on Recidivism in a County Jail."
10. Bellamy et al., "Peer Support on the 'Inside and Outside.'"
11. Strobel et al., "Beyond Revenge."
12. Klimecki, Sander, and Vuilleumier, "Distinct Brain Areas Involved in Anger Versus Punishment During Social Interactions"; Brüne, Juckel, and Enzi, "'An Eye for an Eye'?"; Fourie, Hortensius, and Decety, "Parsing the Components of Forgiveness."
13. Strobel et al., "Beyond Revenge."
14. Ibid.
15. Brüne, Juckel, and Enzi, "'An Eye for an Eye'?"
16. Crockett et al., "Serotonin Modulates Striatal Responses to Fairness and Retaliation in Humans."

CHAPTER 3: THIS IS YOUR BRAIN ON REVENGE

1. Rowe et al., "Pilot Study of Motive Control to Reduce Vengeance Cravings."
2. Ibid.
3. Hadlock and McClam, "Hasan Found Guilty of Premeditated Murder in 2009 Fort Hood Rampage"; Campoy, Sanders, and Gold, "Hash Browns, Then 4 Minutes of Chaos."
4. Chester and DeWall, "Pleasure of Revenge."
5. Bushman, Baumeister, and Phillips, "Do People Aggress to Improve Their Mood?"
6. Ibid.; Pinker, *Better Angels of Our Nature*, 299.
7. Ramírez, Bonniot-Cabanac, and Cabanac, "Can Aggression Provide Pleasure?"; Bushman, Baumeister, and Phillips, "Do People Aggress to Improve Their Mood?"
8. Sanfey et al., "Neural Basis of Economic Decision-Making in the Ultimatum Game"; Singer et al., "Empathic Neural Responses Are Modulated by the Perceived Fairness of Others"; Brüne, Juckel, and Enzi, "'An Eye for an Eye'?"
9. Chester and DeWall, "Pleasure of Revenge."
10. Bushman, Baumeister, and Phillips, "Do People Aggress to Improve Their Mood?"
11. Chester and DeWall, "Pleasure of Revenge."
12. *Resolution on Violence Motivation Research and Prevention*, Pennsylvania Psychological Association.
13. Chester and DeWall, "Combating the Sting of Rejection with the Pleasure of Revenge."
14. Ibid.
15. Chester et al., "Neural Mechanisms of the Rejection-Aggression Link."
16. Ibid.
17. Ibid.
18. Ibid.
19. Yau and Potenza, "Gambling Disorder and Other Behavioral Addictions."
20. Threadgill and Gable, "Revenge Is Sweet."
21. Lembke, *Dopamine Nation*, 47–68.
22. Ibid., 59.
23. Gollwitzer and Denzler, "What Makes Revenge Sweet"; Gollwitzer, Meder, and Schmitt, "What Gives Victims Satisfaction When They Seek Revenge?"

24. Funk, McGeer, and Gollwitzer, "Get the Message."

25. Foulkes, "Sadism."

26. Chester, DeWall, and Enjaian, "Sadism and Aggressive Behavior."

27. Takahashi et al., "When Your Gain Is My Pain and Your Pain Is My Gain."

28. Sussman and Sussman, "Considering the Definition of Addiction."

29. Ibid.

30. Leshner, "Addiction Is a Brain Disease, and It Matters"; Volkow, "What Does It Mean When We Call Addiction a Brain Disorder?"

31. Volkow, Koob, and McLellan, "Neurobiologic Advances from the Brain Disease Model of Addiction."

32. Yau and Potenza, "Gambling Disorder and Other Behavioral Addictions"; Wakefield, "Addiction and the Concept of Disorder, Part 1."

33. Blum et al., "Dopaminergic Dysfunction."

34. Kotyuk et al., "Co-occurrences of Substance Use and Other Potentially Addictive Behaviors."

35. McCullough, Kurzban, and Tabak, "Cognitive Systems for Revenge and Forgiveness."

36. Lee, *Violence*, 32.

37. Benton et al., "Influence of Evolutionary History on Human Health and Disease"; Karnib and Van Staaden, "Deep Roots of Addiction."

38. Golden et al., "Compulsive Addiction-Like Aggressive Behavior in Mice."

39. Anthony, Warner, and Kessler, "Comparative Epidemiology of Dependence on Tobacco, Alcohol, Controlled Substances, and Inhalants"; Tremblay, "Early Development of Physical Aggression and Early Risk Factors for Chronic Physical Aggression in Humans."

40. Schumann and Ross, "Benefits, Costs, and Paradox of Revenge."

41. Golden et al., "Compulsive Addiction-Like Aggressive Behavior in Mice."

42. Golden et al., "Nucleus Accumbens Drd1-Expressing Neurons Control Aggression Self-Administration and Aggression Seeking in Mice."

43. Kimmel and Rowe, "Behavioral Addiction Model of Revenge, Violence, and Gun Abuse."

44. Brown, Ramchand, and Helmus, "What Prevention and Treatment of Substance Dependence Can Tell Us About Addressing Violent Extremism."

45. Stern et al., "Practices and Needs in Reintegration Programs for Violent Extremist Offenders in the United States."

CHAPTER 4: THIS IS WHAT REVENGE ADDICTS WANT YOU TO KNOW

1. World Health Organization, "Injuries and Violence."

2. Sataline, "Gunman Kills 2 in Crowded Restaurant."

3. For example, according to the Centers for Disease Control, 26,031 people were murdered in the United States in 2021. National Center for Health Statistics, "Assault or Homicide." Of them, according to the *USA Today*/Associated Press/Northeastern University Mass Killing Database, 172 were murdered during mass killings of 4 or more people, excluding the offender. Fox, "Mass Killing Database."

4. Garbarino, *Listening to Killers*, 2. What I've uncovered about Michael's motivation to kill Salgado and Abate comes from extensive conversations with him and from the official investigation report prepared by the Connecticut Office of Adult Probation prior to his sentencing for the crimes.

5. Hendrix, "In the Army and the Klan, He Hated Muslims."

6. Maresville et al., "How an Undercover Grand Knighthawk Foiled a Murder Plot

Concocted by KKK Law Enforcement Members"; Anti-Defamation League, "Ku Klux Klan Robes."

7. Bernhardt and Blankenship, *Refuge.*
8. Hendrix, "In the Army and the Klan, He Hated Muslims"; Buckley, "Never Lose Faith in Hope and Healing"; Barker, "How a Former KKK Member and a Muslim Refugee Became Friends"; Buckley, "Former White Supremacist"; Allam, "'We Were Blindsided.'"
9. Buckley, testimony.
10. Buckley, "Never Lose Faith in Hope and Healing."
11. Buckley, testimony.
12. Sutherland and Chakrabarti, "U.S. Military Promised to Counter Extremism."
13. Buckley, testimony.
14. Ibid.
15. Ibid.
16. Ibid.
17. Hendrix, "In the Army and the Klan, He Hated Muslims"; Maresville et al., "How an Undercover Grand Knighthawk Foiled a Murder Plot Concocted by KKK Law Enforcement Members."
18. Buckley, testimony.
19. Murdoch, *KKK.*

CHAPTER 5: THESE ARE THE SCREAMS OF REVENGE ADDICTS IN PAIN

1. Fox, "Mass Killing Database."
2. Peterson and Densley, "Key Findings." The Violence Project uses the Congressional Research Service's definition of mass shootings as involving the murder of four or more people, not including the shooter, in a public location and not related to a robbery, gang warfare, or other underlying criminal activity.
3. Lee, *Violence,* 32; Knoll, "'Pseudocommando' Mass Murderer: Part I, The Psychology of Revenge and Obliteration."
4. Girgis et al., "Mass Murders Involving Firearms and Other Methods in School, College, and University Settings."
5. Steadman et al., "Violence by People Discharged from Acute Psychiatric Inpatient Facilities and by Others in the Same Neighborhoods."
6. Lee, *Violence,* 32.
7. Silver, Simons, and Craun, "Study of the Pre-attack Behaviors of Active Shooters in the United States Between 2000 and 2013."
8. National Threat Assessment Center, "Protecting America's Schools."
9. Schwartz, "Mind of the Mass School Shooter"; Knoll, "Mass Murder."
10. Ibid.
11. Calhoun and Weston, *Contemporary Threat Management.*
12. Lankford and Silver, "Why Have Public Mass Shootings Become More Deadly?"; Meindl and Ivy, "Mass Shootings"; Woodcock, "Archivists Are Putting Terrorist Manifestos Online."
13. Garbarino, *Listening to Killers,* 2.
14. The harrowing account of the massacre that follows is based on the official investigation conducted by the governor of Virginia's Review Panel after the incident. Virginia Tech Review Panel, *Mass Shootings at Virginia Tech, April 16, 2007.*
15. Windrem, "Va. Tech Killer's Strange 'Manifesto.'"
16. Cho, Manifesto, April 16, 2007.
17. Knoll, "'Pseudocommando' Mass Murderer: Part II, The Language of Revenge."

18. Knoll, "'Pseudocommando' Mass Murderer: Part I, The Psychology of Revenge and Obliteration."
19. Rosen, "Revenge—the Hate That Dare Not Speak Its Name."
20. Knoll, "'Pseudocommando' Mass Murderer: Part II, The Language of Revenge."
21. Sood, "Getting into the Mind of the Killer."
22. Ibid.
23. APA, *Diagnostic and Statistical Manual of Mental Disorders: DSM-5-TR.*
24. Sood, "Getting into the Mind of the Killer."
25. Virginia Tech Review Panel, *Mass Shootings at Virginia Tech, April 16, 2007,* app. N.
26. Ibid., 46–49.
27. McAuliffe et al., "Motives and Suicide Intent Underlying Hospital Treated Deliberate Self-Harm and Their Association with Repetition"; Johnson-Migalski, "Paradoxical Strategy for Suicidal Clients"; Knoll, "'Pseudocommando' Mass Murderer: Part I, The Psychology of Revenge and Obliteration."
28. Brandon and Finley, "'Bodies Drop' as Walmart Manager Kills 6 in Virginia Attack."
29. Finley, "Witness: Walmart Shooter Seemed to Target Certain People."
30. Finley and Barakat, "Walmart Shooter Left 'Death Note,' Bought Gun Day of Killing."
31. Nassauer, "Walmart Investigated in Early 2020 Complaints About Chesapeake Shooter from Co-workers."
32. City of Chesapeake (@AboutChesapeake), "As the investigation has progressed, detectives conducted a forensic analysis of the suspect's phone, which was located at the scene."

CHAPTER 6: THESE ARE THE DEADLIEST REVENGE ADDICTS IN HUMAN HISTORY

1. Keynes, *Economic Consequences of the Peace,* 199–200.
2. Hitler, "Speech of 18 September 1922," 107–8.
3. Simms, "Against a 'World of Enemies.'"
4. Gilligan, *Violence,* 110–11; Kelty, Hall, and O'Brien-Malone, "You Have to Hit Some People!"
5. Hitler, *Adolf Hitler Collection of Speeches.*
6. Simms, "Against a 'World of Enemies.'"
7. Kershaw, *Hitler,* 10–40.
8. Flood, "Lance Corporal Adolf Hitler on the Western Front."
9. Ibid.
10. Ibid.
11. Hitler, *Mein Kampf,* 163.
12. Hunt, "Myths, Guilt, and Shame in Pre-Nazi Germany."
13. Hitler, *Mein Kampf,* 167.
14. Ibid., 479.
15. Shrier, *Rise and Fall of the Third Reich,* 226.
16. National WWII Museum, "Research Starters: Worldwide Deaths in World War 2."
17. Montefiore, *Young Stalin,* 295.
18. Tucker, *Stalin in Power.*
19. Montefiore, *Young Stalin.*
20. Ibid., chaps. 1 and 2.
21. Ibid., chap. 3.
22. Jalabadze, "Resurgence of Blood Feud in the Georgian Lowlands"; Useinova and

Bazarbaeva, "On the Question of the Relationship Between the Institutions of 'Blood Feud' and 'Talion'"; Ericksen and Horton, "'Blood Feuds'"; Walsh, "Valley of Death."
23. Montefiore, *Young Stalin,* chap. 3.
24. Ibid., chap. 4.
25. Ibid., 51.
26. Ibid., 66.
27. Ibid., prologue.
28. Ibid., 3–4.
29. Davies and Wheatcroft, "Years of Hunger," 326–28.
30. White, *Atrocities,* 383.
31. McNeal, *Stalin,* 129.
32. White, *Atrocities,* 383–84.
33. McNeal, *Stalin,* 143.
34. White, *Atrocities,* 384.
35. Graziosi, "Political Famines in the USSR and China."
36. White, *Atrocities,* 385.
37. Shipler, "Anatomies of a Murderer."
38. White, *Atrocities,* 386.
39. Lanchin, "Trotsky's Grandson Recalls Ice Pick Killing."
40. McNeal, *Stalin,* 201.
41. Montefiore, *Stalin,* 197–99.
42. McNeal, *Stalin,* chap. 10.
43. Tucker, *Stalin in Power,* 165.
44. Ibid.
45. Nagorski, *Greatest Battle.*
46. White, *Atrocities,* 388.
47. Remme, "Battle for Berlin in World War Two."
48. Djilas, *Conversations with Stalin,* 110.
49. Best, *Five Days That Shocked the World,* 198; McNeal, *Stalin,* 251.
50. Chang and Halliday, *Mao,* 6.
51. Spence, *Mao Zedong,* chap. 1.
52. Chang and Halliday, *Mao,* 7.
53. Ibid., 28.
54. Spence, *Mao Zedong,* chap. 6.
55. Chang and Halliday, *Mao,* 13.
56. Spence, *Mao Zedong,* 17–18; Pines, "Legalism in Chinese Philosophy."
57. Spence, *Mao Zedong,* chaps. 4–5.
58. Ibid., 70–71; Chang and Halliday, *Mao,* 78–79.
59. Chang and Halliday, *Mao,* 79–80.
60. Spence, *Mao Zedong,* chap. 6; White, *Atrocities,* 347; Gregory, Lin, and Nguyen, "Chiang Chooses His Enemies."
61. White, *Atrocities,* 376–77.
62. Ibid., 378–80.
63. Spence, *Mao Zedong,* 107.
64. Xun, "Violence in Revolutionary China," 409.
65. Javed, *Righteous Revolutionaries,* 2, 27–31.
66. Ibid., 16–17.
67. Ibid., 16–17, 43, 189–93.

68. Xun, "Violence in Revolutionary China," 411.

69. Mao, "Report on an Investigation of the Peasant Movement in Hunan," 29.

70. White, *Atrocities*, 437.

71. Mao, "On the Correct Handling of Contradictions Among the People," 409–15; Spence, *Mao Zedong*, chap. 9; Graziosi, "Political Famines in the USSR and China," 51; White, *Atrocities*, 430–31.

72. Xun, "Violence in Revolutionary China," 411.

73. Spence, *Mao Zedong*, chap. 9; Chang and Halliday, *Mao*, chap. 40; White, *Atrocities*, 433.

74. Bernstein, "Mao Zedong and the Famine of 1959–1960"; Chang and Halliday, *Mao*, 627–30; White, *Atrocities*, 433.

75. Spence, *Mao Zedong*, chap. 10; Graziosi, "Political Famines in the USSR and China"; Bernstein, "Mao Zedong and the Famine of 1959–1960."

76. Spence, *Mao Zedong*, chap. 10; Bernstein, "Mao Zedong and the Famine of 1959–1960."

77. Graziosi, "Political Famines in the USSR and China."

78. Spence, *Mao Zedong*, chap. 10; Bernstein, "Mao Zedong and the Famine of 1959–1960."

79. Spence, *Mao Zedong*, chap. 11; Bernstein, "Mao Zedong and the Famine of 1959–1960"; White, *Atrocities*, 433; Xun, "Violence in Revolutionary China."

80. Xun, "Violence in Revolutionary China," 411.

81. Chang and Halliday, *Mao*, 630; Wemheuer, "Dealing with Responsibility for the Great Leap Famine in the People's Republic of China"; Graziosi, "Political Famines in the USSR and China."

82. Bernstein, "Mao Zedong and the Famine of 1959–1960"; White, *Atrocities*, 437; Graziosi, "Political Famines in the USSR and China."

83. Wemheuer, "Dealing with Responsibility for the Great Leap Famine in the People's Republic of China"; Graziosi, "Political Famines in the USSR and China."

84. Graziosi, "Political Famines in the USSR and China."

85. Dikötter, *Cultural Revolution*.

86. Dikötter, preface to ibid.

87. White, *Atrocities*, 435–37.

88. Dikötter, preface to *Cultural Revolution*; Kristof, "Tale of Red Guards and Cannibals."

89. Chang and Halliday, *Mao*, 703; Graziosi, "Political Famines in the USSR and China."

90. Chang and Halliday, *Mao*, 781; Spence, *Mao Zedong*, chap. 11.

91. Chang and Halliday, *Mao*, 777–79.

92. Dikötter, preface to *Cultural Revolution*.

CHAPTER 7: THIS IS AMERICA ON REVENGE

1. The original animated version of *The Lion King*, released in 1994, pulled in $968.5 million, the 2019 live-action remake of the film brought in $1.67 billion, and the stage musical earned a whopping $9.1 billion. Beech, "Disney's 'Lion King' Tops $11.6 Billion on Anniversary, Most Successful Franchise Ever."

2. Denham, "'Lion King' Has Been Clouded by Intellectual Property Controversy for 25 Years."

3. Nash Information Services, "Box Office History for Bambi Movies."

4. McIntyre, "This Is the Most Profitable Kids Movie of All Time."

5.   Nash Information Services, "All Time Worldwide Box Office for Walt Disney Movies."
6.   "Markets: Meta Platforms Inc."
7.   Wells, Seetharaman, and Horwitz, "Is Facebook Bad for You?"
8.   Horwitz, "Facebook Whistleblower, Frances Haugen, Says She Wants to Fix the Company, Not Harm It."
9.   Hagey and Horwitz, "Facebook Tried to Make Its Platform a Healthier Place."
10. Ibid.
11. Ibid.
12. Horwitz and Scheck, "Facebook Increasingly Suppresses Political Movements It Deems Dangerous."
13. Javed, *Righteous Revolutionaries.*
14. "Chilling Images from the Capitol Riot," *USA Today.*
15. O'Sullivan, Subramaniam, and Duffy, "Not Stopping 'Stop the Steal.'"
16. Silverman et al., "Facebook Hosted Surge of Misinformation and Insurrection Threats in Months Leading Up to Jan. 6 Attack, Records Show."
17. Wells, Seetharaman, and Horwitz, "Is Facebook Bad for You?"
18. Office of the Surgeon General, *Social Media and Youth Mental Health.*
19. Guess et al., "How Do Social Media Feed Algorithms Affect Attitudes and Behavior in an Election Campaign?"
20. Cox et al., *Social Media in Africa*; Al-Masaeed, "Islamic State E-caliphate on Twitter"; Williams and Evans, *Extremist Use of Online Spaces.*
21. Evans and Williams, *How Extremism Operates Online*; Al-Saggaf, "Online Radicalisation Along a Continuum," 429–39.
22. X, "Update to the Twitter Transparency Center."
23. Williams and Evans, *Extremist Use of Online Spaces.*
24. Brown, Dustman, and Barthelemy, "Twitter Impact on a Community Trauma."
25. Runions, "Toward a Conceptual Model of Motive and Self-Control in Cyberaggression."
26. Nicholson, Keeling, and Black, *Countering Violent Extremism Online,* 25–26.
27. Hickey et al., "Auditing Elon Musk's Impact on Hate Speech and Bots."
28. "Musk Says Twitter Is Losing Cash Because Advertising Is Down and the Company Is Carrying Heavy Debt," Associated Press.
29. Morrow, "With Antisemitic Tweet, Elon Musk Reveals His 'Actual Truth.'"
30. Flint and Haggin, "Apple and Disney Among Companies Stopping Ads on X."
31. Ibid.
32. Stewart, Buckley, and Bloomberg, "Elon Musk Is So Irate at Disney for Pulling Ads from X That He Says CEO Bob Iger 'Should Be Fired Immediately.'"
33. Isaacson, *Elon Musk,* 2–3.
34. Ibid.
35. Ibid., 4.
36. Ttofi, Farrington, and Lösel, "School Bullying as a Predictor of Violence Later in Life"; DeCamp and Newby, "From Bullied to Deviant"; Copeland-Linder et al., "Retaliatory Attitudes and Violent Behaviors Among Assault-Injured Youth"; Fluck, "Why Do Students Bully?"
37. Ott and Hoelscher, "Digital Authoritarian"; Guerrero, "Guerrero: Why Elon Musk, the Bully, Is Seen by Many, Including Liberals, as a Hero"; Reich, "Bullying Adversaries. Demeaning Critics. Craving Attention. Who Does Musk Remind You Of?"
38. Kimmel, "What the Science of Addiction Tells Us About Trump."

39. Rubin, Malin, and Steakin, "By the Numbers: How the Jan. 6 Investigation Is Shaping Up 1 Year Later."
40. Phillips, "Full List of Capitol Rioters Jailed So Far and the Sentences They Are Serving."
41. Ibssa and Cathey, "Trump Will Stay in 2024 Presidential Race Even if Indicted."
42. Lee, *Dangerous Case of Donald Trump*.
43. Zenko, "Obama's Final Drone Strike Data."
44. Halperin and Heilemann, *Double Down*, 55.
45. Holder, statement.
46. Bush, "Address to a Joint Session of Congress and the American People."
47. Bush, "President Delivers 'State of the Union.'"
48. Bush, "President Discusses the Future of Iraq."
49. Watson Institute for International and Public Affairs, "Costs of War."
50. Obama, "President Obama on Death of Osama bin Laden."
51. U.S. Department of Justice, Office of Justice Programs, "U.S. Correctional Population Continued to Decline in 2021."

CHAPTER 8: THIS IS HUMANITY ON REVENGE

1. Glatter and Finkelman, "History of the Plague."
2. Duff, "Plagues and Concern for the Neighbor."
3. Glatter and Finkelman, "History of the Plague."
4. Sala et al., "Sima de los Huesos Crania."
5. Jackson, Choi, and Gelfand, "Revenge."
6. All Bible quotations are from the King James Version. Quran quotations are from the Muhammad Muhsin Khan and Muhammad Taqi-ud-Din al-Hilali translation.
7. Sjöström, Magraw-Mickelson, and Gollwitzer, "What Makes Displaced Revenge Taste Sweet."
8. White, *Atrocities*, 109.
9. Ibid., 22.
10. Ibid., 99.
11. Ibid., 100.
12. Ibid., 101.
13. Ibid., 103.
14. Ibid., 109.
15. Ibid., 159.
16. Kramer, *Hammer of Witches*, 25–27; Larner, *Enemies of God*, 3.
17. Kramer, *Hammer of Witches*, 159–70.
18. White, *Atrocities*, 159.
19. Ibid., 554.
20. Not all deaths resulted from deliberate killings by aggressors. White includes in his totals all "man-made death tolls" related to an atrocity (ibid., 186). These may include unintentional human-caused deaths and killings committed by non-aggressors in self-defense. For purposes of understanding the burden and harm caused by revenge addiction in human history, I adopt White's approach and include all human-caused deaths related to revenge-initiated and revenge-fueled atrocities. My table indicates the role of revenge in killings caused by the aggressors in each atrocity, gleaned from the evidence cited by White (and other historical sources for atrocities covered elsewhere in this book).
21. Ibid., 87.

CHAPTER 9: THIS IS YOUR BRAIN ON FORGIVENESS

1. Kimmel, *Suing for Peace,* 32–56, 77–83; Hughes and Warmke, "Forgiveness."
2. McCullough, Kurzban, and Tabak, "Cognitive Systems for Revenge and Forgiveness."
3. Webb et al., "Clinical Correlates of Dispositional Forgiveness."
4. Tabibnia, Satpute, and Lieberman, "Sunny Side of Fairness."
5. Ibid.
6. Sanfey et al., "Neural Basis of Economic Decision-Making in the Ultimatum Game."
7. Brüne, Juckel, and Enzi, "'An Eye for an Eye'?"
8. Fourie, Hortensius, and Decety, "Parsing the Components of Forgiveness." One study of adolescents that combined social exclusion during Cyberball games as the grievance with an opportunity to retaliate or forgive during follow-up dictator games reported increased activation of the dorsal striatum during forgiveness among adolescents with a history of chronic social rejection. Will et al., "Neural Correlates of Retaliatory and Prosocial Reactions to Social Exclusion." By comparison, dorsal striatum activation was not observed among stable adolescents without such a history. The researchers interpreted this not as reward circuitry (GO!) activation for revenge but rather as the brain accessing greater resources necessary to active executive function (STOP!) circuitry needed by chronically rejected adolescents to forgive.
9. Billingsley and Losin, "Neural Systems of Forgiveness."
10. Toussaint and Worthington, "Forgiveness and Mental Health"; Toussaint et al., "Forgiveness, Rumination, and Depression in the United States and Korea"; Kshtriya et al., "Exploring the Association Between Forgiveness, Meaning-Making, and Post-traumatic Stress Symptoms"; Toussaint et al., "Hostility, Forgiveness, and Cognitive Impairment over 10 Years in a National Sample of American Adults."
11. Toussaint et al., "Let It Rest"; Toussaint et al., "Effects of Lifetime Stress Exposure on Mental and Physical Health in Young Adulthood"; Schuttenberg et al., "Forgiveness Mediates the Relationship Between Middle Frontal Gyrus Volume and Clinical Symptoms in Adolescents"; Fourie, Hortensius, and Decety, "Parsing the Components of Forgiveness"; Toussaint et al., "Relationship Between Forgiveness and Health Outcomes Among People Living with HIV."
12. Worthington et al., "Forgiveness, Health, and Well-Being"; Fourie, Hortensius, and Decety, "Parsing the Components of Forgiveness."
13. Fourie, Hortensius, and Decety, "Parsing the Components of Forgiveness."
14. Ibid.
15. Ibid.
16. Ricciardi et al., "How the Brain Heals Emotional Wounds."
17. Billingsley and Losin, "Neural Systems of Forgiveness."
18. Ricciardi et al., "How the Brain Heals Emotional Wounds."
19. Ibid.
20. Clarkson, "Autopsy Report Details Scope of Injuries from Beating That Killed Rancho Student."
21. Yamat, "Judge Orders Las Vegas High Schoolers Held on No Bail in Classmate's Deadly Beating."
22. Ibid.; Yamat, "Las Vegas High School Grapples With How a Feud over Stolen Items Escalated into a Fatal Beating."
23. Magdaleno, "Welcome to the Youth Murder Capital of California"; Langley and Sugarmann, *Lost Youth;* Reynolds, *Blood in the Fields.*

24. The army's anthrax vaccine had been widely reported to have serious safety concerns. Johannes and Maremont, "U.S. Army Is in Bind over Worries About Safety of Its Anthrax Vaccine."

CHAPTER 10: THIS IS HOW TO KICK THE REVENGE HABIT

1. Worthington, *Science of Forgiveness*, 4–6, 18–22.
2. Lembke, *Dopamine Nation*, 76–80, 234.
3. Ibid., 71–206.
4. Petry, Zajac, and Ginley, "Behavioral Addictions as Mental Disorders"; Yau and Potenza, "Gambling Disorder and Other Behavioral Addictions"; Lembke, *Dopamine Nation*, 94–98.
5. Leggio et al., "GLP-1 Receptor Agonists Are Promising but Unproven Treatments for Alcohol and Substance Use Disorders"; Klausen et al., "Role of Glucagon-Like Peptide 1 (GLP-1) in Addictive Disorders."
6. Mahoney et al., "Low-Intensity Focused Ultrasound Targeting the Nucleus Accumbens as a Potential Treatment for Substance Use Disorder."
7. Zafar et al., "Psychedelic Therapy in the Treatment of Addiction."
8. Wakefield, Loken, and Hornik, "Use of Mass Media Campaigns to Change Health Behaviour"; Stead et al., "Mass Media to Communicate Public Health Messages in Six Health Topic Areas"; Noar, Chabot, and Zimmerman, "Applying Health Behavior Theory to Multiple Behavior Change"; Bernhardt, "Communication at the Core of Effective Public Health."
9. Hahn et al., "Effectiveness of Universal School-Based Programs to Prevent Violent and Aggressive Behavior."
10. Kimmel, *Suing for Peace*, 77–83.
11. Ibid., 57–92.
12. Ibid., 84–102.
13. The original version of the NJS in *Suing for Peace* had nine steps. These have since been condensed and simplified into the current five-step version.
14. Van der Kolk, *Body Keeps the Score.*
15. Van der Kolk, "How Trauma Lodges in the Body, Revisited."
16. Ten Boom and Kuijpers, "Victims' Needs as Basic Human Needs."
17. Lundahl et al., "A Meta-Analysis of Motivational Interviewing: Twenty-Five Years of Empirical Studies"; Hofmann et al., "The Efficacy of Cognitive Behavioral Therapy: A Review of Meta-analyses."
18. Rowe et al., "Pilot Study of Motive Control to Reduce Vengeance Cravings."
19. Bellamy et al., "Peer Support on the 'Inside and Outside.'"
20. The chart contains my analysis of the raw NJS Study 2 data and does not reflect the analyses or opinions of my Yale colleagues. Both Yale studies used the nine-step version of the NJS, which has since been replaced with the current five-step version. Participant identification numbers in the chart do not match the numbers assigned in the study. The study was approved in advance by the Yale Institutional Review Board, and participants provided informed written consent to participate in the study.
21. Schumaker, "Is It Possible to Cure the Desire for Revenge?"
22. Connecticut Violence Intervention and Prevention. "Home Page." Accessed October 30, 2024. www.ctintervention.org.
23. Barber, *Citizen Outlaw.*
24. Schumaker, "Is It Possible to Cure the Desire for Revenge?"

25. Ibid.
26. Connecticut Violence Intervention and Prevention. "Home Page." Accessed October 30, 2024. www.ctintervention.org.
27. Chernyak et al., "Paying Back People Who Harmed Us but Not People Who Helped Us"; Hamlin et al., "How Infants and Toddlers React to Antisocial Others."
28. Copeland-Linder et al., "Retaliatory Attitudes and Violent Behaviors Among Assault-Injured Youth"; Fluck, "Why Do Students Bully?"; Varjas et al., "High School Students' Perceptions of Motivations for Cyberbullying."
29. Grites, *Step Back or Get Back?*
30. Kimmel, "Website for Would-Be Killers"; Briquelet, "Would-Be Killers, Click Here for Help"; Volsky and Fleisher, "This Effort to Prevent Mass Shootings Is So Obvious"; Venosa, "Mass Shootings on the Rise."
31. American Heart Association, "Warning Signs of a Heart Attack."
32. Silver, Simons, and Craun, "Study of the Pre-attack Behaviors of Active Shooters in the United States Between 2000 and 2013"; National Threat Assessment Center, "Protecting America's Schools."

CHAPTER 11: THIS IS THE NONJUSTICE SYSTEM FOR SETTING YOURSELF FREE

1. Gandhi, *Young India,* 1182.

CONCLUSION: A REVENGE RECOVERY STORY

1. Kuklick, "Division of Germany and American Policy on Reparations."
2. Ibid.
3. Ibid.
4. *Berlin (Potsdam) Conference, July 17–August 2, 1945, (a) Protocol of the Proceedings, August 1, 1945.*
5. Hinnershitz, "Marshall Plan and Postwar Economic Recovery."
6. Harry S. Truman, "August 9, 1945: Radio Report to the American People on the Potsdam Conference."
7. Center for Preventive Action, "Global Conflict Tracker."

INDEX

ABOUT THE AUTHOR

JAMES KIMMEL, JR., JD, is a lecturer in psychiatry at the Yale School of Medicine, the founder and co-director of the Yale Collaborative for Motive Control Studies, and a researcher, lawyer, and novelist who focuses on neuroscience, psychology, revenge, addiction, forgiveness, and violence. A breakthrough scholar and expert on revenge, he first identified compulsive revenge seeking as an addiction and developed the behavioral addiction model of revenge and the brain disease model of revenge addiction as public health approaches for preventing and treating violence. He is the creator of The Nonjustice System, the Miracle Court app, and SavingCain.org for recovering from grievances and revenge desires and preventing mass violence. He maintains an active legal practice and speaking calendar and is the author of two other books on revenge: *Suing for Peace: A Guide for Resolving Life's Conflicts* and *The Trial of Fallen Angels*, a novel.

jameskimmeljr.com

ABOUT THE TYPE

This book was set in Caslon, a typeface first designed in 1722 by William Caslon (1692–1766). Its widespread use by most English printers in the early eighteenth century soon supplanted the Dutch typefaces that had formerly prevailed. The roman is considered a "workhorse" typeface due to its pleasant, open appearance, while the italic is exceedingly decorative.